B.C.

GOD AND CAESAR
IN EAST GERMANY

THE MACMILLAN COMPANY
NEW YORK · CHICAGO
DALLAS · ATLANTA · SAN FRANCISCO
LONDON · MANILA

IN CANADA
BRETT-MACMILLAN LTD.
GALT, ONTARIO

GOD AND CAESAR
IN EAST GERMANY

THE CONFLICTS OF CHURCH AND STATE
IN EAST GERMANY SINCE 1945

RICHARD W. SOLBERG

Foreword by Bishop Otto Dibelius

NEW YORK   **THE MACMILLAN COMPANY**   1961

First Printing

The Macmillan Company, New York
Brett-Macmillan Ltd., Galt, Ontario

Printed in the United States of America

Library of Congress catalog card number: 61-8759

To fellow members of
the Communion of Saints
in East Germany, with
the prayer that their
faith may not fail

FOREWORD

The struggle between faith and unbelief moves inexorably through all of human history. In our time this struggle has assumed the form of a spiritual conflict of world-wide dimension. The crucial question is whether the character of coming generations shall receive the stamp of atheistic materialism, or whether those values which came into the world with the Christian faith shall be the foundation of human society.

The decision in this struggle will be made in Germany.

Whoever desires to understand the time in which he lives must follow this struggle closely, and eventually choose for himself one side or the other. For proper understanding he must have reports concerning the things which have happened and are happening day by day. These must be sober and factual reports, from which one can learn, as the great German historian Ranke has said, "the way things actually were."

It is best that such reports not be written by Germans who are directly involved in the struggle, but rather by those who have made a careful firsthand study on the scene, and yet who as outsiders have maintained an objective and nonpartisan view.

Such a report is to be found in Dr. Solberg's book. He has presented the course of events with astonishing accuracy and insight. His love for the Christian churches of Germany can be sensed on every page. The final judgment, however, must be formed by the reader himself.

This is exactly the kind of presentation we need today.

The author deserves thanks for daring to undertake such a task before the details of significant events have been forgotten. This book will open the eyes and awaken the consciences of many people.

DR. OTTO DIBELIUS
Evangelical Bishop of Berlin

In New York, November 14, 1960

PREFACE

The dramatic story contained in the following pages is an unfinished one. With each passing day new chapters are being enacted in the heroic struggle of Christian men and institutions in East Germany to maintain their integrity in the face of a totalitarian Communist State. The writing has been undertaken in the conviction that the past fifteen years of this struggle have provided data and insights which can contribute significantly to a fuller understanding of the present great world conflict.

There is information here of crucial importance to the Christian world concerning the methods and extent of the Communist attack upon one of the historic fronts where Christianity has flourished for a thousand years. To the Communist assertion that the Church is a decadent institution that has outlived its relevance in the modern world, the Church has responded with a vigorous proclamation of the Gospel from its pulpits and a striking witness from its laymen in the market place. Though many of its external forms and patterns of activity have undergone changes under the pressures of a militantly atheistic State, the Church has not yielded either its identity or its integrity in East Germany.

Beyond Church history, this conflict has much to say regarding the nature and objectives of the entire Communist program in eastern Europe. It is extremely difficult to follow the developments of the past decade and a half and still hopefully anticipate any permanent commitment on the part of the Communists to a policy of peaceful coexistence. Their tactics have changed frequently, but the Church struggle in East Germany has clearly demonstrated the Communists' dedication to their own moral principle that "whatever serves the cause of Socialism is right."

Research was carried on in Germany in 1959 with the assistance of a grant from the Social Science Research Council while the author was on leave of absence from teaching duties in the Department of History at Augustana College. The broader resources for the project, however, have been accumulated over the course of a twelve-year personal acquaintance with the Churches of Germany, dating from 1949, and including almost five years of residence and work in their midst. Close associations with pastors, leaders, and laymen have afforded opportunities for observation and for involvement in the special postwar problems of the Church in both East and West. It would have been impossible to write this particular story without the facilities placed at the author's disposal by many official agencies of the Churches, especially in Berlin. The Berlin offices of the Federal Republic of Germany also extended both courtesy and assistance. Illustrations used in the book were furnished by the Bundeshaus in Berlin and by the Evangelical Hilfswerk.

Permission was graciously extended by Harper & Brothers to quote from Stewart Herman's *The Rebirth of the German Church* (1946), and by Association Press for a quotation from *How to Serve God in a Marxist Land*, by Karl Barth and Johannes Hamel (1959).

It would be an impossibility to single out all the individuals who have given assistance in the preparation of this book, but a word of special appreciation must be reserved for members of my own family who have shared so enthusiastically in the associations of many years with the Churches and people of Germany, and especially for my wife, June, who also listened as a patient and discerning critic to each successive chapter of the manuscript. At every stage there have been other persons and agencies that displayed both kindness and generosity. In so doing they have materially identified themselves with the mission the author has intended that the book should perform.

R. W. S.

CONTENTS

ILLUSTRATIONS

GOD AND CAESAR
IN EAST GERMANY

ONE

THE DAILY ENCOUNTER

Hansi Wendler wanted to be a teacher in East Germany.

One morning early in March, 1958, she was summoned to the headmaster's office of the Teachers' College in which she was enrolled. When she arrived two other persons were already present—members of the local Communist Party.

Introductions were made. Interrogation followed.

"You wish to be a teacher in the public schools of the German Democratic Republic, Miss Wendler?"

"Yes, sir," replied Hansi. "This is what I have wanted all my life."

"You are a pastor's daughter?"

"Yes, sir."

"And a member of the Christian Student Association?"

"Yes, sir."

The headmaster continued: "You are aware that it is expected of every teacher in the German Democratic Republic that she teach faithfully the doctrines of Marx and Lenin and that she lead the youth of our Farmers' and Workers' Republic into a fuller understanding and a deeper loyalty to Socialism?"

"I am only aware," replied Hansi, "that every citizen of the German Democratic Republic is guaranteed freedom to believe as he wishes and that, according to our constitution, admission to the public service is not dependent upon one's religious beliefs."

"You may certainly have a religion of your own, Miss Wendler," said the headmaster, "but if you want to become a teacher you cannot be bound by outworn superstitions and unscientific ideas. Make your decision. Either recant your Christian faith or leave the school. We shall be waiting for your answer."

As Hansi Wendler left the headmaster's office, she was confronted by the latest poster display on a wall of the corridor outside the room. A huge placard depicted a prospective teacher looking up at a Bible and a cross. Facing the young woman on the poster was the huge, menacing, bearded figure of Karl Marx, surrounded by a host of Communist Youth.

Beneath the picture was a caption summarizing what Hansi had just heard spoken in the headmaster's office: "This we will not tolerate!"

While Hansi Wendler's case was pending, she was required to hand over her passport and identity card, lest she flee to the West before a decision was reached. On the 19th of March the verdict was handed down:

Hansi Wendler has failed to dissociate herself from her basic idealism, from her religious faith and from her church. Though she was given a thorough instruction in Marxism and Leninism, she has only become firmer in her religious conviction. . . . Her fellow students are without exception agreed that she must not become a teacher in the German Democratic Republic.

A public notice appeared one week later, signed by nineteen members of the faculty:

The aims of this Teachers' College and those of the Christian Student Associations are contradictory to each other. The Faculty Council demands that all students resign from these organizations. Those who fail to comply make it obvious that they continue to acknowledge the claim of the church to educate. Such students will be dismissed from the college.

Two days later Hansi Wendler and ten other students were expelled. Protests of the student chaplain to the States Attorney had no effect whatever.

In a hotel in Western Germany, a leading East German Churchman was approached by a waiter who, until a few days before, had been a worker in Thuringia, in East Germany. His wife had been employed in the town hall. Shortly before their daughter was to be confirmed, the mayor of the town called him in and asked why the girl had not been registered for the Communist Youth Dedication.

"We are a Christian family," said the man. "Our daughter is going to be confirmed."

"You evidently forget that your wife is a civic employee," rejoined the mayor.

The father replied, "Our Christian faith is not to be bargained for by State employment."

On the following day the wife was given immediate notice, and he, too, was fired from his job. The whole family fled to West Germany.

A printer preparing samples and sketches of post cards and devotional mottoes paid his required visit to the government licensing office in a Saxon city. The official in charge sorted the samples, and discarded one which contained the verse from Psalm 127, "Unless the Lord builds the house, those who build it labor in vain."

"Anyone knows," she said, "that here in the German Democratic Republic we Socialists can build as good houses as anyone. And we don't need God's help to do it."

A pastor sought approval to reprint a Bible-text card for the Christmas season with the verse from Isaiah 9.2: "The people who walked in darkness have seen a great light; those who dwelt in a land of deep darkness, upon them has light shined."

Across the face of the Bible text an official rubber-stamped, in black ink, the words "Printing permit denied."

Reason for the denial: The verse contained concealed political implications!

The following is an excerpt from a divorce decree handed down by a court in East Germany:

The applicant asserts that his originally happy marriage was disrupted by his wife's joining the church in 1946. Thereafter she became increasingly active in it. Every Sunday morning she attended service, and took part in church functions at least twice a week in addition. . . .

In our Workers' and Farmers' State a progressively thinking man cannot be expected to remain with a marriage partner whose loyalty to the church is steadily increasing. . . .

In such a situation even the policy of our Supreme Court, established on July 1, 1957, making divorce in cases of long-standing marriages very difficult, cannot be applied. . . .

The divorce is granted, because the wife's attitude to the church has led to an inner separation of the married couple, and this is sufficient ground for divorce.

It was June 2, 1957, Confirmation Sunday, in the city of Goerlitz in East Germany. Trinity Church was crowded with parents, sponsors, and friends of the confirmands. Just as the pastor ascended the pulpit to begin his sermon, a column of Communist Young Pioneers marched into the square in front of the church, to the accompaniment of military music played by a brass band. Three times the marching column circled the church, while the congregation strained to hear the pastor's voice above the din. Stirrings and murmurings of protest were audible in the congregation.

Scarcely had the column disappeared and the music faded away when a second group arrived from another direction, and repeated the performance.

By the time a third group had appeared and also circled the church three times, the twenty-five minutes allotted for the pastor's sermon were gone. Just before the pastor concluded his sermon, a stone crashed through a side window of the church, scattering broken glass over a wide area, but fortunately falling in a corner under the balcony where no one was sitting.

In his letter of protest to the City Council, the pastor exercised exemplary restraint in attaching responsibility for the disturbance, but asked for a thorough investigation of the entire affair. Such occurrences, he observed, "tend to undermine confidence in the sincerity of the Communist professions of peaceful coexistence with the Church in the German Democratic Republic."

In a small city near Frankfurt an der Oder, a mass assembly had been called by the local committee of the Communist Party for the purpose of publicly discrediting the pastor. The party press had prepared the way for the meeting, at the conclusion of which a previously composed resolution would be read, denouncing the pastor as an agent of NATO and a saboteur of Socialism. Since no one would dare to speak up against it, the resolution would be declared as the unanimous opinion of the community, and would so be publicized in the following day's newspaper.

A person who attended this particular mass meeting wrote a graphic account of an unexpected turn of events:

"We were all assembled in the big hall belonging to the party," he wrote. "Everyone was looking around to see whether the pastor was present, too. One of the party functionaries from Frankfurt spoke first. He explained that since Sputnik had circled the earth and made it perfectly clear that there was no heaven, faith was out of date. Man could do everything, and he simply didn't need a god. Faith and the Church had nothing more to offer to modern man. He quoted the words of the great 'middle-class' humanist Johann Gottfried von Herder, who in 1798 had declared, 'Every child must study natural science and physics in order to have a happy life, to make use of the good deeds of nature, and at last to break with the superstitions which have never been able to make the human race happy.'"

Our informant wrote that the functionary then began to attack the pastor, who, he claimed, had recently thrashed a youngster in confirmation class so badly that the child had been taken to the hospital. Furthermore, the pastor had required the children to learn by heart a confession of faith that he himself had written.

By the time the speaker had finished, the pastor had been painted as such a degenerate individual that it was only through the goodness of the mayor that he was even permitted to remain in the village. The pastor's account looked bad: He was a convinced NATO supporter, an opponent of the peace movement, and a tyrant!

Another man from Frankfurt then took the floor. "After all we have heard about this pastor," he said, "anybody who still would entrust a child to his care makes it perfectly clear that he is also on the wrong side. As you leave the hall, you will find lists on which all of your names have been entered. If you wish to take your child out of the confirmation class and send him to the Youth Dedication, just make a cross beside your name."

After this, those in the hall were very still for a long while. Finally, the mayor inquired whether anyone else had anything to say.

To the amazement of everyone the schoolteacher stood up and asked hesitatingly why the pastor had not been invited to attend this meeting. All marveled at the man's courage, because such an indiscretion could cost him his job as a teacher. But he went on to point out that the pastor also had a son who was fourteen years old. Moreover, he asserted, in a democratic state anyone who is attacked ought to have the right to defend himself.

A tremor went through the hall. The villagers who until then had been slouching on their chairs like sacks of meal sat up straight. The teacher, warming to his task, went on: "The pastor has never yet disciplined anyone in the confirmation class so severely that he had to be taken to the hospital. I have all the children in the school, and I ought to know. And one more thing. You just talked about Herder, who is such a strong advocate of natural science. But you didn't quote him in full. Let me give you the rest of the quotation. He also said: 'True faith can never be rooted out. The gates of hell cannot overpower it, and the Antichrist with all his power can only drive men to believe more strongly.'"

It was magnificent! The party men up front squirmed, and didn't know what to say. At last the mayor spoke up and tried to save the situation.

"Good people," he began, "you must know that this teacher is a newcomer in town and that he is a supporter of the pastor besides. The main thing is what we home folks want—and we don't want anything further to do with the pastor or the Church and its outmoded faith."

Then a Mrs. Hennig stood up and called for the floor. She had a fourteen-year-old son, and after he was born she was sick for a long time, and endured many of the hardships life has to offer. She was not very old, but everyone in town respected her.

"There have been a lot of evil things said about our pastor here this evening," she said. "And because none of us has spoken up against them, it has appeared that these are also our views. However, while I was sick, I had many conversations with our pastor, and if there is any man in this village for whom we should have the highest regard, that man is the pastor. And I want to say to you all that I am ashamed that of late I have been so seldom in church. It is true that I have often been tired and discouraged, but I should have known that in his sermons I would find renewed strength."

In the spring of 1953 the Churches of East Germany were undergoing their most bitter persecution since the days of National Socialism. Primary targets of the Communist terror were the youth of the Church and the pastors who conducted the youth ministry. More than three thousand boys and girls were expelled from the high schools of East Germany. Seventy-two pastors and youth leaders were arrested and imprisoned. Specially staged public court trials provided the sounding boards for scurrilous and blasphemous attacks on the Church and even on the Gospel itself.

In the midst of these dark days there appeared a small booklet written by Professor Martin Fischer of Berlin, entitled "The Witness of the Imprisoned," introducing some of these men and the work they had been doing that had caused their arrest. He raised the question whether it was wise, in the midst of a cold war, to present, as he had done, people who had been arrested and who were still in prison. His conclusion was that the Church has a responsibility to bear witness through those who are brought into jeopardy for their faith. Arrest and imprisonment and persecution, said Fischer, can be a form of Christian service. Christians have a responsibility to demonstrate that their Churches and pastors are not maintained simply for their own sake. This is not an artificial, emotional kind of heroics. It is a quiet and convinced certainty, in the spirit of Martin Luther at Worms, professing before God and man and before his own quavering heart that no other way was open to him except the way of a firm confession of faith.

A clear witness of this kind, before the eyes and ears of the world, is also necessary for the strengthening of the Church in every generation. "If a person is to pray for someone," said Martin Fischer, "he must be informed! The information he needs is not the political data to be found in the newspapers or heard from the man on the street, but rather knowledge concerning the situation and work of the Church. . . .

"Our concern at the moment is especially the Church in East Germany. In that part of Germany which was placed under Soviet occupation by the Potsdam Agreement, deep-seated sociological, economic, and political changes are taking place. In this part of Germany, however, just as elsewhere, lives the Evangelical Church. It lives in the congregations, and in the word and the witness of its people."

Just as Fischer was concerned about this witness in 1953, there is also a profound concern in many parts of the Church today that the true story of the embattled Christians behind the Iron Curtain be known. The following pages are intended to draw back the curtain and to make clear to American eyes the manner of witness that has been borne for fifteen years by men and women seeking to fulfill, in a Marxist land, the Christian's responsibilities both to God and to Caesar.

TWO

THE END AND THE BEGINNING

When the Russian armored divisions smashed across the Oder River in the early months of 1945 and surged forward across eastern Germany to meet their British and American allies, they were certainly not consciously making Church history. Their military objective was Berlin—their political objective the crushing of Nazism—but, unconsciously or not, they were also helping to shape the religious development of eastern Germany for many years to come. The presence of the Russians on the Elbe, the Evangelical Bishop of Berlin would presently declare, "determines our whole thinking."

Since the Reformation this part of Germany had been a strongly Protestant land, and the Churches of Prussia, Saxony, and Silesia were among the largest Protestant Church organizations in the world. Here Martin Luther had lived, and here the central acts of the Protestant Reformation had been carried out. This had been the theological armory for a substantial part of world Protestantism, and the starting point of the modern Protestant missionary thrust into India in the early eighteenth century.

Within a few short months all of prewar Germany east of the

Oder and the Neisse rivers was to be evacuated by nine million German inhabitants and reoccupied by five million Poles. Several millions had already fled before the anticipated reprisals of the victorious Soviet armies. The rest would be expelled by the orders of the Russian and Polish governments.

In this process the entire Church provinces of East and West Prussia were liquidated, and others, such as Pomerania, Brandenburg, and Silesia, were drastically reduced in size, the latter almost to the point of disappearance. Six million Protestants and almost three million Roman Catholics who were driven from their homes crowded into the immediately accessible lands of refuge, the German territories just west of the Oder and Neisse rivers, where they overtaxed already inadequate and badly decimated housing and food supplies. Many thousands pressed on beyond the Soviet Zone into western Germany, though their exodus only partially relieved the overcrowded conditions in the East. Even in 1960, after losing an additional 2½ million refugees to the West, the population of the Russian Zone remains greater than it was in 1939.

For pastors and leaders of the "resistance Church" in Germany in both East and West, the approach of the armies of the liberation meant the promise of a new beginning for the Church. The ten-year struggle against the Nazis, and their spiritual colleagues, the so-called "German-Christians," was over. As the Russian armies swept in from the East, Nazi hirelings in official Church positions either abandoned or resigned their offices and left the embattled Churches free to attempt a new beginning under the leadership of men who knew what it was to bear courageous witness to the truth of the Gospel.

One of the first new Churches to emerge from spiritual captivity was the Evangelical Church of Silesia. Late in January, 1945, Russian troops crossed the old German frontier between Poland and Silesia and advanced to the Oder River, surrounding the fortress of Breslau, a city of more than 500,000 inhabitants. Although thousands of people managed to leave in time, the Russian advance had been so fast that 200,000 civilians were still there when the artillery bombardment began.

Just before the city was surrounded, representatives of the German Gestapo came to the leaders of the Confessing Church and demanded that all Protestant pastors leave the city. The Church leaders refused to abandon the 200,000 civilians in Breslau, and were able to leave ten pastors within the fortress.

As the Russians crossed the Oder River and moved on toward Berlin, Breslau remained an isolated pocket of resistance until just two days before the final surrender of Berlin on May 8th. On May 4th, with the city 60 per cent destroyed by artillery, the Confessing Church leadership, accompanied by Roman Catholic representatives, went personally to General Niehoff, the commander of the German forces, pointed out the unreasonableness of further resistance, and in the name of the suffering people asked him to call a halt to the hostilities. Pastor Hornig, leader of the delegation, and president of the Silesian Evangelical Church, made it clear that the request was neither political nor military, but was based upon the ordination pledges of pastors who had obligated themselves as shepherds of their parishes in the midst of need.

After asking the pastors to repeat their request to the division commanders, the general made the decision to surrender the city in an effort to spare the loss of further lives. When members of the community understood that the Church had been instrumental in halting hostilities, a sense of confidence and trust welled up in support of the new Church regime. Later on, when Polish occupation authorities took over the city of Breslau, the Church was the only group that could effectively represent the people.

By the time Breslau surrendered, more than 3,000,000 of the 4,700,000 inhabitants of Silesia had fled in panic ahead of the Russian armies. About half had crossed the mountains to the south and entered Czechoslovakia. The other half had fled to the German states of Thuringia, Bavaria, or Saxony, and thousands of them who had crowded into the Saxon city of Dresden were victimized in the saturation air raids upon that city on February 12–14, 1945, which claimed 250,000 lives. Those who had fled to Czechoslovakia were presently driven out again, this time by Czechs, who had not forgotten the treacherous activities of the Sudeten Germans that led to the dismemberment of their nation by Hitler in 1938. Many of these Silesians, driven out for the second time, found refuge in Bavaria and Saxony, but with the fighting over, other thousands sought to return to their homes. Some were able to achieve this, though in most instances they found their homes burned or plundered by Russian troops or by other refugees on the march. Those, however, who attempted to recross the Neisse River into Silesia after the end of May, 1945, were prevented by the Polish militia and the Polish administration which had been set up there following the Russian conquest.

At the end of June, the entire Oder-Neisse frontier was closed to returning refugees, while at the same time the first great waves of political expellees were crossing from east to west. The confusion of homeless people on the west banks of the Oder and the Neisse rivers in the summer months of 1945 was incredible. Among these political expellees were about one million Silesians who had been driven out by force three times within a few months, twice from their own homes, and once from a supposed place of refuge. And before they finally found a place of permanent resettlement, many of them would face several more long marches, and the bitter cold and hunger of more than one winter.

In the few weeks of grace before the mass deportation from Polish-occupied provinces began in earnest, the Silesian Church bent every effort to hold its congregations together and to provide ministerial services in areas where there were no pastors. As the year 1946 opened, there were about 250 pastors to serve 950 parishes in Silesia. Many parishes had no pastor at all, and one isolated Protestant congregation asked the local Catholic priest to hold services for them in their church and to give the Sacrament in both forms, according to their practice. One aged superintendent served his parishes east of the Oder River and for a long time received his support through the kindness of the Russian commandant. Another pastor took care of seven congregations in three different counties for a whole year, from August, 1945, to June, 1946, and in spite of a weak heart covered almost two thousand miles on foot, traveling by day and by night. He had learned, he said, what Isaiah meant when he wrote that those who trust in the Lord "shall renew their strength, they shall mount up with wings like eagles, they shall run and not be weary, they shall walk and not faint."

In many congregations lay people rallied around, reconstructed their churches and parish houses, and even took care of their own Sunday services as lay readers. More than two hundred laymen in the Church of Silesia undertook this kind of activity, and one of them, who served twenty-five parishes east of the Oder River, and had long since passed the three-thousand-mile mark in his pastoral visitations on foot, reported: "The hunger for the Word of God and the Sacrament is everywhere very great, and I am the only pastor in the entire Church district. . . . I had to provide my own housing, and at first I had only an empty room. Finally some women provided me with a sack of straw and a chair. Thus far I am my own cook, and porridge is my main dish. Frequently I have slept in bunkers, but this doesn't matter. God the Lord leads me so wonderfully, as he once did the Apostle Paul. I do not know how I have merited such grace and mercy."

Members of the congregations were poor, and many were homeless, some having been driven five or six times from their homes. The men were often picked up on the street by Russian or Polish officials and arbitrarily assigned a job, even though they were engaged at the moment in some other task. Arbitrary imprisonments were daily occurrences, and the danger of immediate dispossession and expulsion hovered constantly over them.

Church attendance was better than it had been in more prosperous times, and since schools with German-language instruction were not permitted by the Polish authorities, the Church sought to organize special classes for religious instruction in every Silesian parish. In one congregation four hundred children were given two hours of religious instruction every day by both lay and trained teachers. Teacher-training classes also were set up wherever possible.

No state subsidies whatever were given to the Church, and all Church support therefore came from free-will offerings. This was especially significant because German money was greatly undervalued in relation to the Polish currency, and much larger sums had to be contributed in marks in order to fulfill the obligations of the Church in terms of Polish zlotys. Yet in addition to supporting their pastors, the people of Breslau managed to gather enough money even to operate an old people's home and an orphan's home.

Just as the Silesian Church gathered its scanty resources together and deployed about 250 pastors and 200 laymen to serve its 950 congregations, the mass evacuation of Silesia began. Beginning with Breslau and the more heavily settled areas, and extending out onto the more sparsely settled plains, native-born families were given orders to abandon their homes and farms immediately and to move across the Oder-Neisse Line into the German provinces to the west. The expulsions were carried out in different ways. Some Germans were simply rounded up, placed in camps, and loaded onto trucks or railroad cars and moved out. Others were denied food-ration cards. Still others were simply evicted from their houses and thus forced to leave. In many instances they were required to sign statements that they were leaving Poland voluntarily for Germany. Homes, farms, and factories, churches, and public buildings were taken over by Polish authorities.

In the midst of this forced evacuation, the Synod of the Evangelical Church of Silesia met for the last time in Breslau on July 22 and 23, 1946, with forty Church districts from east of the Neisse River represented. On the Sunday just before this, each congregation had conducted a special commissioning service, in which its delegate had been sent out with prayer and with the laying on of hands. Meeting for the last time as a complete Church family, the synod received the report of the Church leadership and passed resolutions concerning the new order of the Church. It directed a special message to the few parishes that remained within Silesia, and also to the people who, like the ancient Israelites, were about to leave their Jerusalem for the land of exile.

After greeting the congregations with the words of the apostolic blessing, the synod called upon them to look back in gratitude as the undeserving heirs of a thousand years of the proclamation of the Gospel in Silesia. Four hundred years had passed since the Reformation, and during these centuries their people had been permitted to build churches and chapels, parish houses and institutions of mercy. God had sent generations of spirit-filled pastors and teachers, hymn writers and church musicians. Pastor's wives and deaconesses, Church elders and parishioners had served in faith and in patience, in times of suffering and need.

In spite of this ministry of grace and goodness which had been so richly present through the years, the synod confessed that the Name of God had not always been hallowed as it ought to have been, that there had been too much seeking of self, and too much confidence in earthly instruments of security. In humble repentance the Church professed itself ready to be subjected to the hidden will of God.

In the afflictions of the present times echoed the words of the eternal God, spoken to Abraham: "Go from your country and your kindred and your father's house to the land that I will show you."

With a realism tempered by faith in God, this Church on the threshold of exile declared, "We know that we are ensnared by sin and death, and that we have here on earth no abiding city." Such knowledge and such faith would bind together the believing brethren of Silesia wherever they might be, whether they remained in their homes, whether they had already gone into other lands, or whether they were yet to go.

Those who were to remain in the homeland received a special greeting, and the promise that the Church would continue to preach the Word and administer the sacraments, and would stand by the faithful, whether in the joy of the marriage altar or in the solemn moment of bereavement. The fellowship of faith would be carried on in churches and in homes, in stables and in barns, in cellars and in every hidden corner. Even if there should no longer be pastors, the Church would summon its elders, its laymen, its baptized members—every person whose heart was aflame for the Lord Christ. To such as these the Church sent out its farewell challenge: Put your hand to the plow! Do not look back! Plow a new furrow!

The Silesian Church, in the words of one of its own leaders, was learning the "great art of dying."

This was, in fact, the fate of the Evangelical Churches in the entire German area east of the Oder-Neisse Line. By the end of 1946 only a few scattered groups of Germans were left, where nine million had been a few months earlier. For the Protestant Church this represented one of the most serious territorial losses since the Reformation. Provinces such as East Prussia and Pomerania had been well over 90 per cent Protestant, and the combined population that replaced the Germans was practically 100 per cent Roman Catholic. Church buildings and other property which had been Protestant since the Reformation were taken over by the Roman Catholic Church. Though the Potsdam Agreement stated specifically that the areas east of the Oder-Neisse Line were simply to be placed under Polish administration, pending the completion of a treaty of peace with Germany, it seems clear that in the minds of both Poles and Russians the matter is closed. The legend of the voluntary resettlement of these nine million Germans is still maintained, buttressed by a strict prohibition by the Soviet Military Government, dated October 8, 1945, against the use of the word "refugee" in connection with the "emigrants" from the eastern provinces.

For whatever reasons they came, these millions contributed substantially to the chaotic conditions prevailing at the time of the surrender and for many months thereafter, particularly in East Germany, but also in many parts of the western zones. Governmental machinery, from the national to the local level, ceased to function. Postal and transportation systems were paralyzed. Hundreds of thousands of soldiers were taken as prisoners of war, and still other thousands were rounded up and sent to Russia and Poland in labor battalions. With the military structure in complete collapse and a large part of the manpower either under military or political detention, the entire productive economy ground to a halt. Cities and towns lay in ruins, and even the countryside and the farmhouses had been plundered and looted by the onrushing troops. Into the midst of this utter confusion and chaos streamed the millions of refugees and the hundreds of thousands of people who had been evacuated from the cities, and who now sought to return to their homes after the fighting was over.

In Berlin, where the resistance of the Nazis continued until the Russian troops entered the city on April 22nd and fought through rubble-choked streets into the very heart of the capital, death stalked through smoking ruins and toppling walls, making little distinction between civilians and men in uniform. Surrender on May 8th was a welcome relief, but violence and death remained long after as the grim supervisors of the conquered city. Plunderings and rapings and murders of civilians went on for days, until the Russian military administration could tighten the reins on the victory-crazed troops. This was not only true in Berlin, but in village and farm communities as well, as attested by hundreds of documented firsthand accounts.

Although the victorious Allies wasted no time in making administrative arrangements for the conquered areas and restoring law and order, it was impossible to prevent the despair, the physical suffering, and the widespread toll of disease and starvation. The destruction of the war, the indiscriminate foraging and plundering of the invading troops, the swollen populations, and the complete breakdown of the economy in East Germany rendered the problem of food supply acute. The rationing schedule adopted by the Soviet Military Government on November 1, 1945, varied from a minimum of 1,050 calories per day to a maximum of 1,520, depending upon the opportunities available for people to secure supplementary unrationed commodities.

Card V was known in Berlin as the "cemetery card," and was designated for housewives, unemployed, ill and aged people. Its daily one pound of bread, ¾ ounce of meat, 2 grams of fat, one ounce of cereal, ¾ ounce of sugar, and one pound of potatoes totaled theoretically 1,500 calories. One cup of milk a day was made available for children, but even at best, half of Berlin's 490,000 school children got no breakfast whatever, and only 30 per cent got a single warm meal a day. The death rate in Berlin rose from a normal figure of 150 a day to 2,000 a day in May, 1945, and 4,000 a day in August. If the death rate of August, 1945, had continued for a year, half of the city of Berlin would have been wiped out.

Conditions in Berlin were bad enough, but in comparison to the Russian Zone it was virtually an oasis. The worst distress area of all was the fifty-mile zone around Berlin, where the refugees surged back and forth without food and without shelter. A city such as Frankfurt an der Oder, just thirty miles east of Berlin and a gateway for the endless stream which poured in from the East, placed a forty-eight hour time limit upon all refugees. There had to be room for tomorrow's transients. By the end of October, 360,000 refugees had passed through this city, which was described by an Evangelical Church superintendent who returned there in September as nothing but "cauterized walls." One medical doctor, equipped with a single operating knife and a pair of scissors, but no bandages, tried to care for the two hundred to three hundred patients who slept on the straw-littered floor of the "hospital." In the month of November alone, 4,500 people died in Frankfurt an der Oder, and most of them were unknown. Only three pastors of the original fifteen were left, and in the two remaining church buildings on the edge of the city, they conducted one hundred funerals a week.

Even the farmers in Pomerania lived on rations. Harvests were 100 per cent requisitioned, and no fat was available. In one village only one cow was left of five hundred, and in another, two out of six hundred. At the end of November, 35,000 people in Mecklenburg had typhus, and hospitals simply couldn't take care of the patients. Suicides mounted, and the dead were stripped to provide clothing for the living. In Rostock a two-horse dray made the rounds to collect bodies, which were wrapped in blackout paper for want of caskets.

It was in a ministry of mercy to these masses of suffering and dying people that the Churches and pastors of East Germany found their first great opportunity for service as they emerged into the postwar era. During these first weeks there was no problem of prohibitions against Church work. In fact, in many communities the Russian commanders summoned the leading ministers and either ordered or requested them to proceed with their work. The Communist mayor of Dresden, where twenty-seven Protestant churches were destroyed, called Pastor Lau and said, "Now the Churches must resume their work, too." To be sure, there were also reports from those who claimed they had to hold worship in secret, with neither singing nor organ music, because worshippers would be hauled off to work in the fields, and others reported that their homes were looted while they were in church.

More than 60 per cent of all German clergymen had been inducted into regular military service during the war, mostly as common soldiers or officers rather than as chaplains. As the war ended, therefore, the parishes were badly undermanned, and often served either by older men or by laymen, or in some cases by the pastors' wives. In any case, these pastors gave themselves unstintingly to the relief of the misery which surrounded them on every hand. The spacious parsonages of Pomerania and Mecklenburg, insofar as they remained standing, were turned into refuges for homeless wanderers. Near Greifswald, in Pomerania, Superintendent Liesenhof established a center for refugees, which developed into one of the very fine Church institutions of the East Zone, called the Suessow Homes.

"The German population," reported Stewart Herman after his first visit to postwar Berlin in 1945, "found its only consolation and aid in the pastors who stood fast and were permitted to continue their Christian services. From the very first days after the Russian entry the pastors saw to the care of the ill and the children, as well as to the burial of the dead who lay about in the houses or on the

streets." The pastors of Pomerania, testified one of the leading laymen of that Church, truly acted as "shepherds of the flock."

But these Churches in East Germany had also to rebuild their
organizations in the midst of all of this suffering and confusion. The
constitutions and the synods which had been in operation before
1933 were not functioning. New synods would have to be chosen,
but such elections could hardly be held in the confusion of the
weeks following the surrender. Fortunately, there had been in existence all during the Nazi period an "illegal" organization of pastors
called the Council of the Brethren, representing the "Confessing
Church." This group had actually managed to hold synods and to
carry on a Church administration beside that of the official one,
which was under Nazi control. Since the finances of the Churches
were also under State control, these "illegal" organizations were supported entirely by free-will contributions of loyal Church members.

Some felt these organizations should simply continue their functions and become the official Churches. They enjoyed the confidence
of the people, and because of their unofficial character they had been
able to emphasize a congregational fellowship among the Christian
people of a community much more than had been possible in the
official Church, with its rather ponderous institutional structure and
its close ties with the State.

However, the older traditions prevailed, and in each of the so-
called Landeskirchen, or Provincial Churches, pastors and lay leaders
of the Confessing Church, many of whom had been ousted from
positions in the pre-1933 Provincial Churches, stepped in to replace
the "German-Christian" or Nazi leadership, which was now completely discredited. These temporary structures were accepted by the
congregations, and then later confirmed by regularly elected synods,
most of which met in 1946.

The constituent provinces of the Old Prussian Church, which had
been the largest of the Protestant Churches in pre-Hitler Germany,
now became separate organizations, retaining only a loose federative
relationship which they called the Old Prussian Union. All the
Churches in the Soviet Zone established the new office of Bishop,
with the exception of the small province of Anhalt which preferred
the title of Church President. Eight separate Churches emerged
from this process. Berlin-Brandenburg, Pomerania, Silesia, and the

Province of Saxony were all formerly parts of the Prussian Church. Mecklenburg, Thuringia, Anhalt, and the former State of Saxony had been separate Churches before. Pomerania and Silesia were radically reduced in size because of the expulsion of Germans from east of the Oder and Neisse rivers, and Brandenburg, too, suffered some territorial loss. Numerically, the largest of the Churches was Berlin-Brandenburg, with 4,700,000 members and 1,327 pastors; smallest was the tiny remnant of Silesia, with 230,000 members and 81 pastors.

The Church of Berlin-Brandenburg was reorganized at the earliest possible moment after the capitulation of the city. The leading spirit in this movement was Dr. Otto Dibelius, who had been ousted by the Nazis in 1933 from his position as general superintendent of the Kurmark, the highest office of spiritual leadership within the Church Province of Brandenburg. For twelve years Dr. Dibelius had been active in the Confessing Church movement, though much of the time he was under the careful surveillance of the Gestapo, and consequently limited in the functions he could perform.

On May 7, 1945, the very day on which the unconditional surrender of Germany was tendered to General Eisenhower in Rheims, Dr. Dibelius, acting according to the plan previously agreed upon by the Prussian Council of the Brethren, gathered the leaders of the Confessing Church in the parish house of St. Paul's Church in Zehlendorf and formed the new Consistory of the Church of Berlin-Brandenburg. A smaller committee of the consistory was constituted as the Church Leadership, and since the offices of the Church were either destroyed or badly damaged, temporary quarters were secured in the Burckhardt House, YWCA center in the suburb of Dahlem.

One of the reasons Dibelius was eager to reorganize the Church structure so quickly was to prevent any possible attempts to bring the Evangelical Church under political control. This motivation was fully in keeping with the principles of the Confessing Church, whose Synod of Barmen in 1934 had adopted the ringing declaration that the Church of Jesus Christ should never again be made the tool of the State for the carrying out of political objectives.

As chairman of the new Church Leadership, Dr. Dibelius then presented himself to General Bersarin, the Russian commandant, and was recognized by him as the official representative of the Evangelical Church in Berlin. Since the other general superintendencies of the Province of Brandenburg were vacant, Dibelius also assumed the right to speak on their behalf, and therefore employed the title of Evangelical Bishop of Berlin. This was a completely new office, and it was not until a vigorous discussion had taken place in the first Provincial Synod of Brandenburg in October, 1946, that it was given final approval by the Church. As head of the largest of the old Prussian Church provinces, Dibelius also was called upon to advise in the selection of the consistories in the other provinces, and subsequently became the president of the Evangelical Church of the Old Prussian Union.

In July and October, 1945, the two Confessional synods of Berlin and Brandenburg met and gave their approval of the new Church Leadership, thus returning the Church functions which the Councils of the Brethren had exercised temporarily for the past ten years. These synods, composed of the men who had fought the good fight of faith against the attempts of Nazism to dominate the Church, might pardonably have felt some satisfaction in the dramatic collapse of the "German-Christians" and the reemergence of the faithful after the long night of persecution.

There was none of this, however, in the opening sermon preached by Superintendent Albertz at the Brandenburg Synod in October. Instead, he admonished the assembled congregation to see, in the darkness of the ruins and the death that covered Germany like a pall, the righteous judgment of God. The patriarch Jacob, returning to his homeland following the deception of his father and the betrayal of his own brother, had wrestled all night in such darkness with an unknown power; and then, as the dawn broke, had discovered that he had been contending against God himself. This had also been the plight of the German people, including the Church, and now they must recognize their guilt, plead for forgiveness and blessing from God, and then go and seek reconciliation with the brethren they had betrayed.

In its message to its pastors and congregations, the Berlin Synod (also called the Spandau Synod) did officially recognize the guilt of the past twelve years and summon Church and people to repentance. The tragedy and deep humiliation of Germany, it declared, were that the events since 1933 could take place in a country in which 90 per cent of the people were baptized Christians. The active sin of Nazism must be recognized, and likewise the passive sin of all Christendom in Germany, that a more vigorous resistance had not been carried on against flagrant violations of God's Law.

But God in his mercy had also given to the Church a new beginning. The past misuse of God's Word had brought to the Church a greater awareness of its real depth. A new group of young pastors had arisen out of the Confessing Church. Congregations had experienced the meaning of the fellowship of suffering.

This gratitude for a new beginning was not an unrealistic attempt to ignore bitter facts. It would be a long time before anything approaching normality would characterize the life of this or of any of the Churches of East Germany. Eighty per cent of the church buildings in Berlin had been destroyed or badly damaged. Transportation was so paralyzed that it was impossible even to visit all the congregations in the province. Many pastors had received no salary at all since May 1, 1945. But the repentant and reborn Church was ready to see, even in the midst of overwhelming physical and spiritual privation, opportunities for service and for Christian witness that it had often failed to recognize in better times.

Three tasks stood out above all others in the eyes of the Spandau Synod. The first of these was to proclaim the Word of the Gospel to a people which had been torn from its self-created role of the Chosen People and awakened to find itself defeated and despised by the whole world, and to save this people from bitterness, hatred, and despair. The second task was directed toward the youth of Germany, which had been confiscated by a totalitarian State and schooled to pride and arrogance. These young people must be guided to a true understanding of freedom and self-respect in the light of the Gospel. Finally, from its own position in the midst of a people whose families had been decimated, and whose houses and homes were gone, the Church must carry on a ministry of love and mercy.

In one particular respect the Spandau Synod was the bearer of a prophetic word for the Churches of eastern Germany. Just as in America the historical development of the nation had given to the American people the pattern of multiple denominations, each with its own group of voluntary supporters, European history had handed to the German people the pattern of the institutional Church, closely related to, and oftentimes even identified with the State. The confessional character of the numerous small German principalities had since the days of the Reformation been determined by the ruling prince; and the administration of the Church had been handled from above, under the supervision of the prince and his ecclesiastical advisers.

With the end of the German Empire in 1918, the direct union between Church and State in Germany was severed, but responsibility for Church affairs did not pass automatically to local congregations. The thought patterns of several centuries were not so easily changed. The provincial Churches of Germany after 1918 remained as institutional Churches, administered from above. Close relations were still maintained with the State, which continued to make its taxgathering machinery available for the collection of Church dues from every citizen. This benevolent service of the State became the device through which the Nazi government was able to gain control of much of the Church administrative machinery in 1934.

One of the greatest blessings which was brought to the Church in Germany through the "illegal" resistance movement called the Confessing Church was the realization that it was possible to find a self-conscious unity on the level of the congregation. Christian people found their common bond not merely in their residence in a given district or their responsibility to a particular tax office, but in loyalty to the Lordship of Christ and the authority of His Gospel as over against the claims of the totalitarian State.

This unity also found expression in a willingness to undertake the personal direct financial support of the Church organization and the pastoral ministry which resisted the State. One thousand young pastors in the Prussian Church—one-seventh of its entire ministry—had been trained in secret seminaries and supported by an annual contribution from Church members, totaling two million marks a year.

When the Spandau Synod looked forward to a renewal of the Church, it expressed the hope that this principle of congregational responsibility might be retained and enriched. If the Church administrations of an earlier day had been in closer touch with the congregations, and had been truly representative of the lay Christians in the Church, the Nazi government would never have been able to overawe them and manipulate them as it did. "The entire pretension of a secularized Volkskirche," declared the synod, "which demands all kinds of vows and pledges, at baptisms, confirmations, ordinations and installations of Church elders—but fails to be concerned about their fulfillment, and simply rests on the illusion of general custom—was laid open through the Church struggle."

There were some indications that these lessons would be applied in the reconstruction of the German provincial Churches after 1945, perhaps more in the East than in the West. But in spite of such open and bravely prophetic voices as that of the Spandau Synod, which certainly represented a forward-looking rather than a backward-looking spirit, the reorganized Churches of postwar Germany bore a striking similarity to those of the pre-Hitler era. The similarity today, in 1960, is even more striking in West Germany, and such changes as have taken place in the eastern Churches, in such essential areas as Church finance and education, have come about under the continued pressures of a Communist government rather than as the enlightened and forward-looking decisions of Churches eager to break new ground in a new age.

THREE

THE NEW POLITICAL CLIMATE

The Church in postwar Germany, just as every other phase of German life, has been profoundly influenced by the division of the land into four separate zones of occupation. According to both the Yalta and Potsdam agreements, this pattern was to be a temporary one, pending the readiness of Germany to resume a peaceful role in the family of nations. Instead, the past fifteen years have witnessed a hardening of these temporary divisions into a permanent partition of East and West Germany. That it became permanent may in large part be laid to the failure of the western Allies to realize soon enough the serious political intentions of the Soviet Union regarding its own zone of occupation, and indeed, for the whole of Germany and western Europe. Cooperation in reconstructing a conquered land and people, the Americans were to discover, demanded agreement and understanding of a much more fundamental nature than that required in fighting a common enemy. The trusting assumption that such understanding existed between the United States and Russia in 1945 was the tragic blunder of Yalta and Potsdam.

The boundaries of the occupation zones in Germany and the

special joint-occupation status of Berlin had been agreed upon as early as the second Quebec Conference, in September, 1944. When the conquest of Germany had been completed, the Russian armies had taken Berlin, while the Americans had pushed eastward to the Elbe River, more than one hundred miles inside the projected Russian zone of occupation. In keeping with previous agreements, American and British forces withdrew from the Soviet Occupation Zone on July 1, 1945, while the Russians turned over to the western Allies the occupation sectors assigned to them within the capital city of Berlin.

The three-power European Advisory Commission, which had been meeting for several months in London in 1944, had agreed that immediately following the German capitulation the four commanders in chief were to meet in Berlin and issue three documents. The first document would declare that the four victorious powers assumed full governmental authority in Germany. The second would give to each commander supreme authority in his zone. These commanders were to meet regularly as an Allied Control Council, under rotating chairmanship, to deal with matters affecting Germany as a whole, and to administer Berlin as a four-power city. The third proclamation was to announce the boundaries of the four zones of occupation and the joint occupation of Berlin.

These documents were signed and issued in Berlin on June 5, 1945, by General Eisenhower, Marshal Zhukov, Field Marshal Montgomery, and General de Tassigny. Thereafter the way was open for each of the powers to introduce in its zone of occupation whatever measures it felt would best achieve the common purposes for Germany, as agreed at Yalta.

Since the Russians were first in Berlin, it fell to them to take initial steps to secure order. General Bersarin established his headquarters in Lichtenberg on April 28th, and immediately appointed civilian mayors for the various boroughs of Berlin. Dr. Arthur Werner was appointed as lord mayor, and although he was not a Communist, nine of the eighteen city councilors and several of the key officials in the new city administration were members of the old German Communist Party (KPD). Colonel Paul Markgraf, who later developed the People's Police, was made police president. Most of these officials were at first recognized by the western Allies when they entered Berlin on July 1st, though they quickly eliminated the street, house, and block officials who had been set up by the Communists.

Both in Berlin and in their zone of occupation outside the city, the Soviets immediately introduced their program of political reorientation. As organizer they selected an old-line German Communist named Walter Ulbricht, who had spent the war years in Moscow. From the days of his boyhood in Leipzig, Ulbricht had moved in Communist circles. During the period between the two world wars, he had at various times been a district party secretary in Saxony, Thuringia, and Berlin, and a member of both the Central Committee and the Military Committee of the German KPD. He had done agitation work in Austria, and served as the German representative on the Executive Committee of the Comintern in Moscow.

In 1930 he had been jailed for two years for high treason, and after his release migrated to Moscow, by way of Prague and Paris. After the war began, he organized the program for the reeducation of German war prisoners, and helped found the Communist-oriented National Committee for a Free Germany. Berlin had not yet capitulated when he arrived on April 29, 1945, to resume political activity in his native land. The arrival of Walter Ulbricht in Berlin on the very day that his archenemy Adolf Hitler committed suicide was only an ironic coincidence, but it provides a dramatic emphasis to the impatience of the Russians in beginning the serious job of political reeducation in conquered Germany.

Tailored to the needs of the moment was the program of the party, as announced by Ulbricht on June 11th. "We believe that it would be a wrong course of action to force Germany to adopt the Soviet system, because this course is not appropriate to the present state of development in Germany. The best interests of the German people call for a different way—namely, the establishment of an antifascist, democratic regime, a parliamentary-democratic republic with all the democratic rights and freedoms for the people."

Specific facets of the program called for the end of agitation and enmity toward the Soviet Union; free democratic election of labor representatives in the factories; and the confiscation of the property of the Nazis, war criminals, and large landowners.

The close cooperation of all other antifascist, democratic parties was earnestly solicited, and although the Christian Democratic Union (CDU), the German Liberal Party (LPD), and the German Socialist Party (SPD) had their own traditions and programs, they were urged by the Soviet Military Government to form a united front with the KPD. By April, 1946, the SPD had been forced to merge with the KPD to form a new party called the Socialist Unity Party (SED), which thereafter was the official standard-bearer of the Soviet Union. All other parties have since joined in a National Front with the SED, for the purpose of drawing up uniform lists of candidates for all elections.

The fact that this entire program of political reorientation in the Soviet Zone could be introduced under the apparent blessing of the Potsdam Agreement indicates what a deep chasm actually separated the political thinking of eastern and western Allies. More tragically, it also reflected an ill-fated optimistic tendency on the part of the Americans to minimize these differences, and to assume that when the Russians spoke of the "reestablishment of German political life upon a democratic foundation" they put the same content into these terms as did the western world.

For an American a "democratic" government is unquestionably one which is based upon free political expression and free and open elections. The Soviet regime has allowed neither of these, and has nevertheless insisted that it was working toward the "democratization" of East Germany, in keeping with the Potsdam Agreement.

The relations of the Churches with the Soviet regime in these early postwar days were surprisingly cordial. As the armies moved into one community after the other, the treatment of pastors and Churches was naturally very different. Many pastors and priests succumbed to the anticipated terrors of Russian violence, and fled ahead of the armies. Others stayed, and experienced the full brunt of brutality and violence, seeing their churches desecrated and burned, and their parishioners and families robbed and raped and murdered. Still others, however, discovered a respect for Christian symbols among the Russian troops, and in some localities the pastors and Church workers donned white armbands with purple crosses and the word for "priest" in Russian. Out of the confusion of reports concerning the behavior of Russian combat troops toward the clergy and the Church, it seems at least clear that there was no official Russian policy of either liquidation or desecration.

The actions of individual commandants in various sectors occupied by the Russians tend to confirm this conclusion. One pastor in a small community in Mecklenburg recalled the indiscriminate plundering that went on for several weeks after the arrival of the Russian troops. Even an ancient Cistercian monastery in the town was burned, because it had allegedly housed members of the nobility, though the last of them had died or moved away 150 years earlier. The pastor recalled how his books were ripped apart and even his clerical clothes were stolen before order was established by the Russian commandant. But when the commandant arrived, he immediately invited the pastor to his office, asked what complaints he had, and ordered him supplied with a bicycle to replace the one that had been confiscated, so that he could make the rounds in his parish ministry.

A superintendent in Frankfurt an der Oder recalled gratefully the efforts of the Russian commandant to secure the use of a hall for Church services which had been requisitioned as a soldiers' club.

The first city government established for Berlin on May 17, 1945, by General Bersarin, included a special office for Church affairs, and when the time came to open the public schools the general told the newly appointed Lord Mayor Werner that he wanted the children brought up "in the fear of the Lord." Responsible for the Protestant Churches in this office was Dr. Heinrich Grueber, who had spent several years in Nazi concentration camps, because of his unremitting aid to the Jews. The Catholics were represented by Pastor Buchholz, whose dedicated ministry as prison pastor in Berlin-Tegel had earned the gratitude of many other victims of Nazi violence.

Not only in the Berlin city government, but also in the Soviet Military Administration, there prevailed in these early times a very friendly attitude toward the Church. The reason for this is clear. The Russians were aware that within the Church a lively resistance had been carried on against the Nazi State, and that great numbers of churchmen, both Protestant and Roman Catholic, had paid the price of their opposition in the grim fellowship of Sachsenhausen, Buchenwald, and Dachau. In these same concentration camps, though for different reasons, many leading German Communists had suffered similarly.

The men who were selected by General Bersarin for the first city administration in Berlin were, according to Dr. Grueber, largely those who had been in concentration camps or prisons, or who had in some way taken part in the resistance movement: "In the camps we had looked together into the eyes of death; now we wanted to face the problems of life together. The brotherly 'du,' which had bound us together as one during our prison days, had an even deeper and more beautiful sound in the clear air of freedom. The confidence which the occupation powers placed in us was just as great as our own desire to cooperate with them."

This so-called "concentration camp effect" on the relations between the Russian occupation authorities and the Church lasted from 1945 to about 1948. In fact, until 1950 one cannot speak of a real Church struggle in East Germany, except against the physical and spiritual privations which came as the result of Nazism and the war. During these years there were, of course, fundamental differences between the Communists and the Church, but these differences never came into open conflict. In January, 1947, at the Conference on Culture, sponsored by the Communist SED, it was openly declared: "The brave conduct of a part of the clergy in the struggle against the barbarism of Hitler has also earned the recognition and respect of Socialist laborers. Faith and Socialism are not the antagonists that some would arbitrarily make them. The position of the party toward religion is one of absolute tolerance. That which Christianity seeks from faith, Socialism seeks from knowledge. In their efforts to achieve their eminently secular objectives, the Socialists have no desire to misuse the Church in a propagandistic manner."

Most leaders of the Confessing Church, however, emerged from their bout with Nazism with a deep distrust of all government, and would scarcely have been prepared to place the degree of confidence in the Communist-sponsored government that Grueber did, regardless of common sufferings in concentration camps and regardless of the blandishments of party leaders. Lenin's writings on religion were not unknown, nor was the tragic history of the Christian Church in Soviet Russia in the period of the 1920's and the 1930's entirely forgotten.

However, the Churches in eastern Germany, emerging from the rubble and ruin in 1945 and attempting to recover and rebuild, could only be thankful that they had this brief respite before the new totalitarianism was clamped down upon the East Zone. They did have time to reorganize their Church structures, to elect their new synods, and to establish ties with their spiritual brethren in West Germany and in the ecumenical world. They did have time to begin the arduous task of ministering to the physical needs of their own people and of the millions of refugees who came swirling into their midst. All that was accomplished in these respects between 1945 and 1950 appears in the light of subsequent developments as a pure gift of God's grace.

Each of the four occupying powers established a special office within its Military Government Administration for the handling of questions pertaining to the Churches, but made it clear in the Potsdam Agreement that they had no intentions of interfering with their internal operations or with the exercise of full religious freedom. Religious affairs were handled by the Soviets under the supervision of Colonel Tulpanov, chief cultural officer, and directly by Captain Yermolajev, who served for four years as the religious-affairs officer of the Soviet Military Government. It would be difficult to judge whether Captain Yermolajev or Miss Mary Bailey, the British religious-affairs officer, was held in higher esteem by the leaders of the German Churches in Berlin. Both of them displayed a degree of tact and understanding which, together with their knowledge of the German language, enabled them to render outstanding services both to the hard-pressed German Churches and to their own governments. In most instances the religious-affairs offices were able to render their most effective services in facilitating some phase of the Church's work, in solving some individual or special problem such as the securing of a travel permit, or simply in providing a listening ear for some discouraged pastor. The willingness to do this kind of service, and the personal interest shown by an official of an occupation government, achieved more in the easing of tensions and the promotion of peace and harmonious relations than any number of directives and regulations issued without the human touch.

Although the policy of the Soviet authorities toward the German Church was in general one of friendliness and noninterference, they were by no means indifferent to the Church and the potential of its clergy. The two main general themes of Soviet policy in Germany were antifascism and democracy, and within this framework there

was a role which the Russians hoped and expected that the Church
would play.

The common aim of the Allies had been to destroy every vestige
of Nazism in Germany, and measures were drafted to achieve this
goal in all zones of occupation. This was not an easy matter, for although there were complete card files on all members of the Nazi
Party and its affiliate organizations, it was very difficult to evaluate
the degree of allegiance and activity displayed by various party members. Some had joined the party in the early years, before they realized
the direction it would take, and then had subsequently severed their
connections. Others had joined after 1937, and done so in full awareness of their action. In the later years of the war, the whole membership of the Hitler Youth, which was virtually compulsory for all
children, was automatically transferred into the Nazi Party at the
age of eighteen. The question of how to treat these various grades of
affiliation with the movement was a very complicated one, and the
rather arbitrary handling of it by the Allies was not a convincing
demonstration of the operation of democracy under the law.

The Church began the process of eliminating Nazis from the ranks
of its clergy and lay leadership as soon as the fighting was over. The
Nazi leadership in most of the Churches simply collapsed, and members of the Confessing Church took over the reins and continued
the process of self-purification. When the occupation authorities,
therefore, introduced their formal systems of denazification, the
Churches could say that they were already well along in the process.

In the Soviet Zone the official denazification process began with
the order from the Military Administration that all former army
officers or members of the Nazi Party, the SS, the SA, or the Gestapo
should report to the local Russian military commandant before September 25, 1945. This introduced a wave of arrests and deportations
throughout the Soviet Zone which went far beyond that of the western Allies.

On the ground of the resistance record of its new leadership, the
Church demanded and finally secured the right to carry its own denazification process on to completion. The position of the Church
committees was that party membership, since it was not in itself an
offense against the Church, could not be regarded as a ground for
Church discipline. Affiliation with the "German-Christian" move-

ment, however, was a Church offense, inasmuch as this movement involved the betrayal of ordination vows and the confessions of the Church. On this basis the Church commissions operated, with the result that some pastors who had not been members of the Nazi Party were nevertheless suspended from office because of membership in the German-Christian movement. On the other hand, there were some party members, even some who had special distinctions and certifications in the party, but were not affiliated with the German-Christians, who were permitted to retain their pastoral, offices.

The Church was required to give reports to the occupation authorities, but the Soviets never forced their way into the denazification procedures of the Church. Many pastors and lay officials who were disciplined by the Church never again resumed their positions. But on the premise that for the truly repentant the Church should always be ready to extend forgiveness, many pastors were eventually restored to office, and are presently serving congregations in East and West Germany. In the light of the spiritual defection of these mature men, and the consequent harm done, especially to children and young people, by their unfaithfulness, the Churches in Germany might well have exercised more rigid policies toward these men. The Church surely has no right to withhold forgiveness from any truly repentant person. But to restore to the office of teaching and preaching a person who in his mature years has been led astray into open perversion of the Gospel is to render a highly questionable service to the Church.

The friendly noninterference policy of the Soviets toward the Church did not rule out attempts to solicit the support of pastors and Church members in cultural and political programs on the local level. The first organization to appear in the Soviet Zone after the war ended was called Antifa (Antifascist). Claiming to be carrying out the terms of the Potsdam Agreement and to be working to uproot the last remnants of Nazism in the communities, it held conferences, small meetings, and discussions, and offered services and advice to people who needed them during the first days of extreme economic and social chaos. Its leaders were sometimes local Communists, but just as frequently they were people from the outside, brought into the communities. Recognizing that in many communities the pastor was the most influential figure, Antifa tried to win the pastors to the support of its program and thus to extend its influence into the congregations. Generally speaking, these efforts met with small success among the clergy.

Just as denazification belonged to the "antifascistic" phase of the Soviet program for East Germany, land reform expressed its "democratic" objectives. In many of the East German provinces, the large farm, or landed estate, had been the accepted agricultural pattern for many generations. The owner of the farm, which might be as large as twelve hundred to fifteen hundred acres, was frequently a member of the old nobility. He employed several farmers to work his land, provided them with living quarters, and gave them the right to maintain a few cows and pigs, and to feed them in his buildings. In addition to the wages he received from the owner, the farmer also was permitted to maintain a small garden plot of his own. In this old, semi-feudal pattern, the owner of the estate was often also the patron of the Church and, as such, paid the salary of the pastor.

When the Russians moved in, they immediately introduced a reform of this old land system. Landowners either fled to the West or were rounded up and put into camps. Some were deported or even executed as whole families.

In early September, 1945, the State administrations throughout the Russian-occupied zone issued decrees declaring that all farms and estates larger than 250 acres were to be confiscated without compensation, divided into thirty-acre tracts, and distributed among farm laborers and refugees. Arrangements were made whereby these people might farm the land without any payment for five years, and then begin monthly or yearly payments on the land until it should belong to them. The dispossessed owners were given orders to leave the district immediately.

Farmers who owned tracts of less than 250 acres were allowed to keep them, unless they had been active members of the Nazi Party, in which case they were dispossessed, regardless of the size of their holdings. Some landowners who had been active anti-Nazis, but whose holdings were in excess of 250 acres, thought they might have been permitted to retain at least a small tract, but they too were completely uprooted.

The manner in which this land reform was carried through illustrates very clearly the procedural techniques employed in the soviet-

ization of East Germany. In this early stage, immediately following
the conquest of an area of older social and economic patterns, the first
step was to destroy the so-called reactionary class, and to distribute its
holdings among the peasants and workers as their own private possession. Not only was this action expected to rid the land of political
and economic opposition, but it would presumably also gain the support of large numbers of small farmers, who would regard this concern for their individual welfare as evidence of the sincerely democratic character of the new regime.

That this was the official party line for this particular stage of the
process was clearly stated by Edwin Hoernle, president of the Communist Administration for Agriculture and Forestry, in an address
before the Communist Party in Berlin on September 19, 1945.
"Among the secret and open opponents of the land reform," he declared, "are some who call themselves Marxists, and assert that the
land which has been taken from the Junkers ought not to be distributed among the small farmers. They say we should rather create
State farms, or at least large collectively administered farms. Whatever else these people may be, they are certainly not Marxists. . . .
They refuse to understand that the important thing at this moment
is to fulfill at last the old dream of every German peasant and farm
worker, the dream of owning his own little piece of ground. These
men will then be loyal to a democratic Germany as long as they live."

In keeping with the principle that whatever furthers the development of Socialism is morally right, there would be ample time to
extol the virtues of the collective farm system at a later stage of the
economic and political development of East Germany.

In the midst of a situation which affected the lives and possessions
of so many of their members, the Churches in East Germany felt
impelled to speak. This was not an easy decision, for sharp criticism
of the policies of the occupation powers might have the result of
worsening conditions for members of the Church rather than improving them. Moreover, the authorities might well raise the question
why the Church, which had been all too silent during the Nazi times,
should now feel impelled to speak up in criticism of the policies of
those who had finally destroyed the Nazi power. Moreover, many
churchmen felt that the principle of land reform was in itself not an

objectionable one, particularly in view of the influx of the millions of homeless and landless refugees.

The question of the obligation to speak out on public issues in which a moral principle is involved was one which would become increasingly important in the life of the East German Churches in the ensuing years. The tragic silences of the past could hardly warrant additional silences on new issues, else the lessons of the past would have been in vain. Whatever the cost might be, the Church must speak, but it must temper its sharpest critiques with a spirit of love and humility.

The Churches of North Germany: Mecklenburg, Pomerania, and Brandenburg, in whose territory most of the large landed estates were located, were naturally the first to speak on the subject of land reform. The Church authorities in Schwerin, in Mecklenburg, issued a statement on October 1, 1945, which recognized the necessity of providing land for the farmers and refugees, so that they might work and produce food for the swollen populations, but registered sharp disapproval of arbitrary and unjust confiscations.

The Confessional Synod of Brandenburg, which met later in October, discussed some of the practical problems of land reform before issuing its official statement. It noted that in some areas local officials who carried out the reform were calling upon the pastor to give his official blessing to the action. Such a word by the pastor could conceivably involve his public approval of the confiscation of the lands of his own patron, who was the bulwark of the local congregation. Yet if a pastor refused to take part, he might be regarded as a reactionary defender of the "old order," which the Communists identified with fascism and Nazi exploitation.

The Brandenburg Synod also accepted the reform as inevitable, and sought to interpret it as a possible blessing to the landless farmers and laborers streaming in from east of the Oder River. The Church avoided any basic judgment of the political-economic aspects of the question, but strongly emphasized the importance of observing God's laws and commands in the administration of such a sweeping reform.

The State authorities were reminded that an irresponsible use of power carries a curse within itself, and that blessing comes only where righteousness and goodness prevail. In spite of the land hunger of the refugees, the legal rights of the landowners should be respected. To drive out honorable men from their homes as beggars would be a violation of the law of God. If estates were to be divided, proper compensation should be provided, and the whole process should be carried out without the accompaniment of offensive talk and the disparagement and dishonor of a whole class of people.

Recognizing again the inevitability of the action, the Church addressed a comforting word to those who would have to give up their family homesteads. Instead of falling prey to bitterness and despair, they were admonished to recognize that their losses were by no means unique. Refugees and dwellers in the bombed-out cities had lost literally everything they had. Moreover, as Christian people, they dare not forget that the greatest treasure of all, namely, their faith in Almighty God, remained inviolable.

In keeping with the relatively favorable treatment accorded them by the Soviet military authorities, the Churches themselves were exempted from the operation of the land reform and were thus able to retain the considerable amount of landed property they possessed. In another phase of the Soviet program of "democratization," school reform, the Church found itself more directly affected.

The teachers of Germany, as a group, had been notoriously subservient to the slogans and doctrines of the Nazis, and the schools had been quickly appropriated as ideological training centers for the children and the youth of the "master race." When the Allied victory came, therefore, "reeducation," "reorientation," and "school reform" were written in large letters in the plans of all four occupation powers.

In the Russian Zone, teachers who had shown an inclination toward fascism and militarism through membership in the Nazi Party or its affiliates were rooted out, even though the supply of teachers was thereby seriously decimated. More important to the Soviets than a mastery of factual materials was an "antifascistic-democratic" spirit. consequently, large numbers of so-called *Neulehrer,* or "new teachers," between the ages of twenty-five and thirty-five, were appointed, even without pedagogical training. Special six-month courses were hurriedly set up, and those "new teachers" who successfully passed them and subsequently taught for one year were given permanent appointments in the public schools. The special courses began on October 15, 1945.

Of more direct concern to the Churches was the action of the Russians eliminating religious instruction from the public schools. For generations past it had been customary in Germany to regard religion as one of the standard subjects in the public schools. Instruction was given by the regular teachers, except in the upper grades, where the pastors came in to conduct several classes each week. This practice had been confirmed by the Weimar Constitution of 1919, and even during the years of National Socialism religious instruction had not been entirely driven out of the schools.

But Russian policy left no room for doubt. The City Council in Berlin adopted the following resolution, and similar regulations were announced in each of the East German States:

Proceeding from the consideration that German schools should no longer be torn by different creeds and ideologies, school will be separated from church. In the future, the religious or ideological education of the children will be the concern of religious bodies or ideological organizations.

Even the use of schoolrooms for religious instruction was no longer to be considered as normal procedure. In the event that no other facilities should be available, the local political authorities might make temporary provisions for the use of schoolrooms. But such arrangements were to be understood as matters of privilege, and not of right. Religious instruction was to be purely on a voluntary basis, and parents who wished their children to take part were to give written notice to the school authorities. If a regular schoolteacher wished to teach such classes, he might do so under regulations governing the "supplementary employment" of teachers. None of these regulations, declared the president of the Province of Mecklenburg-Pomerania, should be regarded under any circumstances as indicative of a hostile attitude toward the Church, but simply as a clear recognition of the principle that "religious or antireligious instruction is not the affair of the State, but of the ideological group or faith-community."

Principles of this kind have a very familiar ring in the ears of Americans, whose national tradition for almost two hundred years has been that of strict separation of Church and State. In Germany, however, where despite a formal separation very close relations prevailed between Church and State, especially in the field of education, these ideas were greeted with suspicion and some open hostility. Both Lutheran and Catholic bishops in Berlin raised strenuous objection, and even took public-opinion polls which showed that in thirteen of the twenty boroughs in Berlin, 85 to 100 per cent of the parents emphatically wanted religious instruction in the schools. Pastor Hans Lokies, the chairman of the Evangelical Church Committee on Education, wrote a letter to the City Council, objecting to the dereligionizing of the schools as an old Nazi policy which was now being imposed by undemocratic means. Cardinal von Preysing appealed to all Catholic parents to unite on the basis of democratic principles and freedom of conscience. He suggested that if nonreligious parents wanted nonreligious schools, they should ask for them.

Bishop Dibelius directed a pastoral letter to the parents of Berlin children on October 25, 1945, in which he expressed dismay that after a ten-year battle on behalf of the Christian faith the Church should again be confronted with an organized attempt to eliminate from the schools everything Christian in character. "The secular school which is now being introduced," declared the bishop, "is not a religiously neutral school. In education there is no neutrality in respect to the great questions of human life. The children must be given answers to these questions, one way or another! The secular school is clearly and unmistakably a school opposed to the Christian religion. In this we have had ample experience."

That the bishop's fears were well grounded has been attested with frightening clarity in the educational program of East Germany in the years since 1945. Begun under the guise of neutrality toward the Christian religion, the schools of the German Democratic Republic have been completely transformed into confessional schools of materialistic atheism.

The determination of the Russians to separate religion and public education, regardless of the opinions of the Church or of the parents, forced the Church to rethink its entire approach to religious education. In a State in which the ruler had been the traditional protector and at times even the legal head of the Church, the use of State-employed teachers for the giving of religious instruction in the schools could be supported with a certain logic. If, however, such a State should become alienated from the traditional doctrines and values of the Christian faith, and imbued with contrary ideologies, it could use its control of religious instruction with devastating effect upon the children, and thus upon the Church.

This was essentially what had happened during the National Socialist regime. Teachers who themselves were neither thoroughly grounded nor convinced Christians had neither the ability nor the courage to oppose the gradual infiltration of the curriculum with Nazi heresies deceptively couched in Christian terminology. That such a movement as the Confessing Church arose to meet this emergency was a testimony to the courageous faith and alertness of many of the pastors and laymen of the German Church. One could only wish that the experience gained in these critical years could have found a more complete expression in the structure and life of the Church in postwar Germany.

The Confessing Synod of Berlin, which met in Spandau in July, 1945, did seem eager to break new ground in the field of religious education. "We cannot dare to imagine," it declared, "that our tremendous educational problem is to be solved simply by the restoration of religious education in the schools." The whole system of Christian nurture, with its beginnings in baptism and its cradle in the family, needs to be reexamined, and the role of the congregation in preparing the children for the two years of confirmation instruction newly interpreted. Otherwise, the rite of confirmation will continue to be simply a formal termination of religious instruction and a farewell to the Church. If the youth are to be retained for the Church after confirmation, the Church will have to establish firmer ties with the children before confirmation. This could probably be more effectively done if religious instruction were given by the Church itself, rather than by public-school teachers, many of whom are themselves indifferent toward the Church.

In spite of these expressions and the experiences of the Nazi times, the Churches of East Germany would probably have restored the old system of religious instruction in the public schools, just as the Churches of West Germany did. But the arbitrary action of the Soviet Military Administration, in the face of Church opposition, forced them to take a step which has done more to anchor the responsibility for Christian instruction within the individual congregation than any other single event in recent German Church history.

In spite of its poverty-stricken physical condition, with buildings and parish houses in ruins, and with a serious shortage of pastors, the Church was driven to establish a complete program of religious instruction, including materials, teaching staff, and even schoolrooms. If ever external circumstances would seem to have warranted a postponement of such a drastic and expensive reorganization, this would have been true in 1945 and 1946.

But there was no alternative. So the Church squared its shoulders and faced its task. Even to its own amazement, it raised up a staff of twelve thousand lay teachers, and provided them with special training in about forty catechetical seminaries, hurriedly erected and staffed for this purpose. Under the supervision of Dr. Walter Zimmermann, who became Chairman of the Department of Education for the eastern churches, teaching materials were prepared, and a long-range program was actually undertaken to help every one of the seven thousand congregations in East Germany to build or furnish adequate rooms in which to assemble its children for instruction. In both of these crucial efforts the Lutheran World Federation provided valuable financial aid to encourage and supplement local Church contributions.

The launching of this catechetical program by the Protestant Churches of East Germany, in the face of almost insurmountable obstacles, is one of the most brilliant and exciting episodes in the postwar history of European Protestantism. It demonstrated that, although the Church often moves slowly, and must sometimes be pushed into progress, it had the vitality to make use of hardship for the achieving of something truly creative, even at the close of a long period of discouragement and suppression.

It demonstrated further that the Church had the elasticity necessary to make adjustments in its long-standing patterns of operation, when confronted by a hostile governmental regime. The Protestant Churches of East Germany were to operate for a long time to come within a climate of Church and State relationships far different from that to which their earlier history had accustomed them. Whether they could confront subsequent manifestations of this wintry climate with equal courage and imagination remained to be seen. But they had made a good beginning.

FOUR

RESPITE FOR REBUILDING

As a company of discouraged and defeated German soldiers trudged wearily eastward out of the ruins of Berlin toward Russian prison camps in May, 1945, they passed a series of newly painted signboards along the Autobahn. The boards had been thoughtfully erected by the Russian Army for the information and instruction of their troops moving in to occupy Berlin. A German soldier who knew a little Russian helped to punctuate the weary miles by translating the signs for his comrades as they passed.

Fourteen years later, one of these soldiers still remembered a sign which pictured the heroic figures of Lenin and Stalin standing together on a platform. The uplifted arm of each was pointing in the direction of Berlin, and beyond, in the distance, toward the tall spires of the Strassburg Cathedral and the Eiffel Tower. Behind the modern Russian leaders stood two huge and shadowy figures out of the distant past: Attila the Hun and the Mongol emperor Genghis Khan. The Russian caption read: "Westward in the Spirit of the Fathers."

The conquest of Berlin was for the Russians much more than a military victory avenging the invasion of their own soil by the German armies. It represented an opportunity to further a Russian dream of westward territorial expansion, which long antedated the Communist Revolution. But, even more important than this, from the ideological standpoint of Marx, Lenin, and Stalin, a real foothold in Germany was the key to the future. "Whoever controls Germany," Lenin had said, "possesses Europe."

The victory in Europe, which in Russian eyes had not been won by the western powers, but by the Red Army and the Soviet peoples, represented, according to Stalin, the confirmation of the truths of Marxist-Leninist dogmas. The Russians fully expected that with the end of the war, the West would find itself in the throes of economic and social crisis, accompanied by strikes and unrest among the laboring groups, and they were determined to make the best possible use of this expected opportunity.

As a matter of fact, the validity of their theories seemed to be borne out when, as the war ended, one land after the other in eastern Europe passed under Soviet political dominance. Rumania, Bulgaria, Poland, Hungary, Czechoslovakia, and Albania all installed pro-Communist governments within a few months, and in Italy and France Communist strength showed an alarming increase.

In keeping with the accepted technique of emphasizing whatever seemed to make their leadership most plausible and acceptable at the moment, the Communists appeared in all these areas as crusaders against fascism and the apostles of democracy. According to the Potsdam Agreement antifascism and democracy were also to be the guiding themes for the reconstruction of Germany. The Russians went to work immediately in their own zone of occupation, clearly expecting that with the help of the chaotic conditions of postwar Germany and the anticipated economic and social crises in the western capitalistic States, they could eventually establish a Soviet-oriented People's Republic in all of Germany as well.

The first steps were clear. Under the banner of "antifascism," denazification and land reform were carried through, and thousands of German workers and technicians were deported to the Soviet Union. Many factories were dismantled to prevent the revival of German war potential, and 45 per cent of the remaining industrial capacity of the Soviet Zone was nationalized on the ground that the owners were Nazis or war criminals. With most of this program the western Allies had no quarrel, since their own attitude toward the defeated nation also stressed the uprooting of fascism and the destruction of the German warmaking potential.

Politically, the Soviets began by licensing in their zone the same political parties that operated in the western zones. That the German Communist Party, the KPD, was among them, was in no sense strange, since the Communists had always been the bitter opponents of the Nazis, and many of the KPD leaders had been either driven out of Germany or put into concentration camps by the Nazis. Even the merger of the KPD with the old German Socialist Party, though actually carried through under the pressure of the Soviet Military Administration, was confirmed by an apparently democratic vote in the assemblies of both parties. The SED Party (Socialist Unity Party) which resulted proclaimed anew its allegiance to the principles of "democracy," though its Moscow-trained mentor, Walter Ulbricht, made it clear that in terms of elections his kind of democracy would tolerate nothing less than a workers' majority in every city and town in East Germany. After the local and State elections of October, 1946, in which the SED received substantial assistance from the Soviet regime, the parliaments in all five of the newly created State governments were safely in the hands of people whose understanding of democracy agreed with that of Ulbricht.

In cultural matters, the same themes prevailed. In July, 1945, the Soviets sponsored the organization of a Cultural Union (Kulturbund) to promote the collaboration of all democratically oriented movements of religious or ideological character, and to restore a "free" German literature and art. This organization was not confined to the Soviet Zone, but its appeal was also directed to intellectual and cultural circles in all of Germany, in the name of humanistic principles and of peace and understanding.

As might have been expected, the Communists lost no time in seeking to enlist the youth for their program. Throughout the Soviet Zone youth committees were established, with the aim of liberating the young people from the regimentation of the Hitler Youth and helping them once more to "think for themselves." "Our primary purpose," stated the Youth Committee of Berlin at its organization on July 5, 1945, "will not be to play soldier or to train for war, but to pursue peaceful work."

Although these Youth Committees were allegedly nonpartisan, with representation from all political parties, and in some instances even from the Evangelical and Catholic Churches, most of the local leadership was carefully chosen by the Soviets.

In February, 1946, the Central Youth Committee agreed to establish a single youth organization for the entire Soviet Zone, to be known as the Free German Youth (FDJ). This, too, was to be "nonpartisan" in character, but it was from the beginning strictly under Communist leadership. Because the intention was to forbid all other youth organizations except this one, the three western members of the Allied Control Council refused to approve the FDJ, and it was forced to operate unofficially for more than a year.

The experiences of the Churches with the Hitler Youth organization and its tactics had already led them to adopt a new pattern of operation in their youth program. Scrapping the separate organizational structure of the so-called Evangelical Youth, the Churches now simply geared their activities to the local parishes, and assembled the young people of each parish into Youth Congregations, or *Junge Gemeinde*. No separate membership lists were maintained; no one joined or resigned. Youth activities of the Churches were thereby restricted to devotional and Biblical themes, with purely social activities and sports reserved by law for the Free German Youth, but in any event the Church youth were free of the regimentation and control of the FDJ. This pattern of operation was also adapted by the Churches to other spheres of auxiliary activity, such as men's work and women's work, which had previously been carried on through independent societies. By coordinating all of these functions within the framework of the congregation, the Churches were not only able to put themselves beyond the control of the State but were also able to develop a more closely knit congregational structure. This was to become increasingly important as the State assumed a more aggressive attitude toward the Church and toward the Christian faith.

In reorganizing the school system of their zone of occupation, the Soviets were not only concerned about rooting out the vestiges of Nazism: in keeping with the entire cultural emphasis of the years 1945–1948, the schools were also designed as training centers for "real democracy and true humanity." Regardless of differences in background, religious beliefs, or economic position, every child was to be given an education at public expense in keeping with his interests and his abilities.

The school laws governing the erection of the so-called Coordinated Democratic School System were promulgated in virtually identical form in all five of the States in the Soviet Zone in June, 1946. After eight years of elementary school, a child might either enter a four-year *Oberschule* which would prepare him for university entrance, or he might follow a more practical and technical course of three years, which could also lead into an advanced technical school on the university level. Attendance in school until the age of eighteen was mandatory under the law. The task of education was to be the absolute monopoly of the State, and no private schools of any sort were permitted.

In order to assure the support and participation of parents in the educational process, the school laws provided for the erection of Parents' Committees for individual schools, to act as advisory boards for the school administration.

Although there was nothing in these original school laws that was openly hostile to the Christian faith or to the Churches, the danger, as the Churches quickly sensed, lay in the monopolistic claims of the State within the field of education. The Soviets contended that the elimination of religious instruction from the public schools was not in any sense a gesture of hostility, but simply an effort to provide a neutral atmosphere for education. This was quite in keeping with the Soviet technique, which had been applied to youth organization and cultural promotion, and even the organization of political parties. The themes of tolerance and democracy and neutrality were calculated to disarm opposition and quiet fearful hearts. Later on, when the time was ripe, the ideological content of Socialism and Communism would be poured in. And with the principle of the State monopoly on education already established, there would be no escaping the ideological impact of materialistic atheism upon every child, regardless of the wishes of the parents. This was the eventuality the Church sought to prevent, when it bitterly opposed the secularization of the schools and the establishment of a State monopoly on education.

Quite apart from the tactical ground for the disarming stress upon "democracy" as the main theme of the educational program, the

Communists in East Germany were faced with the stern reality that there simply were not enough politically acceptable teachers available. These would have to be prepared first, and it would be several years before the ideological program in the schools could be effectively undertaken.

After the stringent denazification procedures had been completed, only about 25 per cent of the trained teachers remained in their positions, and only a few of these were old-line Socialists. The most that could be expected from the so-called "new teachers," who were given short six-month courses and then placed in the elementary schools, was that they were not fascists.

Virtually a whole new teaching staff had therefore to be constructed, and to this end the Soviets established a series of special courses and offered generous monthly stipends for those who would enroll as prospective teachers. Significantly, candidates were to be accepted only from the so-called "democratic" or "working classes." In 1947, eighty-eight schools of this kind were established for the training of nine thousand teachers. As a more permanent program of teacher training, teachers' colleges were also established at all of the East German universities.

To gear the universities of East Germany into a program of "democratic" education presented a real problem to the Soviets. Institutions such as Berlin, Leipzig, Halle, Jena, Rostock, and Greifswald had deeply rooted and distinguished academic traditions, and their students and professors had come largely from the intellectual and the economic aristocracy. This pattern was not easily changed, and the Soviets were fully aware of this when they permitted the universities to resume operation early in 1946.

Nazi professors were summarily dismissed, but those who were retained sensed no immediate political or academic restrictions. Even the theological faculties were retained, in spite of the fact that nothing of this kind had ever existed in Russia. Dr. Paul Wandel, the Soviet-appointed president of the Central Administration for Education, discussed this matter thoroughly with Evangelical Church leaders, and on their urgent advice allowed this German tradition to remain.

The "democratization" of the universities began rather in a revision of the admissions policies in the interest of the children of farmers and workers. These groups had never had the opportunity for university education, nor had they had the particular academic preparation required for university study. The problem would not be solved by simply admitting such young people to the various faculties and allowing them to flounder helplessly. New faculties were therefore established, and special preparatory courses were designed, to bring the farmers' and workers' children into the universities. Elaborate systems of scholarships were set up, with special preferences given to those of the proper economic background and political viewpoint. Some attempts were made to control the student councils, by urging and supporting the candidacies of SED and FDJ students, but any thoroughgoing ideological assault upon the universities in East Germany was postponed until a later and more convenient time.

While the Soviet Military Administration was busily organizing the East Zone of Germany politically, culturally, and economically, the Churches were hard at work in the program of physical and spiritual reconstruction. Hundreds of church buildings had been either destroyed or damaged, and though a complete rebuilding was in most cases out of the question, the parish facilities had to be made at least usable. War casualties among the clergy had been very high; remaining pastors, therefore, many of them older men, had to assume additional responsibilities in order that even the basic pastoral services could be offered to the people of the parishes. The expulsion of German population by the Poles and other peoples of eastern Europe continued year by year, until by 1950 a total of 11,200,000 additional Germans had been crowded into the four occupational zones. Four millions of these remained in the Russian Zone of occupation. For the spiritual and physical care of these refugees the Churches in both East and West Germany felt a deep responsibility. Local parishes did what they could, and the "basket of mercy," hung upon the church doors to receive small gifts of bread to be shared with the hungriest among the hungry, became a symbol of this brotherly concern. Sisters of the Inner Mission moved in and out of the homes and the bunkers, ministering in the name of Christ and His Church, bringing both physical and spiritual nourishment.

Impulses to share within the framework of the Church in both East and West Germany were mobilized by the Evangelical Hilfswerk, founded by Dr. Eugen Gerstenmaier and given official approval

Ruins of Main Building of Pfeiffer Foundation, Inner Mission in Magdeburg (*Photo H. Dieck*)

Bombed-Out Church in East Germany

Dr. Hilde Benjamin, Minister of Justice in the German Democratic Republic, at Youth Dedication (1958)

Recessional Following Youth Dedication in the Theater of Peace, Letschin/Oder (1957)

at Treysa in 1945 as the emergency relief organization of the Protestant Churches of Germany. On the principle that before turning to others for help, the Church must call upon its own members to share, the Hilfswerk appealed to pastors and congregations all over Germany for food and clothing and money. During the first three years of its operation, more than 550,000 tons of food and clothing, and 180,000,000 Reichsmarks in cash were received from German congregations in all four zones. These gifts were then supplemented by the contributions which poured into Germany from Christian and benevolent groups in all parts of the world. The Hilfswerk also acted as the distributor of foreign gifts.

A wide variety of services was provided through these gifts from Germany and abroad. More than 2,500 homes and institutions of the Inner Mission were given assistance in caring for thousands of men, women, and children. About half of the total food supplies which came from foreign sources in the first three years after the war were used for special child-feeding programs that reached about 3,000,000 children. Local repair shops were set up by the Hilfswerk in many communities to repair the shoes and clothing coming from abroad.

University students, particularly theological students, received scholarships; packages were sent to war prisoners and to their families; medicines were provided for the hospitals and clinics; and local parish distribution centers tried to take care of at least the neediest cases among the refugees.

Where worship facilities had been completely destroyed, the Hilfswerk was able to channel aid from the Lutheran World Federation and the World Council of Churches for the construction of temporary church barracks. Gifts of cellulose and paper from abroad were turned into much-needed Bibles, catechisms, and other religious books, to replace the vast numbers that had been destroyed by fire and bombs. Cash gifts mediated through the Hilfswerk enabled the Churches to establish the catechetical seminaries they needed to train lay teachers of religion, and to provide individual congregations with rooms in which instruction could be given.

The Hilfswerk served as the single emergency relief arm of the entire Protestant Church in Germany, and during these early years experienced no difficulty whatever in transporting its shipments from the western zones to the more crowded and war-ravaged communities of the East. A special central office for the coordinating of distributions in the Soviet Zone was established in Berlin under the direction of Dr. Tillmanns, later a member of the West German cabinet. Dr. Heinrich Grueber supervised the Hilfswerk activities in the city of Berlin. The politically directed relief and welfare organization called the "People's Solidarity," which operated in Berlin and the Soviet Zone under the leadership of the SED, made no objection, because it was in no position to assume full responsibility for the mass of human need pressing in on every side.

These years also gave the Church opportunity to perfect its organizational structure. Only a few weeks after the surrender of Germany and the consequent liberation of the Churches from Nazi control, leaders of the Confessing Church revived their long-cherished dream of an all-German Church, united by a common profession of the lordship of Jesus Christ.

The man who stepped into the leadership in this movement was the venerable seventy-seven-year-old Bishop of Wuerttemberg, Theophil Wurm. After a journey through northwest Germany to determine whether sentiment warranted his taking the initiative, he called for an all-German Church conference to be held at Treysa, a small Hessian village, not far from Fulda, on August 27, 1945. This place was chosen because of its central location and because there were facilities there in an Inner Mission institution for the housing and feeding of the delegates.

The Treysa Conference laid the groundwork for the organization of the Evangelical Church in Germany, which would be formally established at Eisenach in 1948. Charged with the responsibility of preparing a draft constitution and for representing the common interests of the German Protestant Churches until that organization should have taken place, was a Council of Twelve, including such leading personalities as Theophil Wurm, Martin Niemoeller, Hans Asmussen, Hanns Lilje, Otto Dibelius, and Hans Meiser.

During the years 1946 and 1947 energetic discussions concerning the nature of the proposed Church union went on under their direction in all parts of Germany. One group, drawing its leadership largely from the Council of Brethren of the Confessing Church and stressing the unity which had been experienced in the years of the struggle against the Nazis, insisted that the proposed Evangelical Church in

Germany be a true Church, carrying with it all of the blessings of the sacramental fellowship.

Pastors and leaders from the large group of Lutheran provincial Churches, however, though ready to give their full support to an all-German Church federation, stressed the importance of confessional unanimity as the condition for fellowship in the Lord's Supper. Although the theological Declaration of Barmen had been accepted in 1934 by all of the adherents of the Confessing Church, both Lutheran and Reformed rejecting Nazi efforts to use the Church for their own purposes, Lutherans insisted that no new "Church" had been created at Barmen, overarching the confessional positions of more than four hundred years. They reserved the term Church for the association of twelve Lutheran Churches of like confession, which had also laid the groundwork for its organization at Treysa in 1945.

The constituting assemblies of both the Evangelical Church in Germany and the United Evangelical Lutheran Church in Germany were held in Eisenach in July, 1948, just as the political and economic developments in Germany were leading up to an open division between East and West. The currency reform introduced as a part of the program of economic reunification in the western zones took place just as the Eisenach meetings were scheduled to open, and for a time it appeared that they might even have to be postponed.

But on July 10th, with delegates present from all Churches, the assembly constituting the Evangelical Church in Germany convened in the historic city of Luther, Eisenach, in the Soviet Zone. The twenty-eight separate Churches of Germany, embracing more than 40,000,000 Protestants, had found their way together, and were about to achieve a unity which in the political sphere was to be indefinitely denied to the people of Germany. Ecumenical visitors and representatives of the occupation powers echoed the cordial expressions of Major Eichenwald of the Soviet Military Administration at the festival opening of the assembly on the Wartburg, as he wished the delegates "complete success" in their task of uniting the evangelical Churches of Germany.

The establishment of these two all-German Church structures, the EKD and the United Evangelical Lutheran Church, just at the time when political forces were beginning to drive a wedge between East and West, was one of the most significant events in the life of

German Protestantism following the war. The Church thereby achieved an asset in a period of comparative peace and good feeling that would be a strong bulwark in the years of tension and even of persecution lying ahead. When all other organizational ties between East and West Germany should have been severed by the sharp cutting edge of the descending Iron Curtain, the Evangelical Church would continue to hold its synods in both East and West, and to speak for the whole of German Protestantism on the great moral and spiritual issues confronting its people. Similarly, the brotherly bonds that were forged and strengthened through the EKD became the basis for one of the most extensive programs of inter-Church aid in the history of modern Protestantism. The physical and spiritual assistance that has flowed from the Churches of West Germany through the channels of the EKD to the eastern Churches in the past ten years has been a major factor in their energetic witness and in the resourceful ministry they have been able to carry on against increasing opposition from official party and government agencies.

If the all-German organization of the Church had been delayed for even one or two years, it probably would never have been attained. By that time, there would be two German governments, and the Soviet hopes of bringing all of Germany within its political orbit would have passed beyond hope of realization. Consolidation would have become the Soviet policy in East Germany, and under such circumstances the good words of Major Eichenwald at Eisenach, wishing "complete success" to the Churches in their efforts toward unity, would not have been in order.

In the midst of the crying need for physical relief and reconstruction, and for the readjustment of its own ecclesiastical structure, the Church in East Germany showed a strong sensitivity to the moral climate of the postwar years. Both the years of National Socialism and the usual ravages of a war experience had worked severe damage upon moral standards in Germany. Respect for life and property and for the sanctity of personality had been dealt violent blows by the Nazis, and the observance of Sunday as a day of rest and worship had been widely disregarded. False notions of personal and racial superiority had been impressed upon the youth. The provincial synod of the Church of Pomerania pointed to these officially sanctioned violations of the Ten Commandments as the cause of the "greatest collapse in the history of the German people."

In view of the monumental moral defection of the German people, the Church felt a deep obligation to restate the Ten Commandments clearly and to summon the people to a new obedience. This was not an easy matter in the immediate postwar years, when disillusionment and despair filled the minds of great numbers of the youth who had suddenly made the bitter discovery that they had been deceived by false teachers. It was not easy in a time of great physical privation, when a struggle for actual survival was the main occupation of thousands of men, women, and children.

In his report to the Synod of Berlin-Brandenburg in October, 1946, Bishop Dibelius sketched a frightening picture of the moral problems of those bitter days: "The tasks of the Church today," he said, "are overwhelming. It must minister to a people whose inner life has been shaken and desolated through a long and frightful war, and through the hazards of life in the postwar period. Those who view the situation only from the outside often have no idea what conditions are really like. But those who visit in the homes, or in some other way secure a deeper insight into the situation, stand speechless before the actual level to which the German people have fallen in these times. Mothers are ordering their sexually diseased daughters out of the Berlin hospitals because they can't exist without the income these girls have been earning in their sinful trade. All over Berlin great numbers of people are plundering coal trains, claiming that at last they are getting what rightly belongs to them. Cases of exploitation of children are on the increase. Black-market dealings make up the main interest among half-grown boys, many of whom are not more than seven years old. And even among those who have not become involved in gross violations, large numbers still draw the line at subjecting themselves to the law of God. One is constantly faced with the question of just how much the German people must go through before they begin again to take God seriously and to make a new beginning. And over still others who are truly ready to do all this, there broods the spell of unending weariness and hopelessness, which will not allow them to think constructively any more, and whose final word is always simply this: It's just no use!"

Among the casualties of this moral collapse was the observance of Sunday as a day of rest and worship. In many congregations, according to Superintendent Harder of Berlin, Sunday didn't even exist. Nazi party meetings on Sunday and work during the war had wreaked havoc with Church attendance, and with the end of the war there was no sudden reversal of form. Bishop Dibelius feared that many pastors would have to see their task as that pictured in the sixth chapter of Isaiah, where the prophet preached the Gospel, knowing that most people would reject it and go on their way to ruin, leaving only a small remnant as the good seed for future generations.

This hardness and disillusionment and despair which stalked among the congregations of East Germany after the war were in many ways more devastating than the physical privations and hunger. Empty stomachs could be filled, and destroyed homes rebuilt, even though the task might last for years, but the seared souls and the scorched minds of Hitler's "lost generation" seemed to defy even the healing of the Gospel.

These wounds were not healed by official declarations, nor was this the purpose of the Church in making them. But such statements reflect a healthy awareness on the part of the Church and its leaders of the tremendous task of spiritual ministration which pastors and laymen had to face in every parish.

Part of the moral reawakening that had to take place in the communities of East Germany if the population was to survive at all was a revival of a will to work, and of a sense of community responsibility. To this kind of reawakening the Church also felt impelled to summon its members. At the time of the planting of the fields in the spring of 1946, the Church of Brandenburg issued an appeal rich in the implications of Christian stewardship: "The spring work has begun: It requires us this year to summon all the strength we have. . . . not only that we may have just enough bread for our own families. Remember, all of you farmers and settlers, that the saving of millions of Germans from death by starvation in this coming year depends upon you! Work together, citizens and refugees, and make full use of every inch of ground you have. And even if it is work to which you are not accustomed, it will still bear fruit. This doesn't apply only to work in the fields. The work must go forward also in the cities. Houses must be repaired; new dwellings must be built; we must begin to restore our economy. Wherever it may be, in the city or in the countryside—indifference causes weakness, but trust in God is a source of strength!"

In none of the areas of physical relief, internal reorganization, or moral regeneration was there anything in the program of the Church which the Soviet occupation authorities found seriously objectionable in these immediate postwar years. On the contrary, much of what the Church said and did to strengthen the physical and moral standards among the people of East Germany was cordially welcomed by the Soviets.

The earnestness with which the Church restated the Ten Commandments in the midst of the degeneracy of postwar Germany was rooted in a humble awareness that much of the moral decay that was so apparent could have been prevented if the Church had spoken out more clearly when the Nazis were freely flouting the commandments of God. The sincerity of the Church's repentance was reflected in its determination never again to remain silent in the face of a moral obligation. Even if it should mean calling the victorious powers to task for some of their policies, the Church felt compelled to speak.

The first of such issues raised by the Church was that of mass expulsions of populations from eastern Europe and from the eastern provinces of Germany. It was true that Nazi authorities had been guilty of similar forcible expulsions of peoples, but the adding of other millions to the toll of the homeless surely did not correct the earlier injustice. The German Evangelical Church directed a plea in February, 1946, to the United Nations and to the Allied Control Commission for Germany, pointing out the pitiful condition of the expellees as they arrived, half starved, in a ruined Germany which could provide neither housing nor food for them. "It has often been said to us," declared the Council of the EKD, "that the Allied powers did not intend to deliver the German people to a lasting suffering. On the basis of this promise the representatives of the EKD plead with the governments concerned to meet this impending danger in the spirit of humanity before it is too late." Social relief measures would not suffice. The only solution would be to stop the evacuation of Germans from the East and let them stay where they were, and earn their bread as loyal citizens.

A year later, as the terrible winter of 1946–1947 was holding the entire land in its icy clutches, Bishop Dibelius sent a telegram to the Allied Control Commission, pleading for wood and coal for heating, and also urgently requesting that at least during the winter months the process of expulsion of Germans from Poland might be halted.

"It must surely be possible," pleaded the bishop, "that this inhumanity could finally be checked."

The voice of protest was not only directed against inhumanities in East Germany. In the wake of the vindictive policies of the western Allies in the first months after the end of the war, starvation actually threatened many people in western Germany. Martin Niemoeller wrote an open letter to a New York pastor, following his first visit to the United States early in 1947, in which he bitterly assailed what he called the "starvation policy" of the Allied Occupation. The official food ration provided by the United States Army in its zone of occupation in 1945 was 1,550 calories, and not until March, 1946, did the government permit the shipment of any supplementary food supplies by private agencies into the American Zone.

The problem of war prisoners and interned civilians also concerned the Church, particularly as the months stretched into years, and thousands of Germans were still not even in touch with their families. The Brandenburg Synod in October, 1946, directed a plea to the Allied Control Council, calling especially for the release of children under eighteen, many of whom were in Russian prison or work camps. The Roman Catholic bishops in Germany made a similar appeal a year later, adding the ominous note that the number of such internees, including women and children, was increasing from month to month, and that parents in the Russian Zone who had attempted to secure information from the police concerning their children received no information whatever, and in some cases were even threatened with arrest themselves.

The periodic appeals made by various Church authorities to the Soviet Military Administration finally secured a promise from Marshal Sokolowski to take steps to ease the situation of these prisoners and internees. In April, 1948, the Evangelical bishops of the East Zone wrote a letter of appreciation to the marshal, and even asked for the privilege of visiting him personally to convey the thanks of the Church for his willingness to listen. But in spite of small improvements and occasional releases, the number of German prisoners and internees in Russian camps remained in the hundreds of thousands even in 1949.

There were also some instances when the Churches felt their own independence was being endangered, and they made their objections very clear. Most of these instances were local in character, and could be handled through representations to the Soviet Military Administration in Berlin. When word reached Bishop Dibelius, however, that some of the pastors in Berlin-Brandenburg had been ordered to submit advance copies of their sermons to Soviet military commanders, he directed an unequivocal letter to all of the Church superintendents in the province, declaring such practice to be wholly unacceptable.

The Nazis had also attempted, observed the bishop, to compromise the spiritual freedom of the pastors, and the answer of the Church to this attempt had been convincingly given by the Confessional Synod of Barmen in 1934. If a Church ever should permit a censorship of the sermons of its pastors, that Church would already have become merely an instrument in the hands of the State.

No less serious than the attempt to censor sermons was the periodic effort to enlist the political support of pastors and Church leaders. Most pastors were wary of the direction in which the new political order was moving, and avoided any personal commitment which might compromise their pastoral effectiveness. But in order to give them some official support, the Lutheran Church of Saxony placed a letter in the hands of its pastors in July, 1946, defining the political role of a pastor. There was no question whatever about the right and the responsibility of a pastor to function as a voting member of his political community, supporting whatever party he might choose. But open political activity on behalf of any party, warned the Church, might very easily interfere with the sense of freedom which every parishioner ought to feel toward his pastor as a spiritual counselor, and therefore pastors ought not to engage in partisan political activities.

The Church sharply criticized election procedures in the East Zone for the first time in May, 1948, when the Soviet authorities announced a general referendum on the question of "peace and unity." The background of this referendum was the Soviet proposal to the western Allies for an immediate peace treaty and a central all-German government to be set up on the Soviet pattern, without elections. The Allies had rejected this proposal. The Soviets therefore accused them of violating the Potsdam Agreement, but continued to move toward a government for their own zone, claiming for it an all-German character. The manner in which the Soviets proposed to conduct a referendum on this issue was greeted with outspoken protest both by the Church of Berlin-Brandenburg and by Bishop Dibelius.

In the first place, declared the Church leadership in a letter to all the pastors, it was impossible for a conscientious citizen to express his true attitude in this referendum because of the way in which the question was stated. Whoever affixed his signature, and thereby indicated that he favored a treaty of peace and the unity of Germany, would be regarded by the government as a supporter of its particular proposal for achieving this goal. If a person refused to sign, his refusal would be interpreted by the Soviets as a vote of disloyalty.

Against such an unfair statement of the question, which actually gave no fair and clear alternative, the Church protested on moral grounds. In a pastoral letter to all the congregations in Brandenburg, Bishop Dibelius called attention to the dangers involved in exerting any kind of pressure on the consciences of people in making political or other decisions. This kind of action by a totalitarian State had become all too familiar to the German people during the Nazi times, he pointed out, and the result had been a complete obscuring of the virtues of truth and honesty.

The protection of the freedom of conscience, said Dibelius, is a Christian responsibility. Whether attempts were made openly to exert pressures upon the conscience, or whether the threats were concealed; whether such efforts were made in school, in the factories, or in the political parties, the Christian was under obligation to speak out his uncompromising objection. Even if the objective should be one to which the Christian could otherwise give his approval, he must still object to the use of pressures or threats, since in such cases even the best objectives become unrighteous before God.

The most thoroughgoing statement on the relationship of the Church to public and political affairs was contained in a letter written by all the bishops of the East Zone Churches to Marshal Sokolowski, chairman of the Russian Military Administration for East Germany, on May 11, 1948. The occasion of the letter was the increasing tendency of Soviet representatives to approach pastors, requesting their support of political measures. Conferences with the officials who had made these requests of the pastors had demonstrated a lack of understanding of the basic attitude of the Evangelical Church on matters of this kind, and therefore the bishops directed this rather comprehensive statement of policy to the Russian marshal, with the hope that he would honor it and advise his local officials in the Soviet Zone accordingly.

According to Evangelical doctrine, stated the letter, every Christian is obligated under God to obey the laws of the State, insofar as those laws do not contradict the laws of God. The task of the Church, which had been entrusted to it by Jesus Christ, is to proclaim the Gospel, and in fulfilling this task the Church cannot accept the direction of any human authority, whether it be the State or a political party. This position, based upon the Scriptures, had been most recently confirmed by the Confessional Synod of Barmen, in its opposition to the pretensions of the National Socialist Party.

There may be political questions, however, upon which the Church feels impelled to speak. If some proposal or action of a party or of the State deeply affects the moral life of the community, the Church may support it or criticize it. Such an expression on the part of the Church, however, must never be based upon political considerations, but solely upon the duty of the Church to summon men to obedience to God.

The freedom of the Church to express itself positively or negatively toward measures of the State is an absolutely essential element of the religious liberty guaranteed under the State constitutions of the East Zone. The State, in turn, may expect of the Church that its criticisms should not be made in a form calculated to undermine or destroy the authority of the State.

The significance of this letter in the development of relations between Church and State in East Germany lay in the fact that it was the first formal statement directed to the Soviet authorities in which the official position of the Evangelical Church was made clear. Thus far there had been no occasion for such a statement, inasmuch as there had been no serious attempt on the part of the Soviets to mobilize the Church for any political purposes. The Church had been permitted to carry out its own denazification program; the elimination of religious instruction from the public schools in no sense called into question the basic right of the Church to teach the Christian faith to the children; and the land reform did not directly affect the basic functions of the Church's ministry. But when the attempts were made to censor sermons, and when pastors were called upon to give public support to political programs, the fundamental question of the independence of the Church from political agencies was clearly raised. That the Church was alert enough to catch this first attempt on the part of the State was a testimony to the fact that the lessons learned under National Socialism had been taken to heart. It is noticeable also that, after this letter had been written, the tone of relations between Church and State in the East Zone began to take on a sharper edge. The so-called "concentration camp effect" was beginning to wear off, as the Communist program moved beyond its preliminary peaceful "antifascistic and democratic" stage into a more positive and aggressive socialistic stage.

The summer of 1948 also brought the rupture between the Russians and the western Allies, climaxing in the split of the Berlin four-power control and the imposition of the Berlin blockade. The SED announced an intensified "class struggle," and declared that in cultural circles "neutrality" would no longer be possible. The FDJ leadership was "purged," and in public schools and universities the ideological emphasis was increased and administrative controls were tightened.

A definite stage in the process of the sovietization of East Germany had come to a close. The Iron Curtain was beginning to descend, and by 1949, with the establishment of the German Democratic Republic, the Soviets launched seriously their program for the complete integration of East Germany into the Soviet satellite bloc. The letter of the East German bishops to Marshal Sokolowski served notice to the Soviets that the Evangelical Church would resist integration into this system.

FIVE

THE CHURCH BETWEEN EAST AND WEST

In the summer of 1950 the great bronze Freedom Bell was placed in the tall fluted tower of the West Berlin City Hall as a reminder of the common efforts of Berliners and Americans to keep Berlin free. The blockade of 1948–1949 by the Russians had failed, and though the city was hopelessly divided, West Berlin was unmistakably free. American school children contributed their pennies and nickels to purchase the bell, and with high ceremony it was rung for the first time on United Nations Day in 1950. Struck by the symbolism of this occasion, American military authorities approached Bishop Otto Dibelius with the suggestion that on the day of the dedication, all the church bells in West Berlin be rung in unison with the Freedom Bell.

When the bishop refused this apparently plausible and even praiseworthy request, American military channels in West Berlin buzzed with criticism of the bishop. What possible objection could he have? Some even wondered whether he was pro-Communist.

Actually, the bishop was giving dramatic expression to the peculiarly precarious position in which the Evangelical Church of Germany found itself in 1950. "If I should allow the church bells of West Berlin to ring together with the American Freedom Bell tomorrow," declared the bishop, "it wouldn't be twenty-four hours before I'd have a similar request to ring the bells of East Berlin for some Soviet-sponsored celebration."

Whether it wished to be in such a position or not, the Church stood between East and West, between two political powers, each of which was ready to enlist, if it could, the powerful sanction of the Church in support of its program and purpose. The question for Dibelius was not whether one of these powers or the other had a better ground for making such a claim upon the Church. It was rather a question whether the Church could perform its God-given mission of proclaiming the Law and the Gospel to all people alike, if it allowed itself to become the handmaid of any political party or system, no matter what it might represent. This is an issue which faces every Church in every land, but in 1949 and 1950, with their land divided into two widely differing political entities, the Evangelical Churches of Germany faced it in an atmosphere of extremely high tension.

The Church in Germany had been living in the presence of these two political powers since the collapse of Nazism in 1945. One of them had occupied the eastern area of Germany, and the other the western. But in neither area had the work of the Church been seriously hampered. In the West, an initial spirit of vindictiveness soon passed, and the gates were opened to a flood of relief measures. All Churches were left perfectly free to reorganize their internal affairs. In the East, apart from school and land reform, the Church found little to complain about in its treatment by the occupational authorities.

While the Churches had been enjoying their freedom to recover and reorganize, eastern and western occupation authorities had been at work in their respective zones, presumably preparing the way for a peace treaty and for speedy political reunification. Actually the Russians had been systematically pursuing a policy calculated to achieve the ultimate sovietization of all of Germany. For this reason they favored a centralized government of Germany, more easily controlled from above, while the Americans and the British wanted a decentralized federal government. At the Paris Foreign Ministers Conference in 1946, the Russians made it clear that they would not favor the making of any peace treaty until a central government had been erected in Germany which was "democratic enough to root out every remnant of fascism in Germany and . . . responsible enough to fulfill all its obligations to the Allies." This same theme was reiterated by Molotov at the Moscow Ministers Conference in March, 1947, and in addition the Russians demanded Allied approval of their reparations policy, a joint administration of the industrial Ruhr area in West Germany, and the recognition of the Oder-Neisse Line as a permanent Polish-German boundary. The Allies refused all these demands.

Having learned a few things about the political techniques of the Russians by 1947, the western powers had no intention of contributing further to the march of Communism into western Europe. Consequently, when the Russians insisted upon this whole series of conditions for reunification, the Allies seized the initiative. The Truman Doctrine was announced on March 12, 1947; on May 29th England and the United States declared the economic unification of their zones; and on June 5th, George Marshall, American Secretary of State, announced his far-reaching plan for the economic strengthening of the free world.

The Russian reply to this new and vigorous western policy in Germany was another assertion of Allied unfaithfulness to the Potsdam Agreement, and an SED-sponsored appeal in November for an all-German congress. This call was intended to reach all parties and mass organizations in both East and West Germany, and to kindle a spontaneous all-German movement for unity and peace. When the Congress met, however, only the SED was represented; even the other parties in the Soviet Zone declined to participate.

Nevertheless the People's Congress for Peace and Unity sent a message to the London Foreign Ministers Conference in November, urging the reception of a delegation from the congress to plead for the speedy conclusion of a treaty of peace for all Germany. The refusal of the London Conference to receive the delegation was used again to propagandize the apparent unwillingness of the Allies to permit reunification, as opposed to the deep desire of the Soviet Union to secure peace and unity.

While the three western powers were meeting in London in March, 1948, to lay the groundwork for a separate West German government, the Second People's Congress convened in Berlin, claiming to be the only true representative body in Germany. After passing a resolution calling for a popular referendum on the question of peace and unity, the People's Congress "elected" a group of four hundred members to a "German People's Council," which should be a standing representative body for all Germany. From this body a proposed constitution eventually emerged, presumably intended for all Germany, but actually valid only in the Soviet Zone.

On March 6, 1948, the tensions in the Allied Control Council had risen to the point that the Soviet representative, Marshal Sokolowski, walked out of the meeting, and thus brought the four-power administration of Germany and of Berlin virtually to a standstill. Three months later, the Berlin blockade was instituted, and the separation between East and West was made permanent.

Early in 1949, with the blockade still in force, and Berlin now completely divided, the People's Council approved the constitution for the "German Democratic Republic" (GDR), and called for a National Front to support their projected plans for all Germany. By the time the blockade was over in September, all the preliminary steps had been taken for the formation of a provisional government. Without a single popular, free election having been held, this new government was declared to be in effect on October 7, 1949.

Meanwhile, the western Allies, who could scarcely mistake the Soviet intentions of forcibly incorporating Berlin in their sphere of control through the blockade, had also moved quickly toward the establishment of a Federal Republic in the three western zones. A parliamentary council appointed by the minister-presidents of the States met in Bonn on September 1, 1948, and began work on a constitution, which was ready for approval one year later. General elections were held in August, and on September 7, 1949, the new West German Parliament assembled for its first session.

With these developments the artificial unity of the Potsdam Conference collapsed and the wide differences in Soviet and western political aims for Germany became clear. It is not true that in the years 1948 and 1949 sudden power-political differences arose between Russia and the United States which derailed a smoothly developing process of German reunification and divided the country into two parts. Rather, in 1946 and 1947 the Allies realized for the first time what the Soviet intentions really were, and began immediately to register their disapproval. If the Allies had accepted the Soviet terms, the result would have been the unification of all Germany, instead of just the East Zone, within the German Democratic Republic. Italy and France, with their strong Communist parties, might well have followed Germany into the Soviet orbit, in much the same fashion as did Czechoslovakia in February, 1948.

The tragedy was that these Soviet aims were not more clearly understood at Potsdam, where ambiguous terminology fostered the impossible expectation that postwar Germany could be reconstructed in two diametrically opposed economic and political patterns at the same time. For the sake of western Europe, it was a fortunate thing that the Allies awakened as soon as they did. The relative cooperation between the Soviets and the Allies in the Four Power administration of Germany continued as long as it did simply because the Allies did not realize what stakes the Soviets were playing for. Apparently they had not seen the Russian signboards along the Berlin Autobahn, with Lenin and Stalin pointing toward Strassburg and the Eiffel Tower.

The reaction in all parts of Germany when this cleavage became a geographical reality was one of bitter disappointment and chagrin. Actually, by the time the two governments were formed in East and West Germany, the division into two countries had already existed for several months. Politically, the SED had dominated all other East Zone parties ever since its formation at Soviet behest in March, 1946. The FDJ had been organized. The Cultural Alliance was at work. Between the land reform and the nationalization of all mineral wealth and half the industry of the East Zone, economic sovietization was well under way. The schools had been reorganized to prepare for socialistic indoctrination, and a new force of teachers was already in charge. Developments in the West had moved in quite another direction.

The Churches in Germany seem to have paid little attention to the implications of these widely divergent developments in East and West before 1948. This is not entirely strange, since each of the twenty-eight provincial Churches faced a major task of physical reconstruction and internal reorganization in the immediate postwar years. Whatever governmental contacts most of the Churches had were with local German officials, or with some *one* of the occupation powers. There was no all-German organization of Protestant Churches until 1948, and the relative unconcern over the divisive potential of the East-West cleavage for the Church is reflected in the fact that during the conferences in 1946 and 1947 preparatory to the formation of the EKD at Eisenach, the main point of issue was whether the union to be consummated should be a "Church" or a "federation of Churches."

The Council of EKD and the Church of Berlin-Brandenburg had directed messages to both the Moscow and London conferences in 1947, pleading for a restoration of peace after two years of futile negotiation and delay. But the full impact of the divisive political tendencies at work in Germany was not felt by the greater part of the Church until 1948. Ironically, the assemblies constituting the Evangelical Church in Germany and the United Evangelical Lutheran Church in Germany were very nearly postponed because of the currency reform that ushered in the Berlin blockade. And during those very July days, while the Protestant churchmen of all Germany were joining in Eisenach in thanksgiving to God for having permitted them to unite brethren of the faith from the Oder to the Rhine, and from the North Sea to the Alps, a bayonet-studded Iron Curtain was being lowered across every highway and railroad leading into Berlin. As the assembled pastors looked up into the skies above the castle of the Wartburg and saw the silver wings of the American C-54's flying food and coal to the beleaguered residents of West Berlin, it would have been very difficult for them to remain silent about the fate of a divided Germany.

In the message prepared by the Eisenach Assembly on the subject of peace and unity, there is both a wistful and a fearful note. "Three years after the end of a frightful war, the German people are still waiting vainly for peace. . . . Without peace there can be no rebuilding of the life of a people, no moral restoration of men, no opportunity to shape a human life according to the will of God."

The final decision on peace or war rested in other than German hands, but the men of Eisenach, with the memories of bitter years still fresh in their minds, hoped that they might make at least a small contribution to peace. Therefore, they declared, as far as the Christians of Germany were concerned, the war was past; there were no longer any enemies among the peoples of other nations. They urged their fellow countrymen never again to become the tools of any propaganda through which enmity between nations could be stirred up, or acts of military power prepared.

Having achieved its unity in the shadow of the Berlin blockade, with its ominous prophecy of long-lasting tension and precarious peace between the Soviet Union and the western Allies, the Evangelical Church in Germany found itself almost immediately involved in a lively discussion of its role in a divided Germany. In the later months of 1948, and especially during 1949, no theme was so often discussed as that of "The Church Between East and West."

One of the most articulate voices raised in the attempt to interpret the role of the Church was that of Professor Heinrich Vogel of Berlin. Dr. Vogel had been a colleague of Dietrich Bonhoeffer, and one of the "traveling professors" who had kept the Kirchliche Hochschule of Berlin alive and one step ahead of Hitler's Gestapo while this "illegal" theological seminary was training young pastors for the Confessing Church. Great friend and admirer of Karl Barth, and like Barth a Professor of Systematic Theology, Vogel had breathed deeply of the atmosphere of Barmen in 1934, where the Confessing Church had proclaimed its great manifesto on the Lordship of Christ and the independence of the Church from all political overlords. When the Kirchliche Hochschule was reopened after the war in 1945, Vogel resumed his teaching there, holding at the same time a chair in the theological faculty of Humboldt University in East Berlin.

Despite his mild-mannered appearance, Heinrich Vogel has been a formidable controversialist. During the past ten years his theological statements, both spoken and written, have aroused vigorous discussion at nearly every synod of the EKD. Together with his friends and associates in the Brotherhoods of the Confessing Church, he has had a special affinity for political issues, and has been an ardent protagonist for collective guilt, for peace, and for free and open discussion with Communists.

In fact, his readiness to discuss questions of peace and politics with the Communists has made him a regular and enthusiastic participant in the series of Communist-directed peace rallies in Vienna, Stockholm, Prague, and elsewhere. Although he has claimed that his presence in these circles was an essential demonstration of the nonpartisan position of the Church between East and West, and of the sincerity of the Christian Church in its quest for peace, Vogel's public expressions have generally been far more critical of western policies than of eastern. His sharp attacks on atomic rearmament in the West, for example, have not been matched by equally pointed protests against Communist atomic rearmament, although for ten years the uranium produced by East German mines contributed directly to the building of Soviet atomic weapons. In his eagerness to demonstrate to the Communists that the Church has not "written them off," he has too often remained silent in the face of flagrant Communist violations of both Christian and human rights.

It was the Brotherhoods of the Confessing Church that first touched upon the issue of the church's relation to political developments in postwar Germany as early as August, 1947. At that time they issued a sharp warning to the Church not to regard itself as the defender of western culture, but as the proclaimer of conversion to God and service to one's neighbor. The Brethren continued their study, and just at the time of the launching of the two German governments in the fall of 1949 they issued another contribution to the very real issue of the "Church Between East and West."

To this statement, appropriately issued in the divided city of Berlin, Professor Vogel wrote a stirring introduction, which he entitled "The Church in the Breach." He recalled the Biblical story of Abraham, who pleaded with God on behalf of the cities of Sodom and Gomorrah, which were destined for destruction because of their great wickedness. Like some shrewd Oriental trader, Abraham bargained with God until he had secured His promise to spare the cities if there were even ten righteous people to be found within their walls.

Against this background Professor Vogel raised the question for the world of 1949, which was also living from day to day under a threat of destruction. Confident in itself, unrepentant, believing insanely in its own political religions as the way of salvation, and yet failing at every conference to find the formula of peace and security, this world was threatening to wipe itself out with the product of its own research.

Most tragic of all, it threatened to destroy itself over the wrong issues: East versus West, Bolshevism versus Capitalism, Collectivism versus Individualism. That one of these antagonists claimed to be

atheistic and the other the defender of the Christian civilization of
the West did not alter the fact that they were moving like two
mighty trains from opposite directions, heading toward a crash which
could end only in complete annihilation. And, said Vogel, all of mankind was standing between these two giants, with the terrifying feeling that the time of grace was growing very short. Hence the burning
questions: Who will leap into the breach? Who will recognize that
the impending destruction is the judgment of God upon all the
world and that the only hope of salvation is in His mercy? Who will
become the world's advocate—the Abraham who pleads for this
mercy, even while the fire from heaven impends?

Vogel's answer was that the Church must leap into the breach.
The service of Abraham could not be done from any pious vantage
point. The Church must confess that Christ died, not only for its
sins, but for those of the whole godless, power-drunk, hate-filled world.
It cannot call down fire to destroy the world, even though the world
rejects the Gospel. It must not react in self-righteous condemnation.
Rather, it must have an ear for the voices of hunger and thirst, of
hidden longing and seeking after truth.

This Church in the breach would have to withstand serious
temptations from left and right, on the one hand partisanship, and
on the other the avoidance of decision. The Church could not become a partisan of either East or West and identify a political economic program with the plan of God on earth. Jesus Christ could
not be made into a partisan for the western world.

Nor could the Church fall prey to an easy and unrealistic neutrality. It dared not overlook the actual hard facts, for example, that in
the East Zone the true dignity of man was denied and that people
were constantly forced by official policies to lie and deceive. For
these people the Church must be an advocate and defender, else it
did not truly serve as a Church between East and West.

In pursuing this course the Church must expect to earn the thanks
of neither party, but more likely scorn, ridicule, and possibly even
persecution. But regardless of these prospects, the Church could go
no other way. And even for the course of world politics, it could
well be decisive that the Church stepped into the breach to declare the Law and the Gospel. For over its prayers and its deeds
stood the promises of God, to all who believe, statesmen as well as

churchmen, not only for eternal salvation in the next world, but also for guidance in the decisions which must be made in this world.

Following this eloquent introduction, the message of the Council of the Brethren spelled out in more specific terms the appeal to the German people, to the occupation powers, and to all mankind, that God and His Law be acknowledged. Yet though the message was clear and struck deeply into the very real problems of self-righteousness and deceit and lust for power; the spirit of evangelical humility was somehow lacking. Both toward the people of Germany and toward the occupation powers there was a detachment which expressed itself too often in the phrases, "We ask," "We speak," "We admonish."

"We ask," said the Brethren, for example, "Is the atomic bomb the secret God and Savior?"

"We ask, Is the dollar the Savior of the world?"

In neither phraseology nor in spirit was the feeling conveyed that the Church was identifying itself with the world and its problems. Rather, it appeared to be assuming a tone of judgment, slightly tinged with self-assurance and a suggestion of bitterness.

The spirit of a study document prepared by the ecumenical study group of the Berlin-Brandenburg Church for the Amsterdam Conference of the World Council of Churches offered much greater promise of a sympathetic and constructive spiritual service on the part of the "Church Between East and West."

"We have been placed by God at an especially decisive geographical point in world politics," they declared. "Standing upon the boundary between East and West, with their widely differing ways of life, viewpoints, and objectives, under the eyes of the occupation powers who today represent the whole world, we are conscious of the responsibility which rests upon us. We do our service as members of a people which has sunk into political oblivion, but especially in this situation we hear the call of our Lord to declare with great joyfulness His Gospel of Peace."

Another controversial figure, who was to play an exceedingly significant role in the relations of the Evangelical Church to the East German government for the next eight years was Dr. Heinrich Grueber. The ruddy-faced, silver-haired provost of St. Mary's Church in East Berlin had won a distinguished reputation, during the period of National Socialism, as a sturdy friend of the Jews. Having given direct aid to hundreds in Berlin through the famous "Grueber Office," and having aided many others to find safety in other lands, he was twice arrested by the Gestapo and finally sent to Sachsenhausen Concentration Camp in 1940. Brutal guards beat him and knocked out his front teeth, and when he later suffered a heart attack in Dachau his body was thrown for dead upon a pile of corpses in the prison yard.

Released in 1943, Grueber returned to Berlin and resumed his pastorate in the district of Kaulsdorf, where he was during the last terrible days of the siege and destruction of Berlin. Immediately after the capitulation Grueber went to work with more energy than his precarious health would seem to have warranted. He reopened the "Grueber Office," for although there were no more Jews to aid, there were suffering people on every hand. Grueber used to travel more than thirty miles a day on his bicycle through the ruined streets of the city to fulfill his widely varying duties. "My family," he wrote in retrospect, "lived in Niederschoenhausen in the northern section of the city; my parish was in Kaulsdorf in the east; the city offices were in the Parochialstrasse; the church headquarters in Zehlendorf, far in the southwest, and the relief office I opened was in the Bethany hospital."

When the Russians set up the first city administration in May, 1945, Provost Grueber was asked to represent the Protestant Churches in the Office of Church Affairs. In this capacity he worked closely with the Communist officials, many of whom he knew personally as fellow prisoners in Sachsenhausen and Dachau. Because of these relationships Grueber was able to serve the Church in a special way during the first few years of the occupation, years in which the Soviet policy tended to pay real respect to the record of anti-Nazi resistance established by such doughty members of the Confessing Church as Heinrich Grueber.

When the relations between the Russians and the western Allies began to deteriorate after Potsdam, and the cleavage between the eastern and western zones of Germany grew more pronounced, it was quite understandable that Provost Grueber should feel a special disappointment. Though he never tended to minimize the ideological differences between East and West, and surely never found the materialism of the Communist compatible with the Christian faith, Grueber believed it was possible for these widely differing viewpoints to work cooperatively for certain limited objectives such as peace and German unity.

Speaking to his colleagues in the Society of Victims of Nazi Persecution, who elected him chairman in 1948, Grueber said: "We didn't enter the concentration camps and the prisons as North Germans or as South Germans, East Germans or West Germans, but simply as Germans who had resisted injustice and fought for a free and peaceful Germany. The common experience in these years of struggle and suffering is still the source of strength for all the work we have to do today in building bridges. We who spent so much time behind barbed wire want not only to see that barbed wire disappear which now artificially divides our people, but we want to eliminate that spiritual barbed-wire entanglement which is now being purposefully laid in Germany. Therefore we gladly welcome all efforts which have as their aim this quest for unity."

Provost Grueber's entire public service in the Church after the war has been an honest attempt to demonstrate a thesis of dubious promise, namely, that the Church could bridge the political gap between East and West. "The Churches of Europe today," he told representatives of the press in London in 1948, "have a special task. They must guard themselves lest consciously or unconsciously they contribute to making Germany the battleground between two economic systems fighting one another. The Church must rather serve in the role of a bridge builder."

The Provost declared that he himself would never become weary of pointing out the inner meaning of the Latin word for "priest": "Pontifex means bridge builder. The Church, called to the office of Pontifex, can never yield to the role of Partisan."

In his earnest desire for the unity of Germany, Grueber marked out for himself and for the Church a political role, to achieve objectives which many people would regard as eminently desirable in themselves. But in his earnestness he tended to underestimate the fundamental differences between East and West, and especially the seriousness and ruthlessness of Communist determination to achieve a full sovietization of East Germany. In his efforts to avoid political partisanship with the West, he frequently ran the risk of being used as a tool by Communist peace crusaders and politicians. Although his close personal ties with leading East German officials frequently served to solve special problems and to ease many tensions for the Church, these friendships did not necessarily provide a common foundation upon which to build a new Germany. The Provost would come to experience this ten years later, when a far more mature Communist regime in East Germany would no longer even receive him as an official spokesman and negotiator for the Church.

The third contribution to the theme of "The Church Between East and West" in this period of political disintegration came from the Evangelical Bishop of Berlin, head of the Church which more than any other was to feel the physical force of the division of Germany. The entire city of Berlin and the whole province of Brandenburg, spanning the Russian Zone of occupation from East to West, lay within this Church. With the division of Berlin into two sectors during and after the blockade, the Church of Berlin-Brandenburg had to operate within three distinctly different political situations: West Berlin, East Berlin, and the Russian Zone of occupation, later the German Democratic Republic.

From the time he had resumed his ecclesiastical functions in Berlin at the end of the war in 1945, Bishop Otto Dibelius had been one of the most vocal champions of the Church's integrity and mission. But on Pentecost Sunday, June 1, 1949, he sent a pastoral letter to all the congregations of his now divided diocese, which spoke more boldly than his or any other voice of the Church had dared to speak since the war's end. Taking as his text the words of Paul to Timothy, "God has not given us a spirit of timidity, but a spirit of power and love and self-control," Dibelius noted that fifteen years had now passed since the Synod of Barmen had met, also at Pentecost, to declare its opposition to Nazism. Many times since then, he said, the question had arisen at Pentecost whether the Church had the strength to speak again the message it declared in 1934, that it regarded God alone as its Master.

During the years immediately following the war, said Dibelius, all of the German Churches had been reticent about speaking too sharply, both because the occupation authorities were in command and because of all that other nations had suffered at German hands in the preceding six years. But now that responsibilities were being laid more and more on German shoulders, the Church too, would speak more freely. There was much to be said, in request and in warning, both in East and West. Dibelius made it clear that the Church was not a partisan for either West or East, but contended simply for the free and uninhibited course of the Gospel.

He did not see the primary responsibility of the Church as that of a neutral political bridge builder, seeking to close the gap bebetween the two mighty powers over whose differences Germany was being denied its peace and unity. No one desired peace and unity for Germany more than Dibelius, but in the spirit of Barmen he saw that the task of the Church was to resist any attempt by any government to shackle the consciences of men as an assault upon the freedom of the Gospel. Such attempts had to be exposed and resisted when and where they occurred, regardless of political implications. Silence concerning moral violations and encroachments on conscience by a government could be as much an evidence of partisanship as open endorsement of a political course or policy.

The Pentecost letter of June 1, 1949, was the documentation of the letter written by all the East Zone bishops to Marshal Sokolowski in May, 1948. Evidences had been accumulating even by 1948 that the Soviet pattern for East Germany had no room for the Church, except as a willing tool for the futherance of government policies. The letter to Sokolowski laid down the Church's understanding of its role, part of which obligated the Church to speak out when it felt the freedom of the Gospel was being impaired. This Dibelius did in the Pentecost letter, in terms which were unequivocal. "More than anything else," he said, "we are concerned with the fact that the pattern of the State which is arising here [in the East] is already showing signs of the same things which we struggled against under Nazi rule: power which overrules law, inner deception and untruth, and enmity to the Christian Gospel."

In the K-5 Department of the People's Police, Dibelius saw the rejuvenated Gestapo, operating with the same techniques of spies, informers, night arrests, and indefinite imprisonments. In the conduct of elections to the People's Congress he saw the old Nazi technique of a rigged slate and questions posed which could not be answered with anything but Yes.

The Church itself had found in some political offices of the East

Zone Occupation a spirit of understanding and good will, and Dibelius hoped that might continue. But in countless villages and cities Church life had been threatened with breakup by measures of political force. He singled out two examples. Villagers and city dwellers had been regularly ordered to work on Sundays on farms and in factories, and young people had been ordered on Sunday mornings to do work which could just as well have been arranged on weekdays. Thus, without forbidding worship services, the authorities had made it practically impossible for many communities to carry on a normal Church life.

The second area of constant difficulty was the giving of religious instruction. In spite of guarantees and promises, many communities had been left without religious training for the baptized children of Church families, because of interferences. And at the same time the instruction in the public schools was regularly seeking to influence the children from an anti-Christian standpoint.

Against such violations of Christian freedom the Church must raise both a warning voice and a pleading voice. To all those who were concerned they appealed: "Do not be deceived by the illusion that the rule of power and falsehood are the necessary expression of a scientific world view, to which the future belongs. Such a future could only be a future in which man can no longer remain man! We plead with every one in whose breast there dwells a conscience, not to commit yourselves to anything which breathes the spirit of force and falsehood. A courageous 'No' to whatever is contrary to God's law makes a person free, even if it brings him into momentary need and danger."

By the time Dibelius' Pentecost letter was written, the political tensions and divisions had proceeded so far that even less critical statements than his would have been viewed as partisan. From both East and West the propagandists went to work on the bishop's message. The western press saw immediately the sensational political implications of a religious persecution in East Germany. The case of Cardinal Mindszenty in Hungary was recalled, and reports circulated that both Protestants and Catholics would soon be officially notified of an open attack upon them, with the ultimate goal of a State Church, on the Soviet pattern already established in Rumania and Czechoslovakia. Individual instances of the razing of half-ruined churches were expanded into news stories of the dismantling of village churches at government order. Large numbers of pastors were reported arrested.

These reports became so exaggerated and so politically charged that the Roman Catholic Cardinal von Preysing and Dr. Kurt Scharf of the Evangelical Church of Berlin-Brandenburg issued statements warning against circulating false or colored reports concerning the Church situation in the East Zone. The problems which really existed were serious enough without trying to make political capital out of them.

Reactions came from the East with equal vigor and lack of objectivity. Even if the western press had remained silent, Dibelius would have been criticized for his outspoken statement, but the western outcry simply added sharpness. Dibelius was assailed as a tool of western politicians who were seeking to prevent German unity and promote their imperialistic designs on western Europe. Wilhelm Girnus of the Communist *Neues Deutschland* asserted that Dibelius had timed his letter to coincide with the Paris Foreign Ministers Conference in the hope of preventing any positive result from it. Provost Grueber's counter assertion that the letter was timed for Pentecost and not for Paris failed to convince Girnus and his Communist colleagues.

This was the situation in which the Church found itself as the first phase of the postwar period in Germany came to an end, with the division of the country into two parts, one under Soviet control and the other under western leadership. The Church had reorganized in its individual units, and had won a federative, all-German unity in the EKD. But this very unity thrust the Church into the center of the political problem of Germany, since parts of the Church were in the East and parts in the West. With all the best will in the world, it would have been impossible for the Church to remain clear of this battle. Unless the Church were to withdraw completely from the public scene and retire within its ruined buildings—an impossibility for a Church of the Protestant tradition, and only fifteen years removed from the Synod of Barmen—it would have to take a position and speak on important moral and spiritual issues.

As already demonstrated by Bishop Dibelius' Pentecost letter, such expressions would immediately be placed in a political context by one side or the other. The Church stood between East and West, and there it would continue to stand throughout the ensuing decade. As the year 1949 drew to a close, two very dramatic incidents gave ominous indication that in the new period of German-administered government in East and West, this would be painfully true.

The first incident was a visit by Provost Grueber and Bishop Dibelius to a Soviet-administered concentration camp near Berlin. Several of these notorious Nazi camps, such as Sachsenhausen, Buchenwald, and Bautzen, were still being maintained in the Soviet Zone, and were filled with political prisoners and prisoners of war. As Christmas approached in December, 1949, Bishop Dibelius and Provost Grueber were permitted to visit the inmates of Sachsenhausen and to conduct Christmas services for them. Since this was the first such visit permitted by the Russians since the war, great interest was attached to the reactions of these Churchmen. Grueber wrote a report on his visit, which was quoted in nearly every newspaper in both East and West Germany.

This visit was of particular significance to Grueber, since he had last entered Sachsenhausen in 1940 as a prisoner of the Nazis. Memories of the brutality and murder perpetrated in this camp had been refreshed in Grueber's mind and that of the entire German public in 1947, when the Soviets had conducted the special Sachsenhausen Trials in Berlin. Grueber himself had at that time been called in to testify concerning the treatment he had received from a guard known as "Iron Gustav," who was on trial for his life.

But when Grueber entered the grim gates of Sachsenhausen in 1949, he found the domain of Iron Gustav completely changed. The barbed wire was still there, and the familiar buildings, but Grueber was impressed by the great difference in the handling of the prisoners. There were no shaved heads and striped prison suits in 1949. Instead of beaten, silent people, he saw well-fed, well-groomed people, with some of the women even wearing lipstick. As far as physical care was concerned, the new Sachsenhausen appeared to Grueber as good as many refugee camps that he had seen in West Germany. He was allowed to converse with the inmates following his service, and he felt in duty bound to report that those with whom he had spoken had no complaints to make concerning their treatment.

As he walked past a certain building in the camp, Grueber recalled the treatment the Nazis had accorded to certain Russian prisoners confined there back in 1942 and 1943. With shame he admitted that no voice among the German prisoners had been raised in protest against such inhumanity, because to protest would have meant certain death.

After making these favorable comparisons, which he felt compelled to make on the basis of his observations, Grueber went on to declare that concentration camps ought not to exist at all. But if they must exist, then he urged speedy trials for the inmates, correspondence privileges for the families, and a regular spiritual ministry by the Church.

The publication of this report touched off a veritable storm of protest and criticism in the West German press. Frequently without citing more than the portions of his report which supported their contentions, newspapers scored Grueber for "whitewashing" Russian brutality and terrorism. More frequently it was pointed out that what Dibelius and Grueber had been permitted to see in Sachsenhausen was a kind of "Potemkin village," behind the decorated façade of which the real squalor and misery of the camp were concealed. Whether intentionally or naïvely, declared the critics, Grueber and Dibelius had through such reporting thrown the weight of the Church on the side of the Russians in the now ominously teetering balance between East and West.

Lavish words of praise filled the columns of the East German press, stressing of course the portions of the report that were favorable to the East. But not all of Grueber's defenders were Communist sympathizers. A Jewish newspaper in Berlin noted pointedly that far too many of the "courageous voices" now raised to criticize had been painfully silent at a time when Grueber's had been raised against Nazi inhumanity. The implication was clear that much of the "righteous indignation" being expressed in the West concerning Grueber's report had political rather than humanitarian motives. "Only those whose moral conduct during the Nazi times warrants it," declared Der Weg, "are in a position to direct criticisms against the measures of the occupation authorities. One of the few who has such a right is Provost Grueber."

In order to make clear the official position of the churches on these matters, both the Council of the EKD and the Roman Catholic

Cardinal von Preysing issued categorical statements that the operation of concentration camps by any government, regardless of the kind of treatment given to the inmates, was contrary to all principles of humanity.

Three weeks after Christmas, a letter from the Soviet commanding general, Marshal Zhukov, to the deputy premier of the German Democratic Republic, Walter Ulbricht, announced the closing of all Russian concentration camps in East Germany, and the release of 15,000 prisoners. Doubtless the favorable Christmas publicity had provided the Soviets with the best possible opportunity in which to carry out such an act of amnesty. While ridding themselves of an embarrassing symbol of inhumanity, they left at least the suggestion, thanks largely to Grueber's report, that the Russian model of concentration camp was on a higher level than that of the Nazis.

It is also true that 14,000 other inmates of these camps were simply transferred to other prisons. But regardless of the propaganda value the Soviets secured through these developments, it should not be overlooked that 15,000 prisoners were returned to their families. Nor should it be forgotten that, before the amnesty, the Church had made repeated representations to the Soviet military authorities, requesting that such action be taken. But it is characteristic of the position of the Church in the midst of the rising East-West tensions that even such negotiation of humanitarian importance should be used for political purposes by one side or the other.

About the same time as the Grueber report an even more explosive story burst in the German press. This was an interview given by Martin Niemoeller to Marguerite Higgins, a reporter of the *New York Herald Tribune*, on December 13, 1949. Although the interview was given in Wiesbaden, in West Germany, and Niemoeller was president of a West German church, Hessen-Nassau, its reverberations reached Berlin and the East Zone as well, and more dramatically than any other event exemplified the precarious position of the Church between the political powers of East and West.

It was no surprise that Dr. Niemoeller became so thoroughly involved in this strife. His personality and his past record made it almost a foregone conclusion. Son of a Westphalian pastor, Niemoeller had served as a submarine commander in the German Navy during the First World War. Like so many young men of the defeated imperial army and navy, he faced the stormy 1920's without any definite personal direction. His political tendencies were rightist, and he participated in the anti-Communist Kapp *Putsch* in 1920. After an unsatisfactory attempt at farming, Niemoeller decided on the study of theology, and by 1924 was filling an administrative position with the Inner Mission of Westphalia. In 1930 came the decisive move to Berlin and the Dahlem parish, where he was to become the center of the Church resistance against the Nazi regime. To him, as to many others in 1932-1933, the National Socialist regime offered a fleeting hope, and Niemoeller joined the ranks of those who extended congratulations to Adolf Hitler for his energetic program of German revival. The tide changed quickly, however, and Niemoeller found himself leader of the Pastors' Emergency League, resisting the Nazi-dominated official Church government in Prussia. In 1937 he was quietly arrested, and for eight years remained as Hitler's personal prisoner, spending a good deal of time in the concentration camps of Sachsenhausen and Dachau.

He was released in 1945, taken by the United States Army in Italy, and held for questioning in Wiesbaden against his will, until he went on a hunger strike to secure his release to return to his family in Bavaria. He was thrust into the leadership in the postwar Evangelical Church reorganization because of his leading position in the Brotherhoods of the Confessing Church, and, as such, became a member of the Council of the newly forming EKD in 1945 at Treysa.

As one of the signers and ardent proponents of the Stuttgart Declaration of Guilt, Niemoeller won both warm commendation and bitter criticism from his own people. He was elected first president of the newly formed Church of Hessen-Nassau, and from this position plunged into the center of every controversial issue in postwar German life. He bitterly attacked the "starvation policies" of the western Allies in Germany, and denounced the complicated and mechanical denazification procedures of the Americans as productive of deceit and lying, and finally publicly forbade his pastors to participate in any way in the process.

He was extremely critical of the failure of the Allies to reach an agreement on a peace treaty for Germany, but his indignation

Railway Mission Workers Service Returning Prisoners-of-War in Berlin (*Photo Puck Pressedienst*)

78th Annual Katholikentag in East Berlin

Chapel Converted to Barn in East Germany
at Waldsieversdorf (1957)

East Berlin Youth Examining Youth Dedication Certificates and Gift
Books (1958)

reached a high point when the Allies began to take steps toward the erection of separate governments for East and West Germany, and to incorporate these new States into their respective military defense systems.

The prospect of Germany as the battleground of a third world war, as indeed must be the case if the East-West division deepened, to the accompaniment of feverish military preparations, was unthinkable. War of any kind had become bitter for Niemoeller, and one in which German would be pitted against German was most intolerable of all, and contrary to all moral and ethical standards. The possibility of the use of atomic weapons removed the last shred of reasonableness from war of any kind.

These deep feelings were in Niemoeller's mind when he was approached by the enterprising Marguerite Higgins in December, 1949. After an hour's conversation with this very talkative Church president, who obviously said much more than he thought he had, the reporter date-lined a story to her editor which began with the flat assertion: "Pastor Martin Niemoeller said today that most Germans would rather see the reunification of their country under Communism than a continuation of its present division into East and West."

The article explained further that while Niemoeller hoped that a "third way" could be found, he believed that reunification under a foreign dictatorship would provide greater possibilities for continued life as a nation than would a permanent partition of Germany. His own suggestion for the solution of the German problem would be the withdrawal of western and Russian occupation forces and the supervision of a neutralized and demilitarized Germany under teams of the United Nations.

Part of his strong feelings about the division of his country, said Niemoeller, was rooted in the conviction that the new West German government was clearly a Roman Catholic structure "conceived in the Vatican and born in Washington." The cabinet of the new chancellor gave far too much influence to Roman Catholics, far out of proportion to their actual strength. The East Zone of Germany, under Russian control, was more than 80 per cent Protestant. This, claimed Niemoeller, explained why the United States and the western Allies had moved to perpetuate the division. The formation of the Federal Republic, he believed, had been one of the greatest victories of the Roman Catholic Church since the Counterreformation.

Because this interview caused such a storm, Niemoeller felt it necessary to make further explanations—and sought to show that Miss Higgins had quoted his statements out of context. She had asked him first, he said, whether in the event of war a possible new West German army would fight against an East German army. Niemoeller's reply had been that a nation was like a family, which would always find it better to be together even under bad conditions than to live separately, one in a palace and the other in a hovel. He had simply sought to make clear that the Germans didn't want to become a battleground, under any circumstances, since a war would mean the total destruction of Germany.

Since the Russians were currently playing themselves up as the champions of reunification—through the East German People's Congress—while casting the onus upon the western Allies for bringing about the division of East and West Germany, these arguments of Niemoeller's were readily given currency in the East Zone press. Since Niemoeller was a high official of the Evangelical Cheurch, his words carried an official implication, though he insisted he spoke only as a private individual.

This was embarrassing to the Church, for it was thus once again drawn directly into the political aspects of the East-West controversy. When Niemoeller, from his western position, launched his bitter assaults against the western Allies and the West German government and their alleged allies in Rome, it became very difficult for anyone to disagree with him without being accused in the East Zone of being a tool of the imperialist West. Likewise, western Churchmen, and more so, western pressmen who disagreed with Niemoeller, saw him at the worst as an ally of the Communists and at best as a loquacious and bumbling cleric who tended to speak first and explain later. There seemed little question that Niemoeller was most in his element as a member of the opposition, on whatever issue might be under public discussion.

Whatever the merits or demerits of his position, Martin Niemoeller had certainly helped to propel the EKD into the midst of the political cauldron, seething and boiling between East and West

Niemoeller was a member of the Council of EKD and president of its Foreign Office, as well as president of the Evangelical Church of Hessen-Nassau. What he said, therefore, affected the role of this Church in its relation to East and West whether he so desired or not. The controversy became so intense by January, 1950, that the Council of EKD, meeting in Halle, in East Germany, felt impelled to declare publicly that Niemoeller was speaking privately and not on behalf of the EKD. It also attempted to regain something of a position of objectivity by declaring that it was not in harmony with the "Iron Curtain" politics of the occupation powers. Dr. Volkmar Herntrich, of Hamburg, presented a statement on behalf of the EKD, which was broadcast on the Northwest German Radio, in which he urged patience and understanding. He declared that the Church was seeking a "third way," on behalf of all men who had lost their freedom, on behalf of understanding and truth, and *against* the *total* State, wherever it might appear.

In spite of all efforts to quiet the uproar, the discussion continued on into 1950, with Niemoeller adding one statement after another to the growing volume. It was no wonder that when Bishop Dibelius was asked to ring the church bells of West Berlin in unison with the American Freedom Bell, he felt compelled to turn the request down. By this time even the ringing of a church bell conveyed political overtones.

SIX

NOT PEACE BUT A SWORD

The constitution of the German Democratic Republic, which went into operation for the former Soviet Zone of occupation on October 7, 1949, gave ample assurance of religious freedom, both to the Church as an institution and to its members as individuals. These assurances, based in large part on the old Weimar Constitution of 1919, gave no indication whatever of any basic hostility toward the Church or religion by the newly formed government. Beginning with Article 41 and continuing through Article 48 citizens were assured the undisturbed exercise of religious rights. No person could be forced to join any religious ceremony or to take a religious oath, nor was any civic right or privilege to be conditioned by a person's adherence or nonadherence to any religious association.

The constitution specifically declared that there was to be no State Church but that each communion should administer its own affairs independently. Those Churches which had previously enjoyed status as corporations of public law were guaranteed a continuance of this status, which carried with it the right to levy taxes on their own members on the basis of official taxation lists. Any person who wished to give up his membership in the Church was required to make a declaration to that effect before a court of law.

Although religious instruction was not to be the responsibility of the State, the right of the Church to give religious teaching on school premises was explicitly guaranteed. This instruction was to be given by personnel selected by the Church, and no one was to be forced to give, or prevented from giving, religious instruction. The right of parents to decide on the participation of their children was recognized.

Insofar as a demand existed for religious services and pastoral care in public institutions such as hospitals and prisons, this service was guaranteed, though participation was always to be on a voluntary basis.

Somewhat less clear were the references to the public functions of the Church. The right of the Church to take a public stand concerning vital issues facing the people was recognized, but immediately preceding this clause was a statement that religious institutions and religious teachings must not be used for unconstitutional and party political purposes.

Almost immediately discussion began on these ambiguous paragraphs. The Catholic News Service called Paragraph 41 concerning the abuse of religious institutions a "death sentence" for every religious organization which dared to disagree with the State—or the Communist Party. Under this paragraph, said the KNS, the Communist State had secured for itself a legal way to introduce a persecution of the Church whenever it saw fit.

Dr. Lotz of the Thuringian Church spoke more hopefully, pointing out that this paragraph also restrained the State from attempting to harness the Church for any political purposes of its own. But he did admit that the guarantees of freedom and independence to the Church would ultimately depend upon the application of the constitution in concrete cases in a spirit of true tolerance.

Eventually, it was in the spirit, rather than the letter, of the constitution that the relations of Church and State in East Germany were to find their sharpest differences. Aided by the dialectic pattern of thinking, which viewed everything and evaluated it in its relation to progress toward socialistic goals, the leaders of the East German State were able to alter the practical application of almost every one of these constitutional guarantees to the Church without changing the letter of the document in the least. At the 1949 stage of development, tolerance was still more or less a watchword. As time went on, and the party program was expanded and intensified ideologically, practically every guarantee to the Church listed in the constitution was set aside as obsolete. Attempts of the Church to assert "constitutional" rights were fruitless. Laws were passed depriving the Church of its right to use schoolrooms for religious instruction and of its right to examine official tax lists in levying dues upon its own members. Young people have been denied the right of education because of membership in Christian youth groups or student congregations. And teacher-candidates have been expelled from school and denied the right to teach because they have refused to renounce the Christian faith. All of these things have been carried out in East Germany under the alleged authority of the constitution. Socialist Party leaders have stated their basic principle clearly and frequently: "Whatever serves the cause of Socialism is right." On such a foundation of right, a western understanding of the binding character of constitutional law is impossible. Doomed also to failure is every optimistic attempt to find a common meaning for such words as democracy, freedom, peace, and tolerance.

Yet the Church was in the German Democratic Republic. The constitution of 1949 was declared to be the law of the land, and the Church had to live under it. The new government, styled "provisional" until elections were held a year later, was formed by the leaders of the SED. The People's Council, which had also written and approved the new constitution, declared itself to be the "Provisional People's Chamber."

Wilhelm Pieck, old-line Communist, became president, and Otto Grotewohl, prime minister, but the real power in the regime was exercised by Walter Ulbricht, chairman of the SED and deputy prime minister. As a gesture to the other parties "cooperating" in the national front, Dr. Otto Nuschke of the CDU and Dr. Kastner of the Liberal Democratic Party were also named deputy prime ministers. Key positions in the cabinet were filled by members of the SED.

Under the supervision of Dr. Nuschke a Department of Church Affairs was erected, with special liaison offices for Protestants and

Catholics. The Protestant office was filled by Dr. Kurt Gruenbaum, a layman whose lifelong career as an official within the Prussian Church had been terminated by the Nazis, and who, since 1945, had been supervising the landed properties of the Church of Brandenburg. When the Council of EKD appointed Dr. Heinrich Grueber as its official representative for dealing with the German Democratic Republic late in 1949, the liaison structure was complete. A similar representative, Dr. Kunst, was appointed by the council to represent the EKD with the Federal Republic in Bonn.

Far more ominous to Grueber than the fundamentally differing interests of Church and State which were so deceptively concealed in the fine phrases of the new constitution was the bitter fact of the political division of Germany into East and West and the threat to peace which was embodied in it. "The reunification of East and West Germany," declared Grueber in commenting on his new assignment, "is a special concern of the Church." And since he assumed his new responsibilities near Christmas time, Grueber called upon his fellow Christians to prepare the ground for the reality of peace on earth and good will among men. This, he declared, could be done only if honest and sincere cooperation among people of all nations was attempted. Grueber was eager that this cooperation should begin in Berlin.

Actually, there was by the beginning of 1950 a considerable volume of evidence that the interests of Church and State were in more fundamental conflict than Grueber would admit. At its first party conference in January, 1949, the SED had made it clear that it would become more and more a "party of the new type . . . a fighting party for Marxism-Leninism." With the new provisional government firmly under its control, the SED could be counted upon to press the ideology of the class conflict in every aspect of life in East Germany: economic, cultural, and political. Regardless of Grueber's pious hopes and strenuous efforts for common understanding, the Church would eventually find itself in profound conflict with a State whose basic philosophy was an atheistic materialism for which it was prepared to conduct an open crusade.

One of the areas of Church life over which both the Soviet Military Administration and the new regime of 1949 exercised a careful supervision was that of press and radio. At the close of the war all the occupation powers introduced systems of licensing, without which no newspapers, periodicals, or books could be printed. These regulations were in keeping with the stringent antifascist policies of the victors, but they also served the purpose of controlling the distribution of the very limited supplies of paper which were available during the first postwar years.

These licensing procedures were turned over to German committees in the western zones after 1947. In the Soviet Zone they were continued in their original form until 1949 when the German Democratic Republic assumed the responsibility for licensing. Even in 1960 it is still not possible to print even a post card or a page of Church announcements in East Germany without a special permit from the government.

Of the eight Protestant Churches in East Germany with a total membership of about 17,500,000 in 1950, only four Churches had received permission to publish a weekly paper, and their total issue outside Berlin was limited to 65,000 copies. Within Berlin, Bishop Dibelius' paper, *Die Kirche*, operating under both Russian and American licenses, had a circulation of 60,000, and a half-dozen other Church periodicals, including one for youth, one for Christian education, and one for scientific theology, were authorized a combined circulation of some 60,000. In contrast, the 22,400,000 members of Protestant Churches in West Germany were receiving 4,000,000 copies of their Church periodicals. Only a very few of these Church papers were permitted to enter the German Democratic Republic through the mails.

The Roman Catholic Church had not a single Church paper in East Germany until 1951, when a biweekly paper with 100,000 copies was licensed. The weekly *Petrusblatt*, issued in Berlin, was banned from East Germany in 1953, together with the youth publication *Christophorus*.

The publication of books of a religious character was also limited drastically, both through the requirement that every individual book or pamphlet be licensed, and through the restriction of the entire Protestant Church in East Germany to a single publication house, the Evangelical Publishing House of Berlin. Bibles, however, were published, under separate arrangements with the government, by the Altenburg Bible Society and the Evangelical Central Bible Society of Berlin, but both of these houses were severely restricted by the small contingent of paper which they were allocated under the government quota system. Books and pamphlets and papers of a political nature, which followed the Marxian line, on the other hand, received licenses and printing paper with virtually no limitations.

During the first years of the occupation, the Churches were able to conduct Sunday-morning meditations on the radio, without interference. But with the advent of the new German government in 1949, changes appeared here, too. In a series of broadcasts in which Provost Grueber, and General Superintendents Braun and Krummacher of Berlin-Brandenburg were the regular speakers, the names of two so-called "progressive" pastors, Mehnert and Kehnscherper, suddenly appeared. When repeated protests by Church authorities failed to bring any real satisfaction, the Church declined further participation in the broadcast series.

The decision of the SED Party Conference to become a fighting party for the principles of Marxism-Leninism had its effect on religious life and activities in many local East German communities. Pastors found it difficult to gather their congregations for Sunday worship, because political party meetings, rallies of various organizations sponsored by the party, school celebrations and activities, and special community work projects were scheduled for the hour of worship on Sunday mornings. Bishop Hahn of Saxony made this the central theme of his Repentance Day message in November, 1949, and the Church of Anhalt likewise prepared a special appeal to its congregations a few months later, in February, 1950.

The basic attitude of the new SED-directed government toward the Church showed itself also in the instruction, given by the Politburo of the SED to all party functionaries and leaders of related mass organizations in May, 1950, that they were expected to sever their connection with the Church. The same applied to the People's Police, though the commanding officers were instructed to achieve their objectives among the men without giving the impression that such action was the result of any directive from higher echelons. Particularly with the fall elections in prospect and, hopefully, the reunification of Germany also, any direct assault upon the Church was to be avoided. But there was no doubt expressed in the instructions of the Politburo that the maintenance of a Church connection, particularly by an officer of the People's Police, was incompatible with the ideology of a progressive Socialism.

Further evidence of the eagerness of local functionaries to carry out the declared aims of the party was found in a village in Saxony where the motto "Learn and teach to the glory of God" was chipped away from the entrance of the school. Objectors discovered that the District Committee of the Free German Youth had made this a special project throughout the entire district, on the ground that "such mottoes are no longer appropriate to our times." The Thuringian State Minister of Culture declared it to be a mockery for all progressive people, that schools could still exist in which the walls were decorated with religious mottoes and pictures. No progressive person could be expected to study in the presence of such "trash." Every teacher ought to have the ambition to clear his classroom of all such religious "bric-a-brac" and to replace it with pictures of the great political leaders Stalin, Lenin, and Pieck.

In the same category was the government order in 1949 forbidding special holidays and school programs celebrating Christmas, while recommending the celebration of the birthday of Joseph Stalin on December 21st. Christmas vacation was to be renamed "winter vacation," and the "Solidarity Child" was to replace the Christ Child at the center of vacation festivities.

It was among the youth and in the schools that the basic conflict between Church and State was most clearly exposed. The Church had incorporated its youth program directly into the life of the individual congregation, and thus avoided any conflict with the monopolistic claims of the Free German Youth as the only legal organization for youth in East Germany. Nevertheless, overly zealous local leaders of the FDJ, often backed by enthusiastic local party officials, interfered with the youth assemblies of the Church, particularly when more than one congregation was involved. Youth retreats or evangelizations or the presentations of plays were occasionally restricted, and the lapel symbol of the Evangelical Youth, the Cross over the Globe, was declared to be illegal.

But such local interferences were not so serious as the conflicts which were developing in the schools, where it was becoming increasingly apparent that the new Communist State intended to use its educational monopoly as an instrument for the indoctrination of children and youth in the ideologies of atheistic materialism. Annual pedagogical congresses issued statements of policy which reflected clearly the general line of the corresponding party congresses of the SED. Thus, in the late summer of 1949, the fourth Pedagogical Congress, with an eye upon the launching of the new East German government, called for the "education of the youth to a democratic national consciousness . . . to a new morality and discipline, as the condition for a conscious participation in the new society." Every teacher would be expected not only to possess mastery of his special subject matter but also to teach it in the light of Marxism-Leninism. Similarly, every teacher was expected to be a true friend of the Soviet Union.

Such new emphases were immediately translated into action in the schools, in terms of stricter supervision of teachers and increased pressures to conform to the party line. In some places this was reflected in local regulations assigning unfavorable hours for religious instruction, or prohibiting it entirely in the public school rooms. One school principal in Mecklenburg justified such an action with the assertion that the same room could not be used for instruction in both dialectic materialism and an idealistic world view such as Christianity.

Teachers who declared themselves willing to give religious instruction were frequently faced with discriminatory actions within the school. Pastors and catechists who came into the schools to give instructions were often denied access to classrooms because of insignificant or involuntary violations of minor regulations. The pressures were great enough so that on November 13, 1949, the Conference of Evangelical Teachers issued an official statement on behalf of its members.

First, they declared their objection to being used by a political party for its own purposes. Most of them had also been teachers at a time when the Nazi regime had made similar attempts. Silence at that time had been interpreted as approval of those policies, and thereby untruth and injustice had been promoted. For the sake of truth and of their responsibility before God and the government, before their colleagues, their children and the parents, the teachers refused to be silent now.

Second, they objected to being suddenly confronted with pre-pared political statements or declarations and urged to sign them without adequate time to study and consider.

Third, they recognized and accepted their responsibility as teachers to protect their pupils from lies and from force. Finally, as Evangelical teachers, they placed themselves in the service of the Church, and requested Church leaders and congregations, and especially the Evangelical parents, to stand by them and support their efforts.

This the Churches did, without a single exception, declaring their own obligation to speak out against the rising influence of a material-istic world view, which, as the Lutheran Church of Saxony flatly declared, "denies God and leaves no room for the revelation of God in Jesus Christ. . . .

"In contradiction to this materialistic world view, we profess that there is salvation in no other, for there is no other name under heaven given among men, whereby we must be saved, apart from that of our great Chief Shepherd Jesus Christ. We admonish all mem-bers of our congregations to oppose the teaching of materialism, to stand guard that our children do not become its victims, and to confess unafraid that Jesus Christ is the Lord of our lives."

So outspoken were the reactions of both the Evangelical and Roman Catholic Churches to this new political emphasis in the schools that a letter was sent out through confidential channels from the Central Committee of the SED, calling to the attention of the State party leaders the increasing Church opposition. In view of the elections scheduled for October, 1950, and the eagerness of the SED to enlist the support of the Churches for the National Front, party functionaries were advised to refrain for the time being from any overt acts which might give the impression of a State-directed anti-religious campaign. And upon the strong representations of Church officials, a revised edition of the school textbook in history by Michulin omitted a passage which denied that Jesus Christ had ever lived.

In spite of the desire of party politicians in East Germany to pre-vent any appearance of an open break with the Churches, the appli-cation of the new policies in the schools led to increasing tensions between Church and State. Reports continued to flow into the Church offices from communities where children were being politically indoctrinated in the schools, and taught a materialistic viewpoint which was completely contrary to that which they were being taught by their parents and by the Church. In the classes in a subject called "Current Events," children were required to write essays on political subjects. Their grades were made dependent, not primarily on the excellence of their performance, but upon the correctness of their political response on themes such as "Stalin: the Best Friend of the German People," or "The Great War of the Soviet Union for the Fatherland: an Example of a Righteous War," or "The Meaning of the Five Year Plan in the Fight for Peace and Unity."

Since promotions into advanced classes and higher schools were dependent upon the grades received, especially in this subject, children were faced with the alternative of failing because they had written what they really believed or writing what they knew the teachers wanted to find, even though this meant writing a falsehood. One little girl took the second alternative, but at the bottom of every essay she scratched in very tiny script the letters "LL." For weeks her parents tried to discover what this meant, but she refused to say. At last she gave in and confided to her mother that "LL" was an abbreviation for the words "lauter Lügen"—"nothing but lies."

This was one little girl's attempt to preserve some measure of intellectual and moral integrity in the face of pressures which, if openly resisted, might very well mean the termination of future plans for advanced education. Still another youngster told her parents: "We must lie in school, but we must never forget that we are lying."

It was on behalf of these children, who were being deprived of both freedom and integrity, that the Church in East Germany undertook its first serious open conflict with the State. Bishop Dibelius and Cardinal von Preysing directed letters of protest to Prime Minister Otto Grotewohl and Deputy Premier Otto Nuschke, and in March, 1950, Dibelius met with Grotewohl personally to discuss ways of lessening the growing tensions between Church and State. Several suggestions were made by the bishop, but essentially he urged that the government take steps to halt all direct and indirect attacks upon the Christian faith, both in school and elsewhere, and that all kinds of pressures upon children and adults, which deprived them of the right of free decision, should be stopped. He also requested that instead of writing public letters to each other, leading representatives of Church and State should meet together for a basic and thorough discussion of differences. He suggested the Tuesday following Easter as a possible date.

No reply was forthcoming to Dibelius' suggestion until April 18th, several days after Easter, when Grotewohl wrote, confirming the proposed conference, but asking that the Church submit a memorandum with full documentation of its specific complaints, as the basis for discussion.

Obviously irritated by the unwillingness of the State to discuss these matters freely, Dibelius wrote to Grotewohl, reminding him that the Church had asked in the first place for a discussion of basic principles rather than individual cases. It was, as a matter of fact, only the assurance of this kind of discussion that had restrained the Provincial Church of Saxony from issuing a public statement before Easter protesting the situation in the schools.

Dibelius' letter of April 20th to Prime Minister Otto Grotewohl minced no words. He pointed out that of the 20,000,000 people living in the German Democratic Republic, more than 90 per cent were members of the Church. To each of these members the promise had been made at baptism that they should be brought up in the Christian faith. Yet for the past five years these people had lived under constant propaganda for a materialistic world view contrary to the faith into which they were baptized.

It was clearly the right of every citizen to make his own decisions on these matters, the bishop agreed. But the Church could not be quiet when the compulsive power of the State was being used to fight against the Christian faith in the interests of another world view. Any person who wished to do so was at liberty to separate himself from the Church, but it was impossible to secede from the State. This meant that the schools, which were State institutions, were being used to influence the world view of the children whether the parents wished such an influence to be exerted upon them or not.

Concerning the materialistic world view itself, the bishop was no less plain-spoken:

The materialistic world view is not a theoretical matter, but has a very practical effect upon the lives of individuals and of society. Because it recognizes no God, it raises material things to the level of the highest good and the greatest value, and thereby comes into direct conflict with the moral responsibilities of the Christian, which have their eternal foundation in the laws of God. It is not my task to judge how one views the matter from a materialistic standpoint when students write things in political essays which are contrary to their convictions because they don't want to jeopardize their admission to high school or university. According to the commands of God, this is simply a lie. The dialectic materialism may say whatever it wishes when people are forced to take part in political demonstrations which they feel are not right. For the Christian this is an infringement upon his God-given human dignity. When in a constitution it is resoundingly declared that no person shall suffer any subsequent disadvantage if he speaks his opinion freely and openly, and then in practice exactly the opposite becomes a daily experience, this is for the Christian conscience a violation of trust and confidence. The leadership of the Christian Church cannot simply stand by and watch, while its members are subjected to such pressures that they gradually become accustomed to living a split existence, which can end only in general deceit and untruthfulness. Nor can the church simply disregard the pleas for help which are directed to it every day by conscience-burdened Christian people.

Bishop Dibelius wanted to make it clear that his words were in no sense an attack upon the State. Christianity was here on the defensive, and the State had launched the attack. The Church was not interested in becoming mixed up in political matters, but when State actions jeopardized the faith of baptized children and the freedom of Church members to operate according to their Christian conscience, the Church was obligated to speak. On such matters, though the Church sought no battle with the power of the State, it would not shy away from its responsibilities.

Once more Dibelius repeated the suggestions he had made in March for the easing of these deep-rooted tensions between Church and State. It would not be sufficient that individual cases of discrimination or threat against Christian school children were investigated and cleared up. It would not even be enough if the history textbook which denied the existence of Christ were withdrawn, though this would certainly be expected. A garden is not destroyed simply by plucking fruits and flowers, he declared. The trees have to be torn up by the roots. The Church demanded that the State discontinue its propaganda for a particular world view, and leave the decisions on such matters freely to the individual citizen, without fear of reprisals.

The bishop concluded by advising Grotewohl of his intention to publish the letter, but once again expressed the eagerness of the Church to enter into personal discussions with representatives of the State.

On the following Sunday, April 23rd, the opening day of the Synod of the EKD, which assembled in East Berlin, the Churches of Berlin-Brandenburg, Mecklenburg, the State of Saxony, and the Province of Saxony issued declarations that were read from every pulpit. The Roman Catholic bishops of Germany issued a pastoral letter against materialism, both in East and West, and declared that any Catholic "consciously and voluntarily following and propagating the teachings of materialistic atheism" was excommunicated. This letter was read from every Catholic pulpit in East and West Germany. If the government authorities had hoped to prevent an open conflict with the Churches in the election year, they had failed completely. They had also discovered that in the years to come, the new State need not expect to be dealing with docile and easily manipulated spiritual leaders.

The message of the Berlin-Brandenburg Church was typical of all of these Sunday pronouncements that trumpeted across East Germany as the opening blasts in a Church and State conflict that was to continue without interruption, though in varying degrees of intensity, for the next ten years. The message declared:

Our Lord Jesus Christ says: "The truth shall make you free." This truth is none other than Christ Himself, the crucified and risen one, He is our comfort and power. We proclaim Him to all men, also amid the great needs of our time. More than ever we see ourselves today surrounded by harassed and restless consciences. Ceaselessly calls come from parishioners to pastors, elders, and Church administrations. They say: "Help us! We are being required to say things which for the sake of truth we cannot say. We are being forced to participate in activities in which we cannot participate with a good conscience. We are required to approve of decisions which we cannot sanction. We are in constant danger of losing our freedom, our employment, and our daily bread if we decline to go along. . . ." Particularly shocking are the complaints of parents that their children are becoming more and more accustomed, under the pressure of schools, higher education and youth organizations, to speak and write differently than they think; that their Christian faith is despised, and that teachers try to talk them into believing that there is no God and that Christ never even existed.

Since efforts to bring the full seriousness of these matters before the leaders of the government had not been successful, the Church felt itself obligated to state its position publicly. It did so in words which reechoed the spirit of the Declaration of Barmen, and belied any suggestion whatever that the Church of East Germany regarded its antagonist as some political group with which it could clasp hands and work together for the mutual goal of peace on earth and good will among men:

1. The Evangelical Church confesses the truth, whose name is Jesus Christ. This truth cannot be combined with a materialistic world view. We therefore protest that this world view is being propagated in schools, in higher education, in government offices and State-sponsored organizations as the exclusively valid truth. No State authority has the right to impose on someone a world view which contradicts his faith and conscience. We summon the members of our congregations, wherever their faith is directly or indirectly attacked, to confess with firmness and joy that Christ is our Lord and that we belong to Him with body and soul.

2. Jesus Christ, who is the truth, frees us from the power of lies. It is a sin to force people to lie, and to mislead even children to do it. We most urgently plead with all who are in public life not to make themselves guilty of such sin.

3. The truth, who is Jesus Christ, liberates us so that we can love our fellow man, even if he is our enemy. Wherever hate is preached against peoples, races, or classes, or against individuals, the Christian is called upon to love. Under no circumstances may he become implicated in any kind of hate propaganda or violence. And when he himself becomes the victim of such action, he may not answer violence with violence, but should beseech God for power to resist while suffering.

4. The truth, which we confess in our Lord Jesus Christ, unites us into a fellowship of faith and love. Where someone falls victim to violence, it is the duty of others to intercede for him, and to prove in deed

that whoever suffers innocently is worthy of a double share of honor and love.

5. The truth, wherein we comfort ourselves, is the voice of the Lord who does not break the bruised reed nor extinguish the smoking flax. We know how many do not have the power to resist from without. As those who themselves know their weakness, we commit you and ourselves to the forgiveness of God. He is greater than our heart. He can cancel all guilt and help us to a new beginning, if we pray him for it. But let no one permit his conscience to become dull, and discover his life to be daily full of untruths that seem to be unavoidable and thus become a matter of indifference.

6. Finally, we declare to those who today still reject the call of Jesus Christ that His truth would also make them free. Without Him all of us together, even when we do not admit it, are poor and wretched and frightened creatures. He alone liberates us that we may be human beings and brothers toward one another.

Jesus Christ, the Risen One, greets His own with His Easter greeting: Peace be with you! To this peace we commit you and ourselves. He is the victor over fear, sin, and death. He forsakes no one who trusts in Him. To Him be glory forever!

Meanwhile, Prime Minister Grotewohl struck back at the Churches, denouncing the open letters of both Protestant and Catholic leaders as an attack on the constitution, the government, and the republic. These letters, he declared, represented a breach of faith, since they were made public while negotiations between the government and the Church on the subject of a Church Declaration were still going on.

The sharpness of the government response, however, was tempered by the desire of the SED Party to convey the appearance of inner unity in the country through the building of the National Front. The Russian Ambassador Semjonow seems also to have reminded the government of the importance of this sense of unity in the first months of the new government's life. In any event, Deputy Prime Minister Otto Nuschke appeared at the Synod of the EKD in Weissensee and brought a very cordial greeting to the assembled Church representatives. And on April 28th, as the synod came to an end, the desired conference of Church and State leaders was held.

Prime Minister Grotewohl was accompanied by all three of his deputies and by several other leading state officials. With Bishop

Dibelius came Bishops Hahn, Hornig, Mueller, and Beste, representing the Protestant Churches in East Germany. The Roman Catholics were represented by Bishop Wilhelm Weskamm and Prelate Walter Adolph of Berlin. The discussion lasted for six hours, and concluded with ambiguous mutual assurances by Church and State. The Church representatives assured the government that they were deeply concerned about the rebuilding of the life of the German people in peace and freedom. The government assured the Church that its constitutional right to carry on its work within the German Democratic Republic would continue to be respected. Obviously, no clear and definite agreements had been reached in the initial serious confrontation of Church and State in East Germany.

Throughout the entire course of events leading to the founding of the German Democratic Republic in 1949, the Soviets and their German co-workers had sought to convey the impression that they were the real supporters of the German quest for peace and unity. The western Allies were accused of having violated the terms of the Potsdam Agreement. The constitution of the German Democratic Republic was hailed as an all-German constitution, which in time would bring the peoples of both East and West together to rebuild a socialistic Germany in peace and unity.

In order to achieve this objective an organization known as the National Front was established at the time the new government was proclaimed on October 7, 1949. Under the direction of a National Committee made up of three hundred members from the German Democratic Republic and one hundred from West Germany and West Berlin, the National Front declared its objective to be the "assembling of all upright Germans in the fight for the unity of Germany and for the conclusion of a treaty of peace." Under its banner the National Front rallied all of the political parties of the East Zone, and all of the Communist-controlled mass organizations. Its program was so general that unless one understood the basic political purposes behind it, it was difficult to raise objection to its stated aims. Part of the purpose of the National Front was to arrange the "unified lists" of candidates for elections, distributing the positions in advance of the election among the various parties and organizations which cooperated.

No elections were held in October, 1949, when the new government was launched, but preparations were made for parliamentary elections one year later, in October, 1950. These elections should presumably provide the popular ratification of the constitution, and put into office a popularly elected set of officials. During the intervening twelve months, the National Front was given the responsibility of rallying popular support for the "provisional" government and its policies of peace, unity, and reconstruction. These appeals were not limited to the East Zone; a special department was created for the purpose of cultivating connections with West Germany as well.

There was an inherent conflict between this outwardly benevolent and constructive program of good will proclaimed by the National Front, and the sharply realistic platform of the first Party Congress of the SED in January, 1949, proclaiming itself to be a party of the "new type," with strict discipline and faithfulness to the Marxist-Leninist doctrines required of every member. It was this latter emphasis which expressed itself in the more rigid ideological program in the schools, and precipitated the sharp conflict with the Churches which reached its climax in the post-Easter pulpit declarations in both Protestant and Catholic churches.

At the same time the National Front was seeking to win support for its program. It made its first general public appeal in Berlin on February 15, 1950, calling for a reunified Germany, a peace treaty, and the withdrawal of occupation troops from all zones. All parties, organizations, and groups, including the Churches, were urged to associate themselves with this program. Having already been squarely confronted with the ideological aims of the SED, however, which were also the guiding principles of the National Front, both Protestants and Roman Catholics refused to have anything to do with it.

This rejection of the National Front was made clear in several official statements from both Protestant and Catholic leaders. The Berlin Consistory reminded all its pastors of the basic position on political action taken by the Church in the letter of May, 1948, to Marshal Sokolowski. Cardinal von Preysing directed a similar letter to the clergy of the Roman Catholic Church. The Lutheran Church of Saxony recalled the Declaration of Barmen, in which any suggestion that the State might use the Church for political purposes had been emphatically rejected as "false doctrine." The contributions made by the Church to peace and unity could not be made within the political framework of a "National Front." They would have to be made on the basis of the Gospel of Jesus Christ.

No single event set forth more clearly the determination of the Church to maintain this principle, even in the face of political pressures, than the Synod of the EKD in Berlin-Weissensee in April. The theme of this assembly was one that loomed large in the thinking of all Germans in 1950. As the tensions between East and West continued to rise, highlighted in 1949 by the formation of the North Atlantic Treaty Organization and the ousting of Chiang Kai-shek from the Chinese mainland by the Communists, the threat of a third world war seemed all too real. In mid-1950, Russian-equipped North Korean troops burst across the 38th parallel to attack South Korea and plunged the United Nations into a bitter and bloody war in the Far East. Even before the Korean War broke out, the question of the relation of the new Federal Republic of West Germany to NATO and European defense was being discussed, and in the second half of 1950 the issue of German rearmament entangled the new German State in an almost convulsive debate. In this debate the Churches also became deeply involved. Leading churchmen such as Martin Niemoeller and Gustav Heinemann strongly opposed the rearmament policies of Chancellor Adenauer and the CDU Party, which they saw as a direct threat to the peace of Europe. Although this issue was primarily a western issue, the fact that the EKD was an all-German Church federation also involved the Churches in the East. It was only natural that with Church officials of the EKD living in West Germany expressing such strong feelings on these issues, question would be raised as to whether these men spoke for the entire Church.

In the midst of these expressed and unexpressed fears that a third world war, in which atomic weapons might be used, might break out at any moment, and that Germany might again become the battleground, the Synod of EKD proposed to consider the burning question: What Can the Church Do for Peace? Needless to say the politicians of the National Front were very much interested in what the Church would say to this question, inasmuch as peace was one of their major points of emphasis and appeal. In April, 1949, the first World Congress of Fighters for Peace had been held in Paris, and ever since, the East Zone had been blanketed with blue-and-white banners, picturing Picasso's "peace dove," and rallying the people to become "fighters for peace." Part of the campaign for the National Front was the gathering of signatures for peace petitions, rallying support for the coming World Peace Congress to be held in Stockholm in November, 1950.

If the politicians of the National Front were hoping for an answer to the question which could be interpreted as a support for the Communist-sponsored World Peace Movement, they were doomed to disappointment. The Declaration of the Synod of Weissensee spoke with deep feeling of the critical state of world politics, and the earnest desire of the German people that war should be prevented. But instead of laying the blame for the threat to peace upon one nation or another, it pointed out clearly that wars came because of the disregard of the laws and commands of Almighty God. The only way to peace, therefore, was the way of repentance, of subjection to the will and law of God, and of faith in the crucified Christ. The task of the Church was to declare this message as the basis of world peace, even though men and nations seemed to ignore it.

But the Church also had a responsibility to warn men and governments against the forces that produce wars: hatred and injustice, terror and discrimination, irresponsible government, and the creation of a climate of deceit and untruthfulness. These things must be removed, or all talk of peace among nations would be empty and futile. The respect of a government for the individual person and for his conscience could be most clearly shown in the readiness of a government to protect even those who for the sake of their consciences could not perform military service.

The statement did not neglect to lay before the occupation powers the urgent plea for amnesty for the war prisoners who were still being held, for the speedy conclusion of a peace treaty, and for the removal of the Iron Curtain dividing Germany. But there was nothing in the Weissensee Declaration which suggested even remotely the alignment of the Church with the political peace program of the National Front. In fact, the appeal of the synod to the members of the Church not to allow themselves to become the tools of any peace propaganda "which in reality is sowing hatred and promoting war," was plain enough so that the Weissensee Declaration was given a very cool reception among the "peace fighters" of the National Front. In some places the statement was even torn down from church bulletin boards where it had been posted for the information of the congregations.

The Declaration of Weissensee and the pulpit declarations that had been read on the opening day of the synod demonstrated conclusively that the leadership of the Churches was not open to any blandishments from the National Front. The SED politicians turned therefore to the tactic of appealing to individual pastors not to be misled by a reactionary Church leadership, but to assert their independent support of the "National Front for peace and unity." An SED policy document which was prepared for presentation to the party assembly was printed in the official Soviet organ, the *Taegliche Rundschau*, in which this tendency was clearly set forth. "The overwhelming majority of Church members," blithely asserted the SED, "belong both to democratic organizations and political parties. Together with thousands of their pastors, millions of Church members are within the National Front, fighting for peace."

A few high Church leaders, asserted the article, had repeatedly attacked this movement, but these were the same persons who had always supported the monopolists and the Junkers and who gave their blessing to the weapons of Hitler's war. These leaders did not have the best interests of the Church in mind, but were determined rather to erect within it a monopolistic empire of reaction. It was the intention of the SED to give support to the "progressive pastors" who objected to such tendencies within the Church.

At the third Party Congress of the SED in June, Prime Minister Grotewohl made these intentions official. Not only did he assume a sponsorship for these "progressive pastors," but he declared that the financial commitments of the State to the Churches, which were based on legal agreements, would be withheld if the Church continued to oppose government policies.

Bishop Dibelius was singled out for a particularly bitter attack by the prime minister. He was alleged to be the leader of the forces of reaction in the Church which sought to disturb the peace in Germany. He accused Dibelius of having visited President Truman for the purpose of securing advice on how best to assist the policies of the American imperialists in East Germany. He pointed to Dibelius' long-standing record of opposition to Communism, dating back to 1928, and accused him of having given the blessing of the Church to the Nazis in 1933.

During the party rally, a certain Pastor Schwartze of Mecklenburg, who had been removed from office through a disciplinary action of his Church, raised his voice as the representative of the tiny but vocal group of "progressive pastors" who favored the policies of the SED in East Germany. He urged the party to by-pass the Church leadership and to approach the pastors directly.

Dibelius' reply to Grotewohl's accusations was not long in coming. Concerning his visit to the United States, the bishop pointed out that this was simply a brief transit visit on route to the meeting of the Central Committee of the World Council of Churches in Toronto. The idea of an American President making use of such an occasion to give counsel to a German bishop on the political attitudes of his Church seemed to Dibelius fantastic, worthy perhaps of a place in some detective novel, but not likely to survive as great literature.

Concerning the assertions made by Grotewohl that the Church leaders of 1950 were the same ones who had blessed the weapons of Hitler's war of plunder, Dibelius defied Grotewohl to find a single one of the leading churchmen in Germany who had not been a bitter opponent of Hitler. Such irresponsible assertions, he declared, were "monstrous propaganda lies, and nothing else."

Asking pardon for using such sharp words, the bishop declared it was difficult "to remain quiet, when one watches the battle against the Church being carried on with means such as this." Such lying propaganda touched the leaders of the Church especially closely. "Which of us," he asked, "has forgotten what went through our souls when we saw that war begin on September 1, 1939? Who doesn't remember the 'bitter earnest' conversations with our sons who had to give their lives for something that was in enmity with their inmost being? In the face of this—will someone say to us that we *blessed* the weapons for Hitler's war of plunder? This is outright lying, and done deliberately at that! No prime minister ought to be a party to such open falsehood as this!"

Following the attempt to discredit Bishop Dibelius in the eyes of the clergy, the SED issued hundreds of personal invitations to pastors to attend conferences sponsored by the National Front. These invitations were signed by high government officials, and included the payment of free transportation and all expenses. Of fifteen hundred pastors in the Church of Brandenburg, a total of twenty attended the meeting on August 16th and heard party officials assure them that if their Church leaders should discriminate against them for coming, the government would protect them and guarantee their salaries. Resolutions were presented at this meeting, opposing war and the use of the atomic bomb, favoring the Stockholm Peace Declaration, and approving a common ballot for the October 15th elections. Nine pastors signed these resolutions. The following day East German papers declared that the pastors of the Church of Brandenburg had overwhelmingly approved the Stockholm Peace Declaration.

Another series of such meetings was called in September under the sponsorship of the Christian Democratic Union. Before the proposed pastors' conference in Berlin, in connection with the CDU Party rally, was held, the Church leadership of Berlin-Brandenburg directed a letter to Rudi Jahn, minister-president of Brandenburg, advising him that the Church could not give its approval to this meeting. Reports concerning a similar meeting on August 16th had made it clear that the intention was not to hold a free discussion, but simply to use the pastors for political purposes.

The Church used the opportunity to speak a word to the minister-president concerning the coming elections. One year previously the new government had declared before all the world that it would hold free elections in October, 1950. According to all indications, however, voters would only have an opportunity to approve a previously prepared single list of candidates and to endorse the policies of the government. Such an election, declared the Church, was not the free election that had been promised. Such procedures were neither honest nor fair, nor was it right to put loyal citizens in a position where they must either vote Yes or be publicly assailed as warmongers and enemies of the State.

The CDU pastors' rally in Berlin was a complete failure. Only a few "progressive pastors" attended, and these few repeated the August performance, signing resolutions for peace and the National Front. Similar rallies in other states secured no more than a 1 to 2 per cent participation among the pastors. The party leadership, however, indicated that in the future it would pay much closer attention to the Church, encouraging the "progressive element" whenever possible and attempting to increase participation in political life.

The election on October 15th returned the expected overwhelming endorsement of the policies and candidates of the National Front. The vote was not secret, and the only possibility of voting No was by defacing the ballot completely, and this was likely to bring post-election reprisals. The official reports indicated a 99.7 per cent approval of the National Front. West German and American officials advised East Germans not to run the risks of voting negatively, lest they jeopardize their future. The Roman Catholic Bishop of Bautzen advised Roman Catholic priests to vote for the National Front, since all the world realized that the election was a hoax anyway. The Protestant Churches simply left the matter to the individual consciences, and there were many, including the Bishop of Magdeburg, who made no secret of the fact that they had abstained because their consciences would not permit them to take part in an unfair election.

As might have been expected, once the elections were over and the new "popular" government had been duly installed in office, the Church was made to feel reprisals for its stubborn attitude toward the National Front. Prime Minister Grotewohl included a special section in his message to the government on the subject of the rights and duties of the Church. Constitutional guarantees of freedom in the exercise of religion, he declared, were as certain as ever. But every right carried with it corresponding responsibilities. Freedom of religion did not make it right for a group of Churchmen who lived in West Berlin to campaign for the remilitarization of West Germany, and to nullify the sincere attempts of the East German government to promote peace. The urging of remilitarization, pointed out the prime minister, was militaristic propaganda, and this, under Article 6 of the constitution, was a crime. Against such crimes the Church, too, had an obligation to contend actively.

Two ominous actions of the government at this time indicated that these words of Grotewohl were more than idle speaking. For the first time since 1945 western members of the Council of the EKD were denied entry permits to the German Democratic Republic for the purpose of attending a meeting at Elbingerode, and therefore had to meet in Berlin. The second action was the passage on December 15th of the Law for the Defense of Peace, by the East German

Parliament. According to this law, which was to provide the basis for arrest and imprisonment of great numbers of clergy and Church workers in the coming months of the Church controversy, any expression or agitation against the German Democratic Republic and the Soviet bloc could be punished by imprisonment. "Agitation to boycott democratic institutions" was to become a familiar phrase in the indictments of Churchmen and others who dared to disagree openly with government policies.

More specifically, the SED press launched a direct assault upon Bishop Dibelius as an agent of western militarism and imperialism, and an agitator against the National Front. The minister-president of the State of Brandenburg, Rudi Jahn, sent a letter to the Church administration demanding that such western-controlled leadership be repudiated. Most of the pastors in Brandenburg, asserted the minister-president blandly, were ready to cooperate in local committees for the National Front, but they had been hindered by unconstitutional pressure and mass regulations from the Church headquarters in West Berlin. In order to force the Church to cooperate in this demand, two measures were announced: first, State subsidies would be paid after January 1, 1951, only to a Church leadership which had its headquarters within the State of Brandenburg. These subsidies were contractual obligations dating back into the nineteenth century, when Church properties had been turned over to the State in exchange for permanent annual payments. They constituted about 15 per cent of the Church's total income. Second, the State of Brandenburg would assume the responsibility of paying the salaries of pastors who had been discriminated against by the Church because of their political activities, and they would pay these salaries directly out of the money set aside for State subsidies to the Church.

Bishop Dibelius denied that the location of the Church headquarters in West Berlin reflected an attachment to the western powers. The headquarters of this Church, he said, had been located in West Berlin for more than one hundred years, and there was no relation whatever between political and ecclesiastical boundaries. This situation had been known and fully accepted by the State of Brandenburg in December, 1948, when the Church had put its new constitution into effect. Any attempt to revise this situation would be regarded by the Church as an infringement upon its rights.

As far as the pastors were concerned, against whom the Church was alleged to be discriminating, Dibelius took up their cases one by one. In no instance was any disciplinary action being carried on against a pastor because he participated in the National Front. But, curiously, several pastors who were already under disciplinary action for various inner-Church reasons found themselves being elevated as martyrs by the government, and some of them encouraged this.

Specifically mentioned by the minister-president as a victim of discrimination was a Pastor Dressler, who had been stricken from the clerical roster thirty years earlier but who had been given repeated opportunities for a new beginning. During the Nazi times he was a "German-Christian." Another pastor named Kietzmann had been in constant trouble in his parish, and the Church headquarters had been requested by the Soviet occupation authorities, as well as by the local community, to recall him. Pastor Kehnscherper, one of the most active of the "progressive" pastors, who had also been in trouble in his own parish, had even offered to leave the parish voluntarily if the personal difficulties there could not be settled. But after the October 15th elections, he changed his mind, and for this reason the Church instituted disciplinary action against him. The files of other pastors mentioned by Minister-President Jahn were available in the Church office, but Dibelius saw no reason for airing personal matters in public communications.

There was certainly nothing in this exchange of correspondence that suggested any relaxation of tensions between Church and State. Dibelius left the final decision on the moving of the Church headquarters up to the synod, which was to convene in February, 1951, but there seemed little question as to what position they would take. There was no indication of any softening on the part of the Church on the question of the National Front, in the hope of saving the annual State subsidies.

Yet just at the turn of the new year a surprising change took place.

Shortly after the October 15th elections, a conference of Soviet bloc states in eastern Europe had been held in Prague. The three western powers had met in New York in May and in September and had proposed an all-German constitutional assembly, based upon carefully supervised free elections, as the means for securing German reunification. The answer of the Prague Conference was a counter-suggestion that an all-German "consultative council" should be appointed, on which the two governments of East and West Germany should be equally represented. This council should set up an all-German government and prepare a peace treaty. Since this proposal made no provision for free elections, it was not acceptable to the Allies.

However, the Prague decision determined the policy of the East German government during the ensuing months. On December 3rd Prime Minister Grotewohl sent a letter to Chancellor Adenauer, which substantially embodied the Prague proposals. In this new policy, calling for a more friendly orientation toward the Federal Republic than had been the case during the first year of their parallel existences, an open conflict between Church and State could only be a liability.

The opportunity to ease the existing tensions was offered very conveniently, just as the year ended. An anonymous letter, doubtless penned by Heinrich Grueber, appeared in the New Year's issue of the Berlin Church weekly *Die Kirche*, suggesting that the good offices of the Church be extended to the prime ministers of both East and West Germany. Specifically, Grueber suggested that Bishop Dibelius invite Adenauer and Grotewohl to meet in his home, as a gesture of good will, and that a committee of three be appointed, representing East Germany, West Germany, and Berlin, to carry out discussions leading to the lessening of tensions between East and West.

Bishop Dibelius, as eager as anyone for a lessening of Church-State tensions, immediately declared his readiness to mediate any such conversations. Grotewohl seized the opportunity to extend to the Church the olive branch of peace. He composed a telegram expressing cordial New Year's greetings to the man whom he had accused only a few weeks earlier of being an agent of western imperialists. Dibelius returned the favor.

The year 1950 had marked the opening of the real controversy between Church and State in East Germany. Much more severe tests lay ahead. But for even a purely tactical respite, such as now appeared imminent, the Church could only give thanks.

SEVEN

INVITATION TO SUBSERVIENCE

The Communists have never spared any effort to make clear their fundamental enmity toward the Church and the Christian faith. Whether one chooses to page through the writings of Marx or Lenin or Stalin, or through the innumerable minor prophets of dialectic materialism, the classic formulation of Lenin written in 1905 stands unchallenged: "Religion is the opium of the people." Between the atheistic-materialistic view of the world and society and the Christian view of God in history no true Marxist-Leninist has ever found a common ground.

On the other hand the strategy employed by the Communists in dealing with the Church has varied widely between the two extremes of *laisser mourir* and *faire mourir*, either allowing the Church to die naturally, or taking vigorous measures to liquidate it. At either extreme, as with all the shades of tactic in between, the goal has remained the same: the ultimate elimination of the Church and religion from the patterns of thought and of life in the new socialistic order.

The history of Communism in the Soviet Union and elsewhere

shows numerous examples of such tactical changes in religious policy. For example, in the earliest stages of the Russian Revolution in 1917 and 1918, the Orthodox Church was made the object of stringent repression, bordering on persecution. But when it became apparent that the attacks had overstepped the limits of popular support, the Communist Party shifted its tactic. The ultimate aim remained the same, but the party issued a warning against "offending the religious sensibilities of believers," which would only lead "to the strengthening of religious fanaticism."

When the Russians undertook their long-range program of sovietization in the East Zone of Germany in 1945, they followed an extremely cautious policy toward the Church, with which may have been mixed a certain amount of genuine admiration for the courageous anti-Nazism displayed by many of the churchmen between 1933 and 1945. But Walter Ulbricht, Wilhelm Pieck, Paul Wandel, Anton Ackermann, and the other Russian-trained German Communists who were sent into Berlin even before the fighting was over to begin building the postwar Germany never had any illusions about the ultimate destiny of the Church in the Communist Germany they were to build.

The tactic of the moment was cooperation with the Church, though even between 1945 and 1949 occasional direction markers of another kind were visible, particularly in the educational and political structure that Wandel and Ulbricht developed. By 1950 the tactic had definitely changed, and the hostility of the Communist regime toward the Churches was manifest in the series of sharp disagreements and even open attacks which were focused especially upon Bishop Dibelius.

Had the Church been less decisive in its resistance to these attacks, or simply maintained a discreet silence, the tactic of encroachment would doubtless have been continued, on the theory, expressed by Ulbricht, that "what was going to fall anyway could just as well be pushed over." But the Church demonstrated that it was alert and vigorous, and therefore it had to be taken into account in preparing the over-all political strategy.

There was no basic change in attitude toward the Church and toward religion signalized by the relaxation of pressures against the Church during the sixteen-month period beginning in January, 1951. The plain fact, as reported in a communication of the SED in Berlin,

was that "in view of the increased propaganda for East-West conversations," neither the SED nor the government was interested in
continuing a conflict between Church and State. To avoid embarrassment, they adopted the "politics of the outstretched hand" toward
the Church, much as Lenin had done in the Soviet Union during the
early days of the Communist Revolution.

There were several concrete evidences during the ensuing months
that the government was seriously seeking to avoid unnecessary disagreements and maintain friendly relations with the Church. One of
these involved an item of old business left over from the futile attempt of the previous year either to wheedle or to force the cooperation of the churches in the National Front. In the closing stages of
this battle, Minister-President Rudi Jahn of Brandenburg had issued
an ultimatum threatening to cut off all State subsidies if the Church
did not move its headquarters out of West Berlin into the territory
of the German Democratic Republic where it would be free of western influences. Dibelius had left this decision up to the synod of the
Church which was scheduled to meet early in February, 1951.

Meanwhile, the shift in tactic toward the Church had taken place;
Dibelius and Grotewohl had exchanged their cordial New Year's
greetings, and Jahn's ultimatum had become obsolete. The synod was
fully aware of the minister-president's predicament when it convened,
and therefore did all it could to couch its rejection of the ultimatum
in as friendly terms as possible. Actually, declared the synod, there
was no such thing as a West Berlin Church leadership. There was
only one Church leadership, and part of its membership lived in East
Berlin, part in West Berlin, and part in the German Democratic Republic. It was true that meetings were held in West Berlin, but only
because the only surviving Church administration building was located
there. However, the Church leadership would be glad to arrange
future meetings alternately in East and West currency areas, just as
the Council of EKD had done from the very beginning. The synod
expressed full understanding for the desire of the Brandenburg State
authorities to meet personally with the representatives of the Church
leadership, and observed that with the office of the general superintendent of the Kurmark located in Potsdam, such contacts had been
possible ever since 1946. In order to alleviate misunderstandings because of the use of two currencies, the Church had erected a special
finance administration in East Berlin.

Expressing the belief that it had done everything possible to fulfill the requirements of the State, the newly elected Church leadership assured the State that it was also prepared to do everything possible in accordance with its own confessions to demonstrate its loyalty to the State. Two months earlier a response such as this by the Church to a clearly stated ultimatum by a State official would have brought sharp reprisals. Within the framework of the "politics of the outstretched hand," there was not even a critical word from Minister-President Rudi Jahn. The subsidies to the Church of Berlin-Brandenburg continued to be paid on the regular monthly schedule.

The tone of Prime Minister Grotewohl's voice also took on a different quality in 1951. The government, he declared at a press conference, had no intention of taking any steps that would alter its good relations with the Church. The right of the Church to give religious instruction in public schoolrooms would be safeguarded, and no one would be forced to give up his membership in the Church. To emphasize that this was more than an empty promise, he noted that at least 70 per cent of the members of the SED belonged to a Church.

The Ministry of Justice, with apparent special consideration for the Church, instructed the courts to notify the responsible parish pastor's office without delay concerning all resignations of Church membership. Any inquiries from Churches or pastors, whether certain specific individuals had taken steps to resign, were to be answered as promptly as possible.

The most significant and subtle aspect of the Communist policy of the outstretched hand toward the Church involved the commissioning of the Christian Democratic Union as its spokesman to the Church. Founded in June, 1945, as one of the political organizations approved by the Soviet occupation authorities, the CDU had sought to carry on the traditions of the old Catholic Center Party on a broader interconfessional basis. Its original Statement of Purpose declared that "democratic freedom in the new Germany can be achieved only if we bear in mind the culture-shaping moral and spiritual forces of Christianity."

From the beginning the leadership of the CDU found it difficult to maintain its independence within the so-called "block politics" sponsored by the Soviet Military Administration. Less than six months after the party was founded, its two chairmen, Dr. Andreas Hermes and Dr. Walter Schreiber, were forced by the Soviets to resign because of their opposition to the arbitrary methods of the land reform. The second pair of chairmen, Jacob Kaiser and Ernst Lemmer, lasted two years, but were also forced to resign because they supported East Zone participation in the Marshall Plan and refused to take part in the Soviet-sponsored People's Congress in December, 1947.

More pliable than this early CDU leadership was Otto Nuschke, who did take part in the People's Congress and who was rewarded at the next party congress with election as first chairman of the party, a position which, with the blessing of the Soviets, he retained until his death in 1957.

During the campaign for the National Front in 1950, the last vocal resistance within the CDU was eliminated through a widespread purge of leading members of the party, including the prominent Roman Catholic layman, Professor Hickman, deputy party chairman and head of the CDU in Saxony. At the fifth Party Congress in Berlin in September, Otto Nuschke placed the full support of the CDU behind the National Front, summoning all Christians to become "fighters for peace" together with the Soviet Union, and urging full participation in the single-list elections in October, which he asserted would guarantee the future of a free and democratic Germany. Area committees of the CDU were urged to make special efforts to rally support among the clergy during the weeks preceding the election, and Nuschke even met with a special committee to consider a series of postelection conferences to bring the Churches and pastors more actively into the "new order."

The role which the leadership of the SED planned for an obedient and docile CDU was clearly shown early in 1951. CDU party officials were instructed at that time by the SED to take up contact with leading pastors throughout East Germany, and to quiet the atmosphere of tension with official assurances that the government had no intention of carrying on a further conflict with the Church.

Most revealing of all was the October appearance of the so-called Meissen Theses on Christian Realism, a series of twenty-two propositions prepared by a special working session of the CDU as the theoretical basis of the party's program. These theses represented the efforts of the CDU to justify in Christian terms its participation in a political front with a party which had officially declared itself to be committed to the principles of dialectic materialism.

Such cooperation by no means involved a denial of Christian principles, according to the Meissen Theses. The central doctrines of man's sinfulness and the redemptive work of God through Jesus Christ were reaffirmed, and the historical authority of the Bible was declared to be beyond question. The errors of both idealism and materialism were rejected because they deprived God of His rightful place of authority. But the theses laid a special stress upon the responsibility of the Christian in society, a responsibility which they felt the Christian Church had all too often ignored. If Christians had truly followed in the footsteps of Jesus Christ, and copied his deep concern over social righteousness; if they had heeded his warnings about the dangers of riches; if they had loved their fellow men as He did, without concern over status or class, the Church would have retained the "progressive" stamp given by its founder and its early adherents.

According to the tenth thesis: "Jesus warned of the danger of riches, and opposed the exploitation of the helpless by the ruling strata. He drove the traders and the moneychangers out of the temple with a whip. He warned the rulers of his people that their course must end in dire catastrophe and in the terrible judgment of God. It was the hatred of this ruling group that nailed Christ to the Cross."

At no time, declared the CDU, had the Church failed more miserably in its social obligation than in the nineteenth century. While wealth accumulated in the hands of a few, and the masses of people became mere cogs in the complex machine of the Industrial Revolution, the Church "passed by on the other side," hand in hand with the rich and powerful. Only a few Christian social-reformers, such as Friedrich Naumann, had been aware of this and had called for thoroughgoing revolutionary changes in the whole economic structure. "We have no intention of being guardsmen over a crumbling past," Naumann had declared. "In its first century Christianity was a renewing power, so must a living Christianity be today. There is nothing in this world which is more progressive, more full of promise for the future, more transforming than real Christianity. The Gospel is like a refining fire, the power of a new epoch."

The real analysis of the social and economic problem of the nineteenth century, according to the men of Meissen, had been made by Karl Marx. He had seen that there was no other way of removing the evils of the capitalistic structure except through the destruction of the system itself. To this thesis, particularly as it had been ideally exemplified in the Soviet Union, the "progressive" Christian in East Germany was urged to commit himself, though he need not thereby also embrace Marx' entire system of dialectic materialism.

This commitment, together with others which followed in the final four theses, was the price paid by the CDU for the luxury of professing allegiance to a few basic theological fundamentals. All of the immediate objectives of the Soviets for East Germany were endorsed in the name of Christianity, as if they had no relation whatever to the clearly stated long-range ideological objectives of the Communists.

The last four theses of the Meissen statement on Christian Realism could easily have appeared in a program of the SED, with only a change of the party name. The final appeal called for a continued "fight for peace" as the "central task of the present day." "Two world wars, which have been caused by crises in the capitalistic economic system, have destroyed the well-being of nations and the lives of many millions of people. The preparations now being undertaken by the Government of the United States for a third world war force us to a clear decision. Whoever is not in favor of an imperialistic war must align himself with the World Peace Front. . . . There can be no true Christian who is not a Fighter for Peace, in the conviction that peace can be secured when the peoples of the world take their fate into their own hands."

The Meissen Theses are significant, not only as an evidence of the "politics of the outstretched hand" employed by the SED in dealing with the Church in 1951. It is certainly a curious fact that in 1950 the Church had to battle against the use of schoolbooks which asserted that Jesus Christ was merely a legendary figure, while in 1951 every newspaper in East Germany carried favorable comments on the Meissen Theses in which Jesus Christ was unequivocally declared to be the Revelation of God. But the most significant thing about these theses was that they contained an attempt, analogous to that of the German-Christians in relation to National Socialism, to provide a theological foundation for the political-economic system of Communism in East Germany.

The CDU, because of the word "Christian" in its name, was selected for this dubious task, and the fact that it allowed itself to be used in this way reflects the tragic fact that its best leadership had already been forced into retirement or into flight to the West. Only Otto Nuschke, perhaps too kindly described by friends and colleagues of former days as "a well-intentioned, but weak man," remained to lead his party in this unheroic role. Although the theology of the Meissen Theses on Christian Realism found only a very few supporters among the clergy in either Evangelical or Roman Catholic circles in East Germany, they stand nevertheless as the best example of the creed of a so-called "progressive pastor" in East Germany.

That the conciliatory and even friendly appearances of the government toward the Church in 1951 did not reflect any basic change in direction is shown in the train of political and cultural developments that were going on simultaneously. After Grotewohl's letter to Adenauer late in 1950, suggesting the formation of an East-West German Council to assist the four powers in the making of a peace treaty, the East German Parliament called for a popular referendum. Voters were called upon to vote Yes or No on the question: Are you opposed to the remilitarization of Germany and in favor of a peace treaty with Germany in the year 1951?

As with earlier referendums, this question was posed in such a way that a negative answer was virtually impossible. Voters were urged to cast their ballots publicly, as a symbol of their open and wholehearted endorsement of peace, and the overwhelming majority thus secured was interpreted as an almost unanimous approval of the particular policies of the Soviets and as a denunciation of the policies of the West.

Against this flagrant misrepresentation and travesty on democratic procedures the little provincial Church of Anhalt raised one of the clearest objections. "According to our understanding," the Church leaders observed, with a kind of logic that unfortunately did not fit the dialectic pattern of the Communists, "it ought to be of great importance to a government in such a referendum to ascertain the real wishes of the people." This end, they suggested, might better be achieved through the posing of a genuine policy question and through government insistence upon the use of booths for secret voting.

"The Yes to peace should not be misused as a Yes to other objectives which have nothing to do with the question of peace, and which, properly understood, are a hindrance to it. The Christian, whose natural inclination would be to vote for peace, finds it very difficult to understand how a campaign for peace can be dominated by a propaganda for hate. Wherever hate is at work, peace is destroyed. For the sake of peace itself, which needs no propaganda, we plead that Christian men, who are obligated to love even their enemies, may not be forced to violate their consciences."

In spite of such pointed objections, the government triumphantly announced on June 6th that 96.31 per cent of the voters had declared their support of the peaceful aims and policies of the Soviets and their opposition to the warmongering militarism of the western imperialists.

Meanwhile the Soviets were doing all they could to prevent the incorporation of West Germany into the European Defense Community, and even sought to make this the subject of a Foreign Ministers Conference scheduled for late summer. When this failed, the East German Parliament made another overture to the West German Bundestag on September 15th, urging consultation of representatives of both parts of Germany on the subject of free elections and the speedy conclusion of a peace treaty.

The West German Parliament responded two weeks later with a fourteen-point program for free elections to an all-German constitutional assembly, and declared its intention to submit these proposals to an impartial commission of the United Nations for approval. At the same time they asked the Allied High Commissioners to request permission from all four occupation powers to carry through such an election.

The government of East Germany expressed its general approval of most of the fourteen points submitted by the West German Parliament, but shortly thereafter announced that it, too, was preparing a set of regulations for the election of a constitutional assembly. When its suggestions were ready in January, it was noted that no provision was made for any international supervision of the elections.

Meanwhile the western Allies had requested the United Nations to form a special committee to investigate the conditions for a free election in all Germany. The Political Committee of the UN received statements from both East and West German governments on the matter, and finally recommended to the General Assembly the appointment of a special commission to report back to the Assembly before September, 1952. Members of the commission were Brazil, Iceland, Netherlands, Pakistan, and Poland.

On February 28, 1952, the East German government refused permission to this UN Commission to cross its boundaries to conduct its investigations. Four notes to the Soviet Control Commission were not even answered, and therefore, although the government of West Germany and the Senate of West Berlin had assured the commission of full cooperation and unrestricted movement within their borders, the commission was forced to report to the UN on April 30, 1952, that there was no possibility of carrying out its assignment. If the support of the East German government actually rested on a 96.31 per cent popular majority, as had been claimed after the People's Referendum on Peace and Demilitarization in June, 1951, there need have been no hesitancy in admitting an impartial international commission for the purposes of preparing for another free election six months later. But freedom of political decision was obviously a luxury in which the German Democratic Republic and its Soviet supporters were in no position to indulge.

Even more convincing evidence that no fundamental changes had taken place in the policies of the Communists was found in the school developments during 1951. This was the year in which the first Five-Year Plan went into operation, and both educational and cultural life had an important role to play in it. At the January meeting of the SED Central Committee, Dr. Paul Wandel, Minister of Education, announced that thus far the party had not paid sufficient attention to the schools. The first task in school improvement would therefore be a serious assault on opposing ideologies and a strengthening of the ideological foundations of the teaching staff. Every teacher must be well schooled in Marxism-Leninism and in the basic principles of progressive Soviet education and must understand his role as an exemplary German patriot and a leader in the fight for world peace.

Just how deeply these principles were to permeate instruction in all subjects and classes could be seen in an article dealing with the new lesson plans in history in a 1951 issue of the teachers' magazine *Paedagogik*; "The historical researcher arrives at the knowledge of objective historical reality only on the foundation of historical materialism. He must allow himself to be guided by the principles of the dialectical method, and by the teachings of philosophical materialism. Only if he makes use of them in his study of the process of social development is it possible for him to grasp the complexity and detail of historical events . . . and to advance to a deeper understanding of the nature of historical events."

In close cooperation with youth, labor, and parents' organizations, the schools were also expected to develop in every class and subject a thoroughgoing political consciousness among pupils and teachers. "At the central point," stated the Instructions of the Ministry of Education for the school year 1951–1952, "stands education for democratic patriotism. Democratic patriotism has its source in love for one's own people, in faith in the creative strength of the people. Education for democratic patriotism also includes education to hatred against the enemies of progress, of peace, and of national liberation."

Closely coordinated with the schools in fulfilling the slogan of the year, "We teach and learn for peace," were the politically oriented youth organizations such as the Free German Youth and the Young Pioneers. "It is the primary responsibility of the school," declared the general school law of May 25, 1951, "to assist the Free German Youth and its Pioneer organization with every possible means."

A special law was passed in April concerning the organization and function of Parents' Councils in connection with the elementary schools. Elections to the councils were based on a list of candidates drawn up by a committee of four, including the school principal, a representative of the Communist youth and women's organizations and one representative of the parents, selected by the local county council. Regulations provided that every meeting of the Parents' Council should be attended by the school principal, representatives of these same youth and women's groups, the chairman of the local schoolteachers' union, and a representative of the workers' organization in the factory which had assumed a sponsorship of this particular school. Attendance of council members at "parents' seminars" was required, in order that they might become better acquainted with the basic educational and political problems, and thereby be better able to perform their function on the Parents' Council.

Even in the midst of a year in which the government had plainly declared that it sought to avoid conflict with the Church, and in which the SED and the CDU were attempting to solicit the support of the clergy for the National Front, the program of cultural sovietization moved inexorably forward. The Provincial Synod of the Church of Silesia complained in its June meeting that the schools were developing more and more into "confessional schools of materialistic philosophy." Whether parents wanted their children taught in this way or not made absolutely no difference to the Communist educational planners.

Before the founding of the German Democratic Republic, the Church had experienced very little interference by the Russian occupation authorities in the conduct of its widespread program of institutional and emergency welfare. The SED had organized the Volkssolidaritaet (People's Solidarity) as its official relief agency in 1945, but there had been more than enough work for all relief agencies, and the Inner Mission, the Hilfswerk, and the Roman Catholic Caritas ministered to everyone they could reach.

At a meeting of the Volkssolidaritaet in Weimar, late in 1949, however, it became apparent that a change was impending. Christian Berg, the director of the Berlin Central Office of the Evangelical Hilfswerk, brought a ten-minute greeting, stressing the basic principle of aiding the needy without regard to race, religion, or political affiliation. The restlessness that was apparent among the leaders of the meeting as he spoke bore witness to the shift in policy which had taken place in the Volkssolidaritaet after the creation of the East German government.

During the ensuing months import permits for relief supplies became more difficult to secure. Shipments were delayed on technical grounds. One twenty-ton shipment of used clothing from Switzerland, for example, was detained for six months at a border check point. On December 12, 1950, the blow fell. From the Ministry of the Interior an order was issued confiscating the sizable stores of relief supplies the Hilfswerk had gathered for distribution in Magdeburg, and prohibiting any further entry of bulk relief supplies into East Germany. Shipments from the West, it was claimed, were being used for the purposes of political propaganda. Furthermore, it was asserted that the standard of living of the people of the Republic had risen sufficiently so that outside gifts were no longer necessary, even though the rationing of basic food commodities was to continue for eight or nine years to come.

From this point on, the Hilfswerk and the Caritas received permission to bring in shipments of food only for special occasions such as Christmas or Easter, and the distribution of these supplies was limited to the homes and institutions of the Churches. The general import and distribution of gifts on a regular basis to the needy in the congregations was thereby terminated. The Hilfswerk, however, through its Berlin office under the vigorous direction of Dr. Christian Berg, continued to channel financial assistance to churches and institutions, both for material relief and for physical and spiritual reconstruction. Vigorous protests against this action were made by Protestants and Catholics, especially in the early months of 1951, when the National Front professed to be seeking more friendly relations with the Churches; but apart from the release of a portion of the confiscated supplies, those appeals were without success.

Fortunately, a unique arrangement of sponsorship within the EKD, first suggested by the leaders of the Hilfswerk at a directors' conference in the summer of 1949, could be used to replace the general shipments of relief goods through Hilfswerk channels. Each provincial Church in West Germany established a special relationship with a Church in the East. The Bavarian Lutheran Church, for example, adopted the Church of Mecklenburg; Wuerttemberg adopted Thuringia, and Baden adopted Brandenburg. The idea was carried over into the various functional areas of the Church as well, such as women's work, youth work, student work, and the Inner Mission. The sponsorship arrangement began with the sending of packages to needy families, but was expanded to include visits by pastors, church elders, and youth groups, both for spiritual strengthening and for physical rehabilitation and recreation. Congregations in the East received substantial assistance in this way from their sister congregations in the West, and the western churches in turn received inspiration and encouragement from the East.

At a time when the political forces in Germany were tending to pull the two sections of the country apart, the Church was seeking in this very practical way to maintain unity and understanding and mutual dependence. Such contributions were far more effective than grandly conceived assertions that the Church should build bridges to span the political differences between East and West and thus contribute to the reunification of Germany and the peace of Europe. The fact that after ten years the Evangelical Church is the only organization in Germany which has managed to preserve its unity in spite of the Iron Curtain is a witness to the success of these efforts.

During these months when the government and its dominant party were professing their desire to promote more friendly relations with the Church, Church leaders took the position that such professions ought to show themselves not only in the halting of direct attacks upon the Church but also in a readiness to fulfill certain concrete requests brought by the Church. The almost total lack of cooperation in the fulfilling of these requests spoke a far more convincing language than did the propaganda speeches of Nuschke and Grotewohl, repeating the constitutional guarantees of freedom to the Churches and professing a spirit of friendly cooperation.

This unwillingness to make concrete concessions was most clearly demonstrated in the ban of relief shipments. It was also shown in the persistent refusal of the government to grant entry to young pastors upon the completion of their theological studies in West German universities. The customary pattern for young German students of theology was to attend two or three universities during the course of a four-year period; consequently, many young men from Saxony and Brandenburg were studying in Heidelberg or Tuebingen in West Germany. Although Dr. Grueber, the official Church liaison with the government, negotiated for several months on behalf of fifty young men who were urgently needed to fill vacant parishes in East Germany, he was not even able to secure a clear decision from the government. Finally, in June, 1951, the Council of EKD directed a letter to Prime Minister Grotewohl, pleading for a decision to permit these young pastors to return to their home churches as parish pastors. There was still no response from the government.

One of the most revealing complaints of the Church was raised by Bishop Moritz Mitzenheim in a letter to the minister-president of the State of Thuringia. The letter was motivated, he said, by an alarming increase in the number of midnight arrests by the secret police, as reported to him in private conferences with pastors. The bishop described the usual pattern of the complaints: "Late in the evening or during the night a person will be 'taken away' by two persons in civilan clothes, who identify themselves as members of the criminal police. In most cases no reason will be given for the arrest, nor will an arrest warrant be served. The next day the anxious relatives, wives, mothers, fathers, discover that the person has been 'detained' by the police. The day following they may receive some noncommittal information to the effect that he has been released from police detention. Indications point in the direction of the local branch of the Ministry for State Security. But all efforts of relatives to discover where the person is being held or what charges are being made against him are fruitless. They stand before a wall of silence. Resigned, embittered, and despairing, many then turn to the Church for counsel and help."

Not only were actions of this kind contrary to the constitution, declared the bishop, but they were actions which tended to undermine the confidence of the people in the integrity and honesty of the government itself. At the very moment when they had been campaigning for confidence and friendship through countless mass rallies, through the newspapers, and through mottoes and slogans, the authorities ought to realize the "paralyzing effect" of measures which clearly violated the very goals which they claimed to be seeking.

Still another situation that led the people of East Germany to question the sincerity of their government was the stubborn refusal to grant amnesty to political prisoners who were seriously ill or physically disabled. The bishops of East Germany advised President Pieck that there were actually large numbers in the prisons suffering from tuberculosis and other chronic illnesses, and still others who were blind or amputees. How such people could constitute such a security threat to the State that it was necessary to hold them in prison the bishops could not understand.

These pleas apparently had some effect, since late in the year the government announced the pending release of twenty thousand political prisoners, including many of those who had been turned over to local authorities following the closing of the Soviet concentration camps in 1950. This amnesty, however, by no means emptied the prisons in East Germany, nor did it affect the other thousands being held as political prisoners in the Soviet Union. For the release of these prisoners the Church also continued to plead, both with the German authorities and with the Soviets directly, though with discouragingly meager results. Bishop Dibelius even directed a letter from the Council of the EKD to Stalin himself, pleading for mercy for the prisoners and for the protection of legal and human rights in the penal system of East Germany.

The most dramatic and eloquent answer of the Church to the Communist propaganda for peace and unity was the German Evangelical Kirchentag which took place in Berlin from July 11 to 15, 1951. This mass rally of all Protestants in Germany, begun in 1949 as an annual event sponsored by the laymen of the Church, was a part of the great awakening in German Protestantism after the Second World War. The tragedy of National Socialism and the war had demonstrated the need for the Church to play a much more responsible role in German society, both through its clergy and its laiety. Dr. Reinhold von Thadden-Trieglaff, himself a layman, had conceived the plan of rallying German Protestantism annually about some great theme which came to grips with the living issues of the day.

In 1951 more than 100,000 people from the Churches of East Germany gathered in Berlin with about 12,000 from West Germany around the theme, "We are brothers just the same!" They met for their opening service in the fine old St. Mary's Church in East Berlin, but spread over the entire city for their Bible studies and discussion groups. When the final rally was held in the huge Olympic Stadium in West Berlin, the 100,000 seats were not adequate for the throngs assembled to bear witness to the unity of the Church and the power of the Gospel.

All of the leading politicians of East and West Germany sent greetings to the Kirchentag, and both President Pieck and Deputy Prime Minister Nuschke attended the festive opening and closing services. Some attempts were made to interpret the Kirchentag as a "peace demonstration" in the Communist sense, but the thousands who attended the discussion groups and the public lectures left little room for such an attempt. When the Reformation chorale "A Mighty Fortress Is Our God" echoed across the packed Olympic Stadium and was answered by other thousands standing on the great open May Field close by, it was an unmistakable witness of the spiritual unity which these people found within their Church. Even after the formal service had ended on Sunday afternoon, the stadium remained filled. One chorale after the other rose spontaneously from the vast throng, in a living expression of the Kirchentag theme, which declared their deepest will and wish "to remain as brothers—in spite of everything!"

Just as the beginning of this period of tactical noninterference had been caused by factors unrelated to the Church, and to some extent even beyond the sphere of the East German government, it was also to end for reasons beyond the control of both parties. The respite had been called in order to avoid any possible embarrassment to the Soviet Union while it was seeking to promote East and West German conversations and to prevent the incorporation of West Germany into the western military alliance system. When on May 26, 1952, Chancellor Adenauer signed the agreement which would eventually make West Germany a member of the European Defense Community, all restraints were thrown aside. The division of Germany was recognized as permanent, and a program aiming at the full sovietization of all aspects of life was openly undertaken. As far as the Church was concerned, this new policy signalized the beginning of a year of the most savage persecution experienced in Germany since the Nazi measures of the 1930's.

EIGHT

HARVEST OF MARTYRDOM

On May 26, 1952, the Iron Curtain literally clanked down between East and West Germany. At the moment Chancellor Adenauer placed his signature beneath the European Defense Pact on behalf of the Federal Republic, stringent security measures were announced by the East German government which turned the inner German border into one of the most formidable and closely guarded frontiers in the world. From Luebeck on the Baltic Sea to Hof on the Czech border, a strip of land three miles wide was designated as a "security zone," within which only "politically dependable" persons were permitted to live.

Immediately inside the border a narrow strip about ten yards wide was cleared of trees and brush and plowed up so that the footprints of "border runners" could be clearly seen. Barbed-wire fencing was installed, and border patrols armed with machine guns and stationed in observation towers at frequent intervals were given orders to shoot without warning any person venturing into the plowed strip. Adjacent to this "zone of sudden death" was still another strip, five hundred yards wide, into which no one was permitted entry without special documentation from the border police. A limited number of border crossing points perforated this Iron Curtain, through which authorized persons might enter or leave the German Democratic Republic, but very few entry visas or exit permits were granted.

These security measures, presumably undertaken to prevent the infiltration of imperialist and militarist propaganda and agents from the West, had a profound effect upon the entire population in both East and West Germany. Fear and suspicion were fostered. Families were separated, though in many cases they lived within a ten-minute walk of each other. Communication and cultural exchange were hampered, and often completely cut off. The work of the Church on an all-German basis was severely handicapped.

But the people who were most immediately affected by the security measures were those who lived within the three-mile border zone. Upon orders of the government a mass evacuation of farms and villages was carried out, in some instances with only a few hours' notice. This expulsion took place in accordance with lists of "asocial or politically contrary people," which had been arbitrarily prepared by the police without any previous information to the individuals so blacklisted. Expellees were permitted to take their movable property along, and they were assured that whatever remained behind would be inventoried by the police and held in trust for them by the government. Since farms were not available in the border province of Thuringia, many families were assigned new lands in Mecklenburg or Anhalt, long distances away from their homes and friends.

Churches in the five-hundred meter security zone were closed for worship services; in the remainder of the three-mile zone services could be held only with the special permission of the police authorities.

After receiving numerous personal and written reports on local situations and visiting border communities in person to ascertain what was actually taking place, Bishops Mitzenheim of Thuringia and Mueller of the Province of Saxony directed vigorous letters of protest to both state and national authorities. Bishop Mueller's letter was particularly plain-spoken, warning Minister of State Security Wilhelm Zaisser that he would be held accountable before God for arbitrary actions of injustice and inhumanity such as these. He compared the actions of Zaisser to the irresponsible violence of the Nazi

Expropriation Law of January 30, 1934, and cited no less than four separate articles of the East German Constitution that were being violated.

Apart from the general unconstitutionality of the whole procedure, Mueller pointed out the callousness with which the expulsion took place. Some families had been driven from their homes at night on two hours' notice. No concern had been shown for the aged or the sick. Even in the rain, some families had been forced to carry their furniture and personal belongings out into unprotected trucks. And while this was going on, loudspeakers were blaring assurances that no one need be afraid who didn't have a bad conscience and that the expulsion was actually for the protection of those being removed.

In some cases expellees were required to sign a statement that they agreed to these regulations or that they were moving of their own free will. "We don't know what the government means by 'guarantee of democratic legality,'" declared the bishop, "but we are certain that none of the measures undertaken on the basis of this law contribute to the guarantee of democratic legality, nor strengthen the democratic order, nor safeguard the democratic rights of the citizen."

A few days later Zaisser replied to Bishop Mueller's letter, regretting that the bishop had accepted as his own the "false and agitator-inspired reports" concerning the safety measures of the border. Full respect, he insisted, was being paid to private property and because they understood this perfectly, the citizens "not only welcomed these measures but eagerly assisted in carrying them out." The only ones who were distressed by them were the criminal element which lived on border smuggling or who were opposed to the antifascistic democratic order. It was incomprehensible to Zaisser why the Evangelical Church would want to speak up so warmly on behalf of such groups of people. It would be more in order, he observed, for the Church to protest against the inhumanities and excesses of the West German government in expelling farmers from lands to be used as airfields, and in signing the "war agreement" (EDC) with the western powers.

Although these security measures along the East-West frontier were introduced for the declared purpose of protecting the people from the belligerent militarism of their western brothers, they also served as a very convenient screen behind which the next major step could be taken toward the sovietization of East Germany.

Speaking at the second Party Conference of the SED on July 9th, Walter Ulbricht announced this next step. "The political and economic conditions, as well as the self-consciousness of the laboring class has developed so far," he said, "that the 'building up of Socialism' has become the fundamental task in the German Democratic Republic."

Administratively, this "build-up of Socialism" began with a move toward greater centralization in government. The five traditional State governments were abolished and replaced by fifteen administrative districts under central supervision. Court structure and the administration of justice were correspondingly revised. In the economic sphere socialization was relentlessly pursued, and small businesses were forced to accept State ownership. Production quotas were imposed upon factories and farms, and great numbers of small farmers were thereby forced to join agricultural cooperatives under government supervision. Still others simply gave up their farms and joined the growing stream of refugees fleeing to the West.

In the cultural fields the role of Marxist-Leninist theory was intensified in education, research, literature, and the arts, and the supervision of this prodigious task was assigned to a newly created Office for the Control and Coordination of Instruction, Science, and Art. The goal in the schools was the "construction" of a new generation of technical experts, well trained, well disciplined, and inspired with the "revolutionary spirit." "Polytechnical education" was introduced, laying great stress upon an understanding of the national economy and production and upon the use of simple tools. Authoritarian methods of instruction were introduced, and both teachers and pupils were strictly supervised. Early in 1953 the pupils were equipped with diaries in which their daily tasks and performances were to be recorded, as well as their participation in leisure-time activities.

The universities, which had undergone a complete reorganization in 1951 as a part of the Five-Year Plan, were now given a new constitution under which administratively appointed officials gained decisive positions in the governing bodies. Lectures were carefully supervised, especially in the social sciences, and after July, 1952, a special course was announced in all universities, in which the latest decisions of the SED Party conferences were to be discussed "academically." At the same time the financial rewards for academic specialists and scientists were raised to magnanimous levels, and scholarships increased until about 90 per cent of the students were being subsidized by the government.

There was nothing in this program of the "build-up of Socialism" which was in essence different from the general program which had been going on under SED direction in East Germany since 1946. The ultimate aim was the complete sovietization of East Germany, and this goal was to be achieved in successive stages, each new stage to be undertaken when the previous one was completed. Room had always been left for the reunification of Germany under conditions that would enable the Soviets to incorporate the whole of Germany into their system, but this factor had become progressively less influential as western resistance to Soviet expansionism had stiffened.

The failure of the Soviet efforts to prevent the inclusion of the Federal Republic in a western system of military alliances gave to the new stage of SED policy in East Germany a particularly sharp and bitter character. Since the Church had consistently rejected the "politics of the outstretched hand" and refused to join the National Front in 1951, it might very well expect harsher treatment under the projected "build-up of Socialism." Ulbricht's warning at the second Party Conference was ominous. "The Church," he declared, "will no longer be permitted to conceal its true feelings under the mask of neutrality. It must decisively renounce its connections with all English and American agents."

After a conference with Prime Minister Grotewohl late in July, Bishop Dibelius reported that dark clouds were gathering for the Church, but even he had no expectation of the severity of the storm that was about to break. At no time since the end of the war was such open and bitter hostility toward the Church manifested by the government in East Germany as in the twelve months between July, 1952, and June, 1953. Recalling the terminology of twenty years earlier, men of the Church still single out this year as the year of the *Kirchenkampf,* or the "Church struggle."

The government made it clear that the realities of the Iron Curtain applied to representatives of the Church as well as to other people. Since the Church had refused to join the National Front for peace, the government concluded that the Church supported the "war policies" of the West. Contacts with the West therefore, even within the functional areas of the Church, were treated as security hazards for the State. Interzonal passes to attend Church functions in West Germany were denied, and applications of West Germans for entry visas to East Germany were also rejected. Lectures and conferences of various kinds were canceled or postponed. The Evangelical Kirchentag, which was scheduled to meet in Stuttgart, had to carry on its sessions with only about forty delegates from the eastern Churches present, instead of the twenty thousand for whom the government had originally promised interzonal passes. Even the quintennial Assembly of the Lutheran World Federation which met in Hannover, representing 50 million Lutherans throughout the world, was deprived of representation from member Churches less than a hundred miles away, because of the refusal of the government to grant exit permits even to bishops.

The five thousand interzonal passes which had been promised for this great world rally were denied at the last minute, and in order to give East German delegates at least a partial benefit from the assembly, it was necessary for the federation to arrange a post-Hannover conference in Berlin, to which representatives of the East German Churches could come.

But also in Berlin, which would continue to be the all-important meeting point for East and West when all other opportunities were closed, the government showed signs of its unfriendly new disposition toward the Churches. The seventy-fifth German Katholikentag, Roman Catholic counterpart of the Protestant Kirchentag, was denied the use of the big Walter Ulbricht Stadium and the Werner Seelenbinder Hall for its assemblies in East Berlin. In a spontaneous demonstration of good will, Berlin Protestants offered the hospitality of their homes to Roman Catholic visitors, and the use of St. Mary's Church, the largest Protestant Church in East Berlin, for the sessions of the Katholikentag.

Several West German Church periodical publications which had previously been permitted to enter East Germany through the mails were now stricken from the postal lists. Among those so treated were the Church welfare journal *Die Innere Mission*, the official Lutheran Church organ the *Evangelisch-Lutherische Kirchenzeitung*, and the

Amtsblatt, official information paper of the Roman Catholic Church.

In financial matters, too, the Church was made to feel the chill winds of State displeasure. For the payment of basic costs such as the salaries of pastors and lay workers the German Churches had traditionally depended upon a Church tax. Since 1945 the Church in East Germany had levied and collected its own tax through its own offices, but had been allowed to examine the tax lists of the State in order to ascertain the amount each person should be asked to pay. East Berlin had been an exception to this practice, through a special arrangement whereby city tax offices had collected the Church tax as a friendly service to the Church. This arrangement was now terminated.

By a curious turn of fortune, the old historic installment payments to the Church had been regularly honored by the Communist government in East Germany since 1945. The threat of the government to withhold the payments to the Church of Brandenburg at the close of the year 1950 had indicated that these payments might be used as political levers. But there was no actual curtailment of the payments until 1952, when they were reduced by 20 per cent

Payments to the Churches of Brandenburg and the Province of Saxony had also been withheld because of their affiliation with the Church federation of the Old Prussian Union, an organization which the East German government refused to recognize because its name seemed to perpetuate a political idea the Communists hoped would never rise again. As the year 1953 opened, direct financial payments to all the Churches in East Germany were cut off entirely.

These curtailments forced the Churches to rely more heavily upon voluntary gifts and collections from their members, a development which in the long run would place them upon a far sounder financial basis. But even here the government imposed restrictions, by limiting the number of house and street collections. Whereas normally four street collections were made each year by the Church, largely for the support of welfare and educational programs, only one street collection was approved in 1953, and house collections were prohibited entirely. Local conditions made even this one collection difficult. In Magdeburg it was stopped after two days. In East Berlin the permission was delayed so long that, when it was finally granted, it was too late for the Church to make the technical arrangements to carry it out. Elsewhere the permission was granted with the stipulation that the collections could not be taken on main streets, in railway stations, or on railway platforms.

Although it would be a long time before the Churches of East Germany could operate entirely on the voluntary contributions of their members, it was a very encouraging sign that even when the number of collections was reduced, and when difficulties were put in the way of administering the few that were permitted, Church income from these sources was higher than in other years. Members were apparently ready to rally to the support of their Church when its work was threatened by the curtailment of traditional sources of income.

Occasions were also found by unfriendly local authorities to interfere with public meetings and occasionally even with the worship services of the congregations. During the days of the Soviet military occupation, the Churches had managed to secure an understanding with the authorities exempting traditional and recurring meetings in church from the general rule requiring the reporting of all assemblies. This same privilege had been embodied by the East German government in 1951 in a regulation of the Ministry of the Interior, providing that meetings held in the Church's own buildings or in rented quarters regularly used for that specific purpose need not be reported to the authorities in advance.

The regulation, however, listed the kinds of Church meetings which were to be exempted. As examples, worship services and Masses, Bible studies, classes for religious instruction, and confirmation classes were specifically mentioned. In the summer of 1952 the authorities in many communities began to interpret this regulation narrowly, permitting only those activities which were specifically named. Police officers took it upon themselves to decide what constituted a worship service or an act of religious edification. Consequently, a pastor in one village might be accused of violating this ordinance because he failed to report a Bible Study Week, while another might be permitted to present a religious play without any question whatever. Some local police also forbade the holding of worship services in rooms not owned by the Church, and in the case of many small villages where there was no church, but where services had been held in schoolrooms or inns, this meant that the villagers were simply deprived of the opportunity of worship.

In addition to the confusion as to what Church activities had to be announced to the police in advance and which did not, conflicts often arose when the local police required "authorization" for Church meetings, rather than mere "notification" as provided in the regulations. Limitations of this kind on services of worship or other regular activities the Church simply refused to accept, and vigorous protests were made when such attempts were made by local authorities. More difficult for the Churches to justify were the larger meetings of an intercongregational nature, which often could not be held in church buildings because of the limitation of space. Over such assemblies the authorities were able to exercise as rigid control as they wished, and particularly during 1952–1953, youth rallies, mission festivals, and laymen's rallies had to be severely curtailed because the necessary permits could not be secured.

One of the most far-reaching proposals of the government in its relation to the Church was the suggestion embodied in a letter from Prime Minister Grotewohl to Bishop Dibelius, in August, 1952, suggesting the closing of the historic theological faculties in the East German universities. As the prime minister observed, it did appear to be somewhat inconsistent with the constitutional separation of Church and State that the pastors of the Protestant Churches were trained in faculties of state universities under professors who were officially in the employ of the State. Although Grotewohl did not mention it, the fact that this State was based upon a philosophy which officially denied the existence of God made such faculties seem even more incongruous.

Grotewohl suggested that the Protestant Churches take steps to establish one large theological academy which would be owned and operated by the Church, entirely independent of State control. To facilitate this change the government expressed its willingness to channel the same financial support to the academy as was presently being used for the support of the six theological faculties in the East German universities, and to be of whatever assistance it could in helping the Church find quarters to house the new academy.

Grotewohl very graciously requested Dibelius to give him an answer to this proposal which would have placed the theological training of all pastors in East Germany under the direct supervision of the Church. Dibelius canvassed the leaders of the Churches and the theological faculties themselves, and several weeks later replied that

the Church would prefer to continue the four-hundred-year tradition
which placed the study of theology within the broad cultural atmosphere of the university. The matter was never again mentioned by the
State, very probably because it had been realized in the meantime
that State control of the theological faculties could in due season
provide one of the most effective means of influencing the whole
inner structure of the Church and the attitude of its clergy. As the
years passed and older professors retired, there was an increasing
tendency to replace them with men whose views were "progressive"
enough to make them acceptable to the Communist political authorities. Should a similar offer be made by the government to the
Churches today, their answer would be given promptly and positively.
But such an opportunity is not likely to come again.

In the face of this new party line of separation and socialization,
which bore within it such serious threats both to the unity of the
Church and to its freedom to function normally within East Germany, the leaders of the Church were not silent. Bishops Mitzenheim
and Mueller had protested the arbitrary expulsions of families from
the border security zones. On July 25th, shortly after Ulbricht's
ominous speech at the SED Party Conference, Bishop Dibelius,
Provost Grueber and President Held of the Church of the Old
Prussian Union conferred with Prime Minister Grotewohl and other
government officials to inquire concerning the State's intentions
toward the Church. Although the discussion was carried on in a very
friendly atmosphere, Grotewohl made it clear that the treatment of
the Church depended very largely upon its attitude toward the
State. No special privileges would be granted to the Church in the
matter of interzonal passes, nor would theological students from the
West be admitted to eastern pastorates.

On the day following, Dibelius issued a pastoral letter stressing the
importance of maintaining the unity of the Church, externally as
well as internally. Two weeks later the Church of Brandenburg assembled in an extraordinary synod to consider how best to meet the
impending threats of the State. In his report to the synod, Dibelius
again stressed the unity of the German Church, which, he declared,
the policies of the government were now directly attacking. References to West Germany as a "hostile foreign land," which had been
appearing in the new government propaganda line, could never be

recognized by Christian people. "We as Christians," declared the bishop, "know no 'hostile foreign land,' " and regard it as completely impossible "ever to regard a part of our own fatherland, in which German brothers and sisters are living," in such a way. "Here we as Christians are challenged. And our answer as Christians can only be an 'everlasting No!' "

Replying to Ulbricht's demands that the Church renounce its ties with American and English agents and cease taking orders from the allied occupation officers in West Berlin, Dibelius flatly denied the existence of any such connections. "An evangelical Church," he declared, "takes directions from no one on this earth, either from governments, from parties, or from individual politicians. It knows no directions other than those that come from God, which are written in the Holy Scriptures." Furthermore, said the bishop, "I should like to make it clear that no agency outside the Church, either in foreign countries or in West Germany, has ever attempted to give directions to the Church."

To identify the Church with foreign imperialists and militarists simply because it refused to endorse a particular partisan formula for peace showed no understanding whatever of the nonpolitical nature of the Church. That the Church desired peace was self-evident. Its entire program was directed toward peace between individuals and among the peoples of the world. It yearned for the day when all the nations of the world would commit themselves to peace, and with a sense of mutual responsibility would once for all outlaw the making and using of atomic weapons of war.

The Church, moreover, was deeply concerned over the restoration of German unity, and deplored every new measure that tended to divide people in East and West Germany from one another.

Finally, the bishop sought to make it clear that the Church was not committed to or dependent upon any particular pattern of social or economic life. Its concern lay simply in this, that in any social or economic reorganization human values be preserved, and that it be recognized that it is contrary both to the law of God and the dignity of human life to seek human progress through inhuman measures.

A few weeks later the Synod of the EKD assembled at Elbingerode, and, under the theme of the "Public Responsibility of the Christian," considered some of the same issues Dibelius had singled out as crucial. Curiously, this synod secured permission to meet in East Germany, with representation from both West Germany and West Berlin, when interzonal passes for virtually every other Church assembly were impossible to secure.

Two developments of considerable significance emerged from this synod. Professor Martin Fischer of Berlin delivered an address, on the responsibility of Christians in East and West, in which he offered a piece of prophetic advice. The Churches of East Germany, he warned, must be prepared to stand by themselves and to think through the way they must take in their new situation. It was not enough to follow the lead of western Protestantism and to become dependent upon its leadership, nor to depend upon the continuing possibility of a flight to the West if conditions became too bad. Someday this escape route would be closed. Fischer urged the Church in East Germany to accept realistically the economic and political atmosphere in which it found itself, and to seek prayerfully the guidance of God's Holy Spirit in making its witness boldly and effectively in a Marxist land. It would not be easy in East Germany to find the right course of action and to render to God what belonged to God and to a totalitarian Caesar what rightfully belonged to him, but the Lord of the Church had never promised that discipleship with Him would be a path of ease and comfort.

Fischer was not advocating a separate course for the Churches and Christians of East Germany. He valued the fellowship and the unity of the EKD more highly than many of his colleagues in the Church. But he was afraid that if the eastern Churches did not come to grips with the subject of Christian responsibility in their own peculiar situation, they might one day find themselves entirely cut off from their brethren in the West without having made adequate theological preparation.

The second result of the Synod of Elbingerode was a decision to send delegations to both German governments to express the grave concern that the Church felt over the prospects of setting up military forces in both East and West. Letters were also sent to Churchill, Stalin, Truman, and Pinay, calling their attention again to the deep longing of the divided German people for reunification and peace.

Very much in the consciousness of both these synods was the situation of Christian youth. In a speech before an assembly of the FDJ in Leipzig early in June, Walter Ulbricht had described the Evangelical Youth as agents of the Americans and as an illegal organization guilty of sabotage. With this encouragement the official newspaper of the FDJ, *Junge Welt*, launched an attack upon the Church youth, hoping thereby to divert the attention of party leaders from its own failures to mobilize East German youth successfully. Their opening thrust was directed against the summer camps and district rallies which had been a regular part of the Church youth program since the end of the war.

One of these rallies was scheduled on June 15th in Luebbenau, a small town about fifty miles southeast of Berlin. This event had been held each year since 1947 on the same Sunday, without interference of any kind. An added feature of the 1952 rally was to be an outdoor concert of brass choirs in the Castle Park, and written permission for this had been secured on May 27th from the local police. About 4,600 young people were expected to attend, and overnight quarters had been secured for 1,200, partly in private homes and partly in the barns of neighboring farms. All of the restaurants in town were prepared for the guests, 1,200 of whom were arriving by special train from the city of Cottbus, about twenty miles away. All arrangements had been fully approved.

On June 10th, five days before the event was to open, the headquarters of the People's Police in Luebbenau sent a letter to the Church superintendent by courier, stating that because the youth congregations were illegal organizations, all permissions were withdrawn and the superintendent was requested to cancel the meeting.

The following day the superintendent protested personally at government offices in Potsdam, pointing out that the youth congregations were not organizations at all, but simply meetings of the young people of the congregations. To declare them illegal was to declare the congregations themselves illegal. The superintendent refused to call off the rally, and said they would meet in the Church's own buildings if necessary. He sent a letter of complaint to the State Headquarters of the People's Police, but received only a noncommital reply.

On June 12th, in Luebbenau, the posters announcing the rally, which had been printed with official license, were torn down by the People's Police. Eleven hundred pounds of meat were confiscated.

Police announced that only private homes might quarter youth and that no more than five might stay in any home. No barns or haylofts were permitted to be used as quarters. Mayors in adjoining villages were instructed by police to announce that the rally would not be held. The superintendent entered formal complaints against these measures also, and announced that if there were not adequate places for the guests to sleep in Luebbenau, he would house them in the church.

On June 13th the railroad officials in Cottbus informed the superintendent that because of mechanical difficulties the special train would not run.

In spite of all of these interferences, the rally was held as scheduled. Most of those scheduled to come on the special train got to Lubbenau anyway, on regular trains, bicycles, or automobiles, although many autos were stopped on the way and searched by police. The use of loudspeakers was forbidden. The brass choir was forbidden to play in the open on Sunday morning, so they stood inside the church and trumpeted through the open doors instead. So many families announced their readiness to take in the visiting youth that there were places for all, in spite of the prohibitions on mass quartering. Farmers, however, were awakened at night so the police could count the number of young people sleeping there, and the farmers were informed that they were giving assistance to an illegal organization.

Shortly after the services began in the church at Luebbenau at eight o'clock on Sunday morning, three trucks carrying about 150 members of the FDJ rolled up with shouts for the republic. They jumped down from the trucks and would have forced their way into the service, but members of the youth congregation formed a cordon by locking their arms, and kept them out. Other events were carried out on schedule, though everything was confined to the church buildings in Luebbenau and the neighboring village of Zerkewitz. In these two churches a total of 4,200 young people gathered, and 500 more who were without transportation assembled in Cottbus, twenty miles away. In every meeting the pastors read a statement admonishing the youth to preserve strict discipline on the street and to respect the rules of the police. The day ended without violence or conflict, and the young people returned to their home communities, having laid down a clear witness to their faith and determination even in the face of threats.

One week later a similar interference occurred at Goerlitz in Silesia. As in the case of Luebbenau, all preliminary arrangements had been carefully cleared with police officials, and the local police had even offered their services for the day of the rally, in case they should be needed to direct crowds.

On June 12th two representatives of the government came to the Church headquarters and asked that the rally be canceled because the Church youth were an illegal organization. The next day the same men visited the local pastor and explained to him that they had confiscated a poster announcing the rally because the poster displayed a Church flag, which could be understood as a battle flag against the East. Also on this poster was the silhouette of the towers of Goerlitz, and over the towers a Church flag with a large cross. It was pointed out that the flag was not blowing in an easterly direction, as would apparently befit a loyal flag, but that it was clearly blowing toward the south. In view of the attitude of the government the officials advised the pastor to notify his colleagues that the rally was likely to cause too much disturbance among the people, and should therefore be canceled.

On June 14th, as one of the youth leaders arrived in Goerlitz to complete preparations for the rally, he was received on the station platform by two men who accompanied him to his residence where a third man was waiting. They informed him that the rally had been forbidden, and confiscated all the material which had been prepared, including the lists of participants and the room reservations.

During the week preceding the rally, mayors in all neighboring towns informed local pastors several times that the projected meeting was illegal, and attempted to prevent the confirmed youth from making the trip to Goerlitz. As a result, the schedule of events was curtailed and limited to the church buildings. Government officials asked for a copy of a religious play entitled *Judas*, which was scheduled for the church on Sunday afternoon. After glancing into the text they explained that the play could not be given because it had not been licensed for presentation in the German Democratic Republic. Furthermore, the content was very questionable.

On Sunday, June 22nd, members of congregations from surrounding towns, who wanted to take part in the services of worship in Goerlitz, were subjected to rigid controls by the police on the railway platforms both on the trip to Goerlitz and back. In one town young people were prevented from purchasing railway tickets, although such interference was directly contrary to the rules of the railroad itself. At another point a delay occurred while police ordered all young people traveling to the forbidden rally to leave the train. Police went through the coaches, rounded up all who had refused to leave the train, and marched them to headquarters, flanked by police officers on both sides. Several of the young people were individually interviewed in an effort to discover whether they were an organized unit with leadership for the trip to Goerlitz. On the return trip all young people were checked again at the railway station, and their names were noted in every case, whether they attended the youth rally or not.

Summer Bible camps were alleged to be in conflict with the summer sport and recreation program of the Young Pioneers. Church leaders pointed out that the Bible camps were not primarily recreational in nature and therefore in no sense competed with the other summer camps. In spite of the letter of protest sent by the Synod of Brandenburg to Deputy Prime Minister Otto Nuschke, about half of these retreats had to be canceled in 1952.

During the course of the summer the chairman of the FDJ, Erich Honecker, issued a series of directions to the youth of East Germany for service in the military program of the German Democratic Republic. According to these directions, both boys and girls were to be given training in shooting and in marksmanship. About the same time the youth office of the Church issued a statement urging its youth not to be blindly led astray by slogans, but rather as Christians to make their decisions in the spirit of the Bible. Honecker claimed this was a western-inspired effort to exert religious pressure on the young people and thus to make them unfit for the defense tasks of the republic.

In the closing months of 1952 careful preparations were made by the FDJ for a major assault on the Church youth beginning in the new year. Part of this preparation was the suspension of the only Evangelical Youth publication in East Germany, *Die Stafette,* allegedly because of a shortage of paper supplies. District leaders of the FDJ were given orders to infiltrate the youth congregations with spies and to gather material which would substantiate the charges of western influence. "It is necessary," declared Erich Honecker, "that the FDJ carry out a broad and thorough investigation of the true character of the wirepullers in the youth congregations."

In January the press attack began through the official organ of the FDJ, *Junge Welt*, and through other East German newspapers. Week after week, charges of sabotage and disloyalty and subversion were hurled at the Church youth, and finally, in April, *Junge Welt* devoted an entire special issue to this theme. The lead article opened with headlines "unmasking" the youth congregations as a "Cover Organization for War Agitation, Sabotage and American Espionage." "The correspondents of *Junge Welt* in all parts of the German Democratic Republic," began the article, "are reporting new cases of the hostile intrigues of the illegal youth congregations. These facts, which we feel obligated to transmit to the public, round out the picture which has been given previously through many contributions of *Junge Welt*. It is evident that this hypocritical organization, veneered with Christian appearances, is directed by American agents and spies stationed in West Germany and especially in West Berlin."

The flagrant untruths and open defamations in these articles finally moved Bishop Dibelius and the Church of Brandenburg to submit a formal request to the States Attorney to take legal action against the editors of *Junge Welt* for violating the laws and the constitution of the German Democratic Republic by irresponsible and vicious slander. States Attorney Dr. Ernest Melsheimer replied that since he could find no authorized registration of the youth congregations in the Ministry of the Interior, they must be illegal organizations, and therefore complaints on their behalf were invalid. Dr. Kurt Scharf of the Church of Brandenburg tried to point out that on the basis of an agreement between the Bishop of Berlin and the Russian Colonel Tulpanov in 1946, the youth congregations were not an organization at all, but the free assembly of the youth of the congregations. The very fact that the youth congregations were not registered was evidence of such an agreement. "It would be difficult," declared Scharf, "to make a plausible case for the fact that an illegal organization had existed in the German Democratic Republic for many years and done its work in public view without being registered." Nevertheless, the attempt of the Church to make use of legal recourses to safeguard itself from slanderous and libelous attack was completely fruitless.

The press campaign was simply preparatory for the full-scale attack, which found its most dramatic expression between Easter and Pentecost in the ousting of more than three thousand high-school students because of their loyalty to their youth congregations. Beginning in Holy Week a series of school assemblies was launched, each of which followed an identical pattern. After a speech on the "European Defense Pact," members of the youth congregations in the assembly were singled out and required to express publicly their opinions of the "western war agreement." If their answers were not satisfactory, the inadequacy of the school's achievements was pointed out, and the youth congregations were held responsible because "progressive" ideas had not been more universally accepted. Statements of the Church youth were cited as proof that they had interfered with the growth of "progressive" ideas.

After a catalogue of alleged undercover political activities of the youth congregations was announced, members of the Church youth were called upon by name and asked to decide publicly whether after these "enlightenments" they still wanted to belong to such an "illegal organization." If they refused to give an oral or written statement of withdrawal, they were denounced as disloyal to the republic, unworthy of further education at public expense in any school of the republic, and formally expelled. Many of these young people who were either taking their final examinations or were just completing their preparations for them were thereby deprived of the formal benefits of all their previous school achievements, as well as the possibilities of any further education in the universities and technical schools of East Germany.

The persecutions reached into the universities as well, where student congregations and student pastors were assailed as American agents and as saboteurs of the peace of Germany and of the world.

In the factories and workshops similar procedures were undertaken under the supervision of the committees of the FDJ. Admission to apprenticeships and even employment on jobs was conditioned upon formal separation from the youth congregations.

Press attacks and personal slander were followed by the arrest of more than seventy pastors and Church workers. Some of these were summarily sentenced to prison terms, and others were singled out for special attention in so-called "show trials," from which the maximum propaganda value was drawn. The first of these trials was widely publicized in January, 1953, as the "Case of Pastor Schumann."

Preparation for the arrest of Erich Schumann was made over a period of several months through a series of articles in the party press, accusing him of perverting the youth and undermining the institutions of the German Democratic Republic. Shortly after an article appeared in December describing him as a "pied piper for Eisenhower," and suggesting that he be either arrested or put into an institution for the dangerously insane, Schumann was taken into custody by the police in the Saxon city of Chemnitz. No representatives of the Church were allowed to visit him before or after his trial.

Charges against him were based upon statements he had made in a lecture to the youth congregation in Zwickau in November, in which he had dealt with the subject of films. Schumann had advised the youth that they should base their judgments of all cultural presentations upon the Word of God and had expressed the opinion that when they visited the film theaters they would doubtless find a great deal that was contrary to Christian teaching. However, he said, if the young people learned nothing else from their experience in the theaters than to be critical of themselves and of what they saw, this would make their attendance worth while.

On this information the State charged Schumann with hindering the effectiveness of educational work being presented on stage and screen. He allegedly encouraged the youth to learn nothing from these presentations except the ability to exercise a critical spirit, and thereby to form themselves into a reserve corps for the enemies of the "democratic order."

Further charges were based upon Schumann's admonition to the young people to become "Christian anglers and fishermen," even among the People's Police, and in the socialized factories. He had reported an incident in Dresden where the youth had actually distributed Church announcements in the police station and in factories. Such activity, charged the State, was a violation of Article 42 of the constitution, which protected citizens of the republic against compulsion to participate in activities of a religious nature.

Other charges were made in connection with Schumann's alleged attitude toward a national army. His ultimate conviction was largely based upon the witness of two members of the FDJ who had attended the lecture in Zwickau with the intention of watching for statements that could be used against him. Sentence was passed on January 23, 1953, and Schumann was given a six-year penitentiary term.

Even before the sentence had been passed, an article appeared in the Chemnitz *Volksstimme*, describing Schumann's conviction as a foregone conclusion. After the sentence had been handed down, another article invited the youth to take note of what happened to criminals who attempted to poison youth with conspiratory speeches and lies, and to undermine the confidence of young people in their State.

Shortly after the trial the Lutheran Church of Saxony and the Herrnhut Brethren issued a statement declaring their full support of Schumann. The public addresses he had made, they said, had been made in the regular course of his preaching ministry, and any attempt to interpret them politically as "agitation to boycott democratic institutions" was a complete misinterpretation. The judgment issued against Schumann was not a judgment against an individual person, but against the Church and all those who preached the Word of God. Promising that it would appeal the decision of the court, the Church summoned all members of its congregations to join in intercessory prayer for Pastor Schumann and for all who preached the Gospel. Despite every effort on his behalf, however, Schumann began his six-year sentence under the "Law for the Defense of Peace."

Scarcely a week passed in the early months of 1953 without one or more pastors or youth leaders being taken into custody by the police. Some of them were openly arrested, like Pastor Reinhold George, who was seized at the conclusion of a service at St. Mary's Church in East Berlin, where he served as youth pastor. Others, such as Kurt Aland, professor in the theological faculty at the University of Halle, disappeared while on a trip to Berlin, and the earliest reports could only say, "Presumably arrested."

One of the most widely discussed arrests was that of the extremely popular and effective student pastor at the University of Halle, Dr. Johannes Hamel, on February 12th. He, too, simply disappeared while on a business trip, and only the searching of his home by the police on the night of his disappearance gave indication to his family and colleagues that he had been arrested. Hamel had had great success in his ministry, and students had to come early in order to find a place to sit during his weekly Bible studies. He was almost constantly conducting interviews with students who were concerned about spiritual matters, and he had won the reputation of being both courageous and forthright in these conversations.

One of the members of his student congregation wrote a letter in 1950 describing the consternation created in certain SED and FDJ assemblies by Hamel's ministry among the students. During an FDJ discussion on the desirability of infiltrating the student congregation with convinced Communists in order to sow dissension among the students, group leaders advised moving with extreme caution. "This is dangerous procedure," they warned. "Our agents may come back as Christians!"

There was no suggestion of underground political activity in Hamel's work among the students. He believed everything should be done openly and above board. For example, on one occasion he went directly to the State Secretary for Higher Education in order to complain about the overburdening of the students which followed in the wake of the new ten-month study program. But he also went directly to RIAS, the American-controlled radio in West Berlin, to protest against the propaganda programs which were being broadcast.

Hamel was constantly under threat from the secret police, and on several occasions was warned to leave the city. He was attacked in newspapers and in public assemblies, and shortly after his arrest an article appeared in *Junge Welt* under the caption "An Alleged Student Pastor." He was accused of seeking to establish political influence over the students. As evidence of his subversive activity, the article catalogued items discovered when the secret police had searched his library. Books had been found which allegedly revealed connections with American military agents and with West German propaganda offices. One of Hamel's news sources, declared the article, "is an institute which calls itself the Evangelical Hilfswerk" and has its offices in West Berlin!

As the number of arrests multiplied, the concern of the Churches not only in East and West Germany but even in foreign countries increased. Prayer lists were published and distributed, and revised each week to include the names of recent arrests. Pastors and congregations prayed for these people by name, both privately and in their Sunday services. Bishops and synods protested and pleaded for an end to this clearly directed attempt to intimidate the Church. Dr. Martin Niemoeller, whose bitter opposition to the defense policies of the West German government at least earned him a hearing with the East German leaders, personally visited both Ulbricht and Grotewohl in an effort to secure the release of the arrested pastors.

From Switzerland came a letter from Professor Karl Barth to the Minister for State Security, Wilhelm Zaisser, pleading especially for the release of Pastor Hamel, but also mentioning several others by name. Describing himself as one who stood consistently "for an understanding attitude toward the East," and who had therefore "often been severely attacked as an apparently secret Communist," Barth urged Zaisser not to spoil the record thus far maintained by the German Democratic Republic in permitting the Church the freedom to live its own life and to preach the Word of God. Through such an attack as had now been launched against the Church, observed Barth, the government was simply strengthening the arsenal of anti-eastern propaganda in the West. Zaisser, however, seemed unimpressed.

Dr. Heinrich Grueber, especially distressed at the arrest of his colleague Pastor George in East Berlin, displayed some of the most scurrilous attacks upon the Church in copies of *Junge Welt* in the glass-enclosed bulletin board of St. Mary's Church, and announced to his parishioners that the government had actually launched a full-scale *Kirchenkampf*. "Perhaps greater sacrifices will be required from pastors and congregations," declared Grueber, "than in the first *Kirchenkampf*. We will also make this sacrifice gladly, as we did twenty years ago. . . . We urge all members of the congregation to continue in intercessory prayer for Pastor George, and for all who have been arrested."

Interferences continued to mount during the early months of 1953 in all areas of Church work. Pastors and youth leaders were spied upon, and many were called before the secret police for extended questionings. There were even some cases of open blasphemy, such as the parody on the Aaronic benediction which became the theme of a song taught to a choir of Young Pioneers. When a Saxon pastor protested against such blasphemy, he was attacked in the press for interfering with efforts to teach the children "songs of peace."

The attack on the youth also had its effect on the Church's program of religious instruction. In East Berlin, where instruction was still given in the schoolrooms, all morning classes were prohibited on the ground that the beginning of the day belonged to the FDJ and the State. No Christian instruction whatsoever could be given on days when the Young Pioneers had activities scheduled either in the morning or afternoon. There were individual instances of school principals, Pioneer leaders, or teachers demanding the right to supervise the content of the religious instruction, and in some cases uniformed policemen tried to enter the rooms where the instruction was being given.

Most dramatic of all were the investigations and arbitrary seizures of several of the great welfare institutions operated by the Inner Mission of the Evangelical Church and the Roman Catholic Caritas. Many of these institutions were the direct outgrowth of the great movement for social missions which was fathered by Johann Hinrich Wichern in the nineteenth century and which had established a world-wide reputation for its ministry to the sick and the needy and the homeless.

Although their work was left undisturbed after 1945 because of the great needs among the population, the Communist State had never recognized the fundamental right of the Church to engage in welfare work. Members of the diaconic orders were gradually eliminated from positions in State hospitals and city health services. The nursing schools operated by the Deaconess Mother Houses survived only with great difficulty. The exclusive right of the Volkssolidaritaet to distribute relief goods among the needy had been asserted in 1950, and this had brought the termination of the relief distributions by Hilfswerk and Caritas.

As a part of the sharpened attack upon the Church in 1953, a wave of seizures of key welfare institutions occurred. The procedure followed a fixed pattern, first demonstrated in March in connection with the great Pfeiffer Foundation of the Inner Mission in Magdeburg-Cracau. After initial critical articles in the party press, a committee appeared to examine the account books, library, sanitary facilities, and the social conditions among the employees. A few days later a second examining committee appeared, accompanied by agents of the secret police who looked more sharply at some of the things which had been critically noted in the first visit. The complaints of the patients and inmates were encouraged, even those of the feeble-minded and retarded. When enough material had been assembled, the seizure took place, with some shadowy justification against which legal protest had no effect whatever.

The case of the Hope Valley Institutions in Lobetal near Berlin illustrates the procedure that was followed. Lobetal was one of the institutional complexes founded by the revered "Father" von Bodelschwingh in the nineteenth century. It operated its hospitals, homes for the aged, for children, for epileptics, and for the mentally retarded, and its workshops and schools, much like a small city community. It even had its own mayor.

About nine o'clock in the morning on May 18th a motorized cavalcade of twenty or thirty automobiles and motorcycles roared through the main gate into the quiet wooded campus of the Hope Valley Institutions. To the astonishment of the staff and the patients and inmates, more than a hundred persons, including fifty uniformed policemen, emerged from the vehicles of the motorcade. Moving with military precision they blocked every access to the grounds as if they were occupying an armed and hostile fortification, instead of a hospital for epileptics and complex of homes for the aged.

Without consulting anyone, seven different commissions fanned out, according to the description of the astonished director, "like a swarm of bees," each to a different building, to begin their investigations. In the office of the director, Dr. Braune, the leader of the invasion presently appeared, announcing himself as "Herr Naumann," a member of the East German Parliament and chairman of the Youth Committee of the District of Frankfurt an der Oder. He was accompanied by a man named Stadlow, who was known to Dr. Braune as the State officer for religious affairs in the same district. Dr. Braune protested the entire procedure, and especially the authority of "Herr Naumann" to investigate hospitals and homes for the aged as a representative of the District Youth Committee!

Naumann, however, assured Braune that the purpose of the entire visitation was simply to help the institutions and to remedy a few possible deficiencies, but his friendly assurances were scarcely sub-stantiated by the armed guards covering every access to the grounds.

The individual commissions, each made up of five to fifteen per-sons, none of whom would identify himself by name, showed a special interest in talking with patients and inmates, gathering complaints concerning their care and treatment. In the kitchens and workshops they inquired only whether anyone was forced to work long hours. Anyone who expressed eagerness or satisfaction in his work was dismissed as foolish. The fact that many had been on the staff of the institution for more than twenty-five years and performed their tasks with a sense of service seemed completely beyond the comprehension of the examiners.

In one of the boys' homes a commission photographed a heap of potato peelings in the kitchen, and this picture subsequently ap-peared in the newspapers as an example of the kind of food served at the home. Two elderly men, a wheelwright and a shoemaker, who had asked for the privilege of sleeping in their shops, were photo-graphed as examples of the inadequate housing facilities available for aged people. In the main residences for epileptics and retarded persons, patients were asked leading questions and urged to admit that they were being exploited because they were not being paid according to regular wage scales for work performed as a part of their therapy.

In these conversations frequent irreverent and provocative expres-sions were used by the commission members. Pious old people were told, "We'll soon break you of your habits of praying." Retarded young men who were slowly and painfully being taught a trade in the workshops were asked by an investigator: "How do you ever manage to hold out in this place? You're just being exploited!" The children in the school were advised not to attend worship services. It was not necessary, they were told, for them to be enslaved by the Church. In the home for retarded boys, one of the visitors revealed the spirit of his mission when he advised those he interviewed, "Hit your teachers in their fat bellies if they try to make you do anything!" A police unit, passing a group of patients peacefully working in a garden, shouted loudly, "Stand where you are! Anyone who tries to run away will be shot immediately!"

Such provocative and irresponsible conduct in an institution for the care and training of retarded persons could only have a profoundly disturbing effect on the entire atmosphere, and upon certain individuals in particular. One feeble-minded young man was singled out by an investigator as a special case of exploitation allegedly being prevented from securing independent employment. Without any discussion whatever with the directors of the home, who knew his background and limitations, the investigator assured this young man in the presence of fellow patients that he personally would see that the young man was given a chance. The patient became so excited that he refused to stay any longer in the home. An eighteen-year-old epileptic was so belabored and stirred up by the questioners that he wandered off in complete disregard of all safety regulations of the home and was drowned in a nearby lake. The bewildered old wheelwright, who had been both photographed and intensively questioned by the commission, sought to quiet his unrest in alcohol, and being entirely unaccustomed to drinking, died of the effects of his overindulgence.

The investigation continued throughout the entire day. The concluding conference with the directors of the institution was cut very short, and about four o'clock the entire caravan withdrew. The promised evaluation of the investigation never took place, and the only reports received were the lurid pictorial descriptions carried by the party press in the days following.

In this case, as in other similar seizures, the protests of the Church were unavailing. Dr. Braune sent a nine-page letter to Deputy Prime Minister Nuschke on the day following the incident, describing in detail the entire arbitrary procedure. On behalf of the Church of Berlin-Brandenburg, Dr. Kurt Scharf directed a similar complaint to Dr. Dieckmann, the president of the People's Parliament, inasmuch as the leader of the invasion had purported to be a member of that body. Dieckmann replied that there was no one named Naumann who was a member of the People's Parliament and that since Dr. Scharf himself had not been present to witness the events he described in his protest it would not be possible to request any government office to undertake specific action. Scharf wrote again, supplying full documentation of the events by eyewitnesses, and suggesting that if "Herr Naumann" was not a member of the Parliament, he had certainly been guilty of misrepresentation, which was also a punishable violation of the laws of the land.

Dieckmann's reply was a masterpiece of evasion. It came two weeks after he received Scharf's second letter, and in the meantime the Revolution of June 17th had very nearly overthrown the entire government. This no doubt increased Dieckmann's unwillingness to become involved in such a controversial matter, but his attitude was typical of the problem the Church constantly faced in trying to find some government official who would accept responsibility for specific actions directed against the Church. Dieckmann advised Scharf to write identical letters to Prime Minister Grotewohl, Minister of State Security Wilhelm Zaisser, and Police Chief Karl Maron. He was careful to suggest that any reference to the previous correspondence between Dieckmann and Scharf be omitted. He did promise to investigate personally the ousting of a teacher from the Lobetal school, which had followed the invasion of May 18th, but the more embarrassing arbitrary violations of constitutional and human rights he preferred to let someone else handle.

During these bitter days of persecution, the most serious Church struggle was going on in the individual parishes of the Church, in the schoolrooms, in factories and shops, in the homes, and in the daily life of the communities. Many a young person with great hopes for a future career discovered a very contemporary meaning in the words of Jesus Christ: "He that loseth his life for my sake and the Gospel's shall save it." Many a parent with deep love and great expectations for his son or daughter, but also with unflinching loyalty to the Gospel, saw for the first time what Christ really meant when He said, "He that loveth son or daughter more than me is not worthy of me." Bishop Dibelius observed that when he preached to congregations during these times, he found a greater response than ever before to texts such as that of the 130th Psalm, "Out of the depths have I cried unto thee, O Lord; O Lord, hear my voice!"

But the people on the front lines needed to be reassured, too, that they did not stand alone. Their expectations were amply met by the pastoral letters of their bishops and the messages of their synods. Bishop Mueller of Magdeburg, for example, wrote to all the parishes in the Province of Saxony, pointing out the courageous witness which was being brought to public life by many Christians. He noted the points of special attack, listing the names of pastors who were in prison and institutions of the Inner Mission which had been confiscated. These citations were not made in a spirit of complaint, but in order that all of the facts might be known to the members of the congregations. The main burden of his message was to urge the Christian people to hold together more firmly in worship, to bear one another's burdens, to pray for those in prison and for peace.

The same warm spirit of sympathetic understanding was found in a letter Bishop Dibelius addressed to the members of the youth congregations and their parents. "I know how difficult it is," he said, "to look on while our children are attacked for the sake of their faith, and how natural the wish is to protect them from new attacks. I have watched all of this in my own children in the previous Church struggle. But do not forget that your children will remember few things so clearly, and there will be few things that bring them so much confidence in later life as this, that they remained true to their Church in their youth. More than anything else, do not forget that a free conscience is better than a smooth and easy way of life. It is written, 'What does it profit a man if he gain the whole world and lose his own soul?' Our Church, however, you may be sure, will do everything possible within its power to help those who have been brought under oppression because of their faith."

When the United Lutheran Church in Germany convened in West Berlin on April 20th, after its scheduled meeting in Weimar had to be canceled, its bishops' conference declared that the measures of the government were becoming intolerable. Denying flatly that the youth congregations were illegal organizations, the bishops protested practices which they described as inhuman and clearly contradictory to legal principles recognized in the entire civilized world. Their high respect as Lutherans for the divine institution of civil authority, they declared, only laid upon them a heavier responsibility to speak out when this civil authority was being misused. "We believe," declared the bishops, "that the judgment of God will rest upon those who misuse the divinely ordained office of civil authority and that his judgment will fall with special force upon those who harm or seek to harm the faith of young people."

Out of this brutal persecution of the Church in East Germany in 1953 there also emerged a witness in Christian literature, through two small documents which were almost apostolic in tone and character. One of these was a collection of sermons preached by the dynamic general superintendent in Cottbus, Dr. Guenter Jacob, under the title *The Light Shines in the Darkness*. The other was a small booklet written by Professor Martin Fischer of Berlin, *The Witness of the Imprisoned*.

Neither of these books was marked by a spirit of self-pity or complaint, but rather by a spirit of thankfulness that the grace of God was great enough to sustain His Church even in bitter days of persecution. There was no attempt to minimize the seriousness of the problems, or to gloss over the methods of terror being employed against the Church, especially against its youth and its pastors.

One of the most dangerous aspects of the persecution, declared Fischer, was the attempt to force the Church to withdraw into a spiritual ghetto, where it might assemble a few older people and observe its rituals, but never bear witness in public that Jesus Christ was the Lord of all life. A Church of the Protestant faith in the living Word could never permit this to happen without betraying its fundamental reason for existence; namely, to bear witness to the redeeming and all-embracing love of God in Christ.

Christians, therefore, had no other choice but to bear this witness, not belligerently but in love and patience. "Where a Church is found worthy of this suffering," said Fischer, "the mercy of God is near. There it is springtime. There people begin to sing. There men may lift up their heads, because their salvation is near. There men rise up from sleep, and there the Church rejoices. There love is warm; prayer, living; understanding, clear. There God's Word has free course. There one learns again to sing Luther's hymn 'Still He is with us in the fight, with His good gifts and Spirit.' For this very reason the complaints of the Church are transformed into the praise of God. This the world cannot understand. It had expected just the opposite. But in this situation the mysteries of Ephesians 3:7-13 are made contemporary: 'Of this gospel I was made a minister according to the gift of God's grace which was given to me by the working of his power. To me, though I am the very least of all the saints, this grace was given, to preach to the Gentiles the unsearchable riches of Christ, and to make all men see what is the plan of the mystery hidden for ages in God who created all things; that through the Church the manifold wisdom of God might now be known to the principalities and powers in the heavenly places. This was according to the eternal purpose which he has realized in Christ Jesus our Lord, in whom we have boldness and confidence of access through our faith in Him. So I ask you not to lose heart over what I am suffering for you, which is your Glory.' "

By no means all of the people in East Germany read Martin Fischer's booklet or even shared his views. There were thousands every week who left the unhappy republic behind and joined the massive stream of refugees that had been moving from East to West Germany ever since the end of the war. Since the formation of the two German governments in 1949, official West German statistics placed the average influx of refugees from East Germany at 15,000 per month, or about 500 every day. With the closing of the "green border," as the line between East and West Germany was called, and the sharpened government policies in connection with the "build-up of Socialism," the numbers soared. In September, 1952, 23,337 people sought refuge in the West. After a brief decline at the year's end, the highest point of the entire postwar period was reached in March, 1953, when 58,605 persons fled. This represented an average of almost 2,000 persons every day, most of them young people under twenty-five years of age. In twelve months, 335,441 people left their homes in East Germany, and went west.

Relatively few of these refugees dared to attempt the dangerous crossing of the "green border," which bristled with barbed wire and machine guns. A considerable number secured permits for family visits, crossed legally to West Germany, but never returned. The vast majority made their escape through West Berlin, which in these days of terror and persecution was virtually overrun with refugees who brought practically nothing with them except the clothes they wore. No one was ever sent back to East Germany against his will, though any who wished to return were at liberty to do so. Temporary housing facilities had to be set up for these people; food had to be provided, and some opportunity of beginning a new life. After careful screening, qualified refugees were flown out at government expense to the industrial areas of West Germany, where the federal government had to assume responsibility for their employment and their integration into the society of the West. At each stage of their migration the Churches provided as much spiritual care as they could, but the feeding, housing, and clothing of such a vast number of people was a task which only the resources of the government could master.

Not all of these people left East Germany as a result of religious persecution, although the unusually large number in the early months of 1953 showed the effects of the accelerated assault upon the youth by the FDJ. For world opinion, however, the refugee statistics provided a startling substantiation of the Church reports on religious persecutions in East Germany and called forth sharp protests from many sources. The Archbishop of York, Dr. C. F. Garbett, suggested that the United Nations take note of the religious persecution in East Germany and other Communist-controlled countries and present the facts to the world public. Dr. Carl E. Lund-Quist, Executive Secretary of the Lutheran World Federation, raised his voice in Geneva against the "devilish methods" being used to crush the faith of young people and children. The effect of these expressions of world opinion were not lost upon the Soviet government, which, following the death of Stalin in March, 1953, was preparing to launch a campaign for "peaceful coexistence" with the western world.

The refugee statistics were also an indication to East German politicians that they had overreached themselves in their program of the "build-up of Socialism." A rigid continuation of these policies would have resulted in a fatal drain upon the very manpower essential for a strong economy. Unknown to the Churches, therefore, a drastic reversal of policy was in immediate prospect as the fateful summer of 1953 approached. Once more, as in 1951, for political and economic reasons beyond the control of the Church, a relaxation of the hostile activities of the Communist government was to afford the Church a much-needed period of respite and recovery.

NINE

MOSCOW'S NEW COURSE

The 10th of June, 1953, was a memorable day for the Churches of East Germany! For twelve bitter months the fires of persecution had been burning in the German Democratic Republic. Seventy-two pastors and Church workers were in prison. Thousands of young people had been expelled from schools because of their loyalty to their Church. Libelous accusations had been hurled at the Church and its leaders by the party press, and five major welfare institutions of the Inner Mission had been seized by the State.

Pleas and protests from churchmen both within and without Germany had proved fruitless. Letters had been written. Requests to discuss points of tension had been ignored. The prime minister had even denied publicly that a *Kirchenkampf* existed in the German Democratic Republic.

Yet suddenly, in response to an almost desperate proposal by the bishops of East Germany on June 5th, Otto Grotewohl agreed to receive a Church delegation for a conference on June 10th. Bishop Dibelius hastily summoned all the Evangelical bishops together at his home for supper on the evening of June 9th to plan the strategy.

It was agreed that each of them should present one phase of the Church's complaints: youth and education, the arrest and imprisonment of pastors, the seizures of institutions, and the hindering of Church life.

The following day the heads of all eight Protestant Churches, together with Dr. Krummacher, the general superintendent of East Berlin, and Heinrich Grueber, the official Church representative to the government, filed into the prime minister's conference room in the big gray government building in East Berlin. They were greeted by the prime minister and his aide, Herr Groetschel, Deputy Prime Minister Otto Nuschke, and the ministers of Education and State Security, Paul Wandel and Wilhelm Zaisser.

Formalities were brief, and after a few words of introduction by the prime minister and Bishop Dibelius, the Church representatives were asked to present their materials. To the astonishment of the bishops, when the question of the youth and student congregations and the expulsion of young people from their schools because of participation in these activities had been presented, Grotewohl produced a prepared statement from which he read a full retraction of the government's position and a promise to rectify the injustices that had been imposed. The youth congregations, declared Grotewohl, were not illegal organizations, and no further measures would be taken by the government against them or any other Church organization. All of the pupils who had been expelled from the high schools because of their activity in the youth congregations would be allowed to return. Teachers who had been ousted for their support of such pupils would be readmitted. Limitations which had been introduced since January 1, 1953, upon the giving of religious instruction in public schoolrooms were to be removed.

With growing amazement the Churchmen listened to a similar acknowledgment of error in connection with the welfare institutions of the Church. Grotewohl promised that all would be returned except one building which had been leased to the Church by the government as a youth center in 1947.

Sentences which had been pronounced by the courts against pastors and Church workers were to be reexamined and unjust penalties withdrawn. Regulations concerning the advance reporting of Church meetings and assemblies were to be reexamined with a view to the elimination of unfair requirements. As if to test the reality of the things he was hearing from the lips of the prime minister, Grueber pointed out that since the subsidies to the Church had not been paid for several months, the salaries of the pastors were in arrears. Grotewohl replied that the State was prepared to resume its financial obligations on a regular basis, and asked how large a sum was needed immediately. Grueber replied, "Two million marks." Grotewohl immediately ordered a check for this amount made out in favor of the Church.

At the conclusion of the three-hour conference, all of these concessions on the part of the State were summarized in a nine-point communiqué that was released to the public. No concessions on the part of the Church were even mentioned. This marked the beginning of the so-called "new course" in Church-State relations.

The reaction of Church leaders after their initial shock of surprise had passed was one of overwhelming gratitude that the *Kirchenkampf* had ended and that God had given the Church a new beginning. Even by 1953 the leaders of the Church in East Germany had learned not to expect basic changes in the attitude of the State toward religion, but to live from one reprieve to the next. This new course was certainly the most spectacular and thoroughgoing modification of government policy since 1949. But even in the sweeping concessions which had been made, there was no suggestion of a fundamental ideological shift, and experience had taught that Communist tactics could be changed very quickly to meet the needs of a given situation.

The Council of the EKD, meeting two days after the conference with Grotewohl, issued a statement reflecting this spirit. After expressing its joy that the struggle was over, the council declared: "In this hour it would not be proper to suggest the reasons which have led to this great change. Nor would it be proper to direct our attention to the things which were not achieved. The facts are there. In these facts we can only recognize the answer to the many prayers which have been raised by our congregations. A bitter time lies behind the Churches in the German Democratic Republic. In these times we have experienced much of the merciful help of God. We have experienced anew all the blessing which God bestows upon the

Christian through suffering. Now we gratefully accept this new beginning from His hand."

From one of these village congregations came a confirmation of the council's statement. "Perhaps you can understand what it meant," wrote one of the young people in a letter to a friend, "when after the usual ringing of the church bells for evening prayer, suddenly the sound of trumpets rang out from the tower: 'All glory be to God on high. Who hath our race befriended! To us no harm shall now come nigh, The strife at last is ended; God showeth his good will toward men, And peace shall dwell on earth again; O thank Him for His goodness!' The congregation understood immediately, and within a half-hour the church was filled with people. The trumpets played on in the sanctuary. There were many young faces in the congregation. Then we sang, 'May God bestow on us His Grace.' The pastor spoke on the text of the day, 'Bless the Lord, O my soul, and forget not all his benefits.' Outside, a wild thunderstorm raged, and suddenly the lights failed. Now we sat in the dark church, lighted only by the two huge candles on the altar. The most beautiful of all was the prayer and the ancient benediction, and then in the darkness we sang together once more our glorious old hymn, 'Now thank we all our God.' "

There was no doubt, however, in the minds of even the most grateful Church leaders that the new course in Church-State relations was closely connected with the political and economic policies of the Soviet Union and its eastern European bloc. Joseph Stalin had died three months before, on March 5th, and the inner political turmoil of the Soviet Union demanded an immediate lessening of all international tensions. The new leadership in the Soviet Union would presently formalize these objectives in a policy of "peaceful coexistence" and in the modification of the stringent Stalinist controls within the ranks of international Communism.

Personnel shifts in the Soviet representation in East Germany suggested that these changes were also to be felt there. The Soviet Control Commission in Germany was dissolved, and its head, Marshal Zhukov, himself a close friend and confidant of Stalin, was recalled to the Soviet Union. Vladimir Semjonow, long-time political adviser to the Soviet Control Commission and advocate of closer relations with West Germany, was named High Commissioner of the Soviet

Union in Germany on May 28th. He arrived in Germany on June 5th and on June 8th Prime Minister Grotewohl advised the Church leaders of his readiness to confer with them and to relieve the tensions between Church and State.

Even more striking was the fact that on June 9th the Politburo of the SED Central Committee also decided upon a sweeping modification of the program widely heralded in 1952 as "the build-up of Socialism." In a spectacular demonstration of the Communist practice of public confession, the Politburo flatly declared that the party and the government had made serious mistakes in the past and that because of these mistakes great numbers of people had left the country. In order to overcome these mistakes and to encourage closer relations between the two parts of Germany, the program of rapid socialization would be immediately suspended.

The interests of the individual farmer, the merchant, the craftsman, and the intellectual had been neglected. Procedures leading to the liquidation of private activity in all these areas must therefore be halted immediately, and credits provided to farmers and merchants to enable them to resume operation in the event that they had been forced to give up their land or their businesses. Machine-Tractor Stations were to be instructed to give assistance to individual farmers in carrying out their work. All penalties for failures to fulfill production quotas were to be reexamined, and anyone who had left the country was assured that if he returned he would receive all his property back again and suffer no disadvantages because of his illegal flight.

The undue stress upon the rapid development of heavy industry at the expense of the production of consumers' goods had been a grave mistake. Party Secretary Walter Ulbricht, faithful Stalinist though he was, confessed publicly that the party leadership had attempted "simply to take over the forms and methods which had been built up in the Soviet state." This was a mistake. The building up of Socialism, he admitted, would be a long and difficult task in East Germany, but its achievement must always be closely bound up with a steady improvement of the economic and cultural situation of the workers. Price raises in certain food products were therefore to be immediately withdrawn, and reductions in railroad fares for workers and apprentices and students were to be restored.

The Politburo declared that procedures for the granting of inter-zonal passes should be eased and that mutual attendance on the part of East and West Germans at conferences of all kinds should be encouraged.

In the schools the stringent requirement that teachers be Marxist-Leninists was abandoned. "It is false," declared the prime minister to a teachers' rally shortly after the introduction of the new course, "to believe that the quality of teaching can be raised by investigating thousands of teachers and dismissing them by the hundreds. We should not dismiss them; we should try to win them over." High-school and university students who had already been expelled were permitted to reenter the schools without any disadvantage and were not even required to take the examinations they had missed. In the future no discrimination was to be shown toward the children of middle-class families in the admission policies of high schools and universities.

The real cause of this sweeping change of policy was actually the fear that the government had pressed its program of sovietization beyond the point of safety. The assumption upon which the "build-up of Socialism" had been launched was that enough workers and farmers in East Germany had either been won over to the new system or were prepared to accept it. The alarming rise in the number of refugees in the early months of 1953 demonstrated that this was not the case. A further indication was the general labor unrest following an increase in the work quotas of the laborers in the State-owned factories on May 28th without a corresponding wage increase. Strikes broke out in Chemnitz and Eisleben and Berlin before the government announced its change of course, and since nothing was said in the statements of the Politburo concerning a revision of labor quotas and wages, they continued afterward as well. On June 9th, the day on which the new course was announced, two thousand workers in the steel mills of Hennigsdorf near Berlin protested the increase in quotas, and when five workers were arrested the whole plant refused to work until their colleagues were released and the quotas reduced. Their demands were immediately met.

Encouraged by such signs of weakness on the part of the government and, more than anything else, by the public admission of errors by party officials, the workers pressed their demands for improved working conditions and for the release of political prisoners. By June 14th the State's Attorney had announced the release of four thousand political prisoners serving terms up to three years, and the impending release of fifteen hundred more. But this was only a part of the prison population, and workers by the thousands, both men and women, gathered in front of prisons in East German cities chanting, "Give us back our men!"

Suspicions of the sincerity of the regime deepened when on June 16th an article appeared in the *Tribune*, official organ of the party-sponsored labor union, declaring that the increases of May 28th in the work quotas were right and proper and should be carried through with all possible vigor.

This statement released a flood of pent-up resentment and anger among the ranks of Berlin laborers. Those who were engaged in building the great showpiece of East Berlin, the Stalin Boulevard, struck first, and marched in a body to the government buildings in the Leipzigerstrasse, adding to their numbers as they passed through the Alexanderplatz and the Lustgarten. In massed chorus they voiced their demands in front of the government buildings and were presently answered by the appearance of Fritz Selbmann, Minister for Metallurgy and Mining. He sought to quiet them by assurances that as a laborer himself he could understand their problems, but one of the demonstrators shouted back, "You've forgotten all about that!"

Others shouted political demands, calling for free elections and for the resignation of the government. Pushed from the speaker's platform by irate workers, Selbmann retired to the safety of the building, promising to telephone the leaders of the government. When he failed to reappear, the workers marched back to the Stalin Boulevard, calling for a general strike against the government. SED party symbols and posters were torn down from buildings and kiosks, and crowds swarmed around the Barnim Street Prison, calling for the release of political prisoners. The government sought to reassure the workers of its readiness to cooperate in meeting their demands, but meanwhile called upon the Russians to send military reinforcements to bolster their crumbling authority.

At seven o'clock in the morning of June 17th the demonstrations began again in the Stalin Boulevard and spread throughout East

Berlin. Within an hour the Soviet High Commissioner Semjonow had assumed command of the situation, and the first Russian tanks were driven at thirty miles per hour into the crowded Alexanderplatz, scattering the swarming masses in every direction. About twelve thousand laborers from the steel rolling mills in Hennigsdorf, north of Berlin, marched silently in a body through West Berlin to join the demonstrators in the Potsdamerplatz. Other columns of laborers, office employees, housewives, and students swelled the crowds in the Lustgarten alone to fifty thousand or more. The electric railways ran only sporadically because workers employed by the government left their trains and joined the demonstration. At eleven o'clock a young man scaled the Brandenburg Gate, tore down the red flag and threw it to the cheering crowd below, which trampled and gleefully burned it.

By noon more tanks were in the streets of Berlin, and bursts of gunfire were being heard frequently. At one-thirty General Dibrowa, the Russian commandant, announced a state of emergency in the city and declared all assemblies of more than three persons in any public place to be illegal. Nevertheless, violence increased during the course of the afternoon. The offices of the secret police were stormed by the crowds. The Columbus House in Potsdamerplatz, which housed a unit of the People's Police, was set afire and destroyed. At six o'clock Radio Berlin announced the decision of the government to withdraw the order increasing the work quotas. But by this time the strikes had gone far beyond their original intentions, and Berlin was in the midst of a full-scale popular uprising.

In the face of this revolt Grotewohl's government had shown itself to be completely impotent. The People's Police, largely sympathetic with the strikers, made no attempt to repress the demonstrations, and took only the most limited measures to control the crowds. Many of them actually joined the demonstrations. Had not Russian military force been summoned to the rescue, the government would unquestionably have fallen. But there was little the workers of the Stalin Boulevard, armed only with picks and shovels, could do against the Russian T-34 tanks and machine guns. When at nine o'clock the Russian-imposed curfew cleared the streets of all civilians, a deathlike quiet settled down over the East Sector of the city. A blow for freedom had been struck, but without weapons or outside help it had only rattled helplessly against the cold steel of Russian armor.

Not only in Berlin did this dramatic sequence play itself out. The news of the June 16th strikes spread through all of East Germany like wildfire. In the factories of Magdeburg, Leipzig, Dresden, Erfurt, Rostock, Chemnitz, Halle, Gera, Goerlitz, Cottbus, and Jena, and even on the farms in the rural areas, workers laid down their tools in a massive protest against the government and its policies. Everywhere the pattern was the same: mass demonstrations, demands for better working conditions, storming of prisons to secure the release of prisoners, violent defacement of party slogans, arrests of alleged instigators by the SSD, the appearance of Russian tanks and troops, sporadic gunfire, and finally—silence!

When the smoke had cleared, the shaken government of the German Democratic Republic sought to regain some measure of its self-respect by blaming the entire uprising to western-inspired saboteurs who, they claimed, had stirred up the peace-loving workers. On the order of General Dibrowa, a harmless West Berlin worker named Willi Goettling, who was arrested on June 16th while on his way through the East Sector of Berlin to collect his unemployment insurance, was shot as a conspirator and ringleader of the plot. A great number of arrests and imprisonments in all parts of the East German Republic followed, and the Minister of State Security and other officials were ousted for their alleged failure to detect the sinister plot which had hatched in their midst.

Despite all such theatricals by the party, it was clear to the vast majority in East Germany that the 17th of June had been a spontaneous uprising of a people against a regime of intolerance and oppression. West Berliners and West Germans honored the sacrifice of Willi Goettling in solemn memorial rites and renamed the great boulevard leading through the Tiergarten to the Brandenburg Gate the Street of the 17th of June. The most significant memorial of the day, however, was the quiet but clear voice in the ear of the German laboring man, reminding him that the guns and tanks that had been turned against him and his colleagues in the streets of Berlin were those of a power that claimed to be the friend and saviour of workers everywhere. This was a memorial which would endure for a long time to come.

The Churches of East Germany were not involved in the uprising of June 17th. The demonstrations were spontaneous reactions of the laboring groups which began as specific demands for limited economic benefits and broadened into a general uprising against the whole governmental system. Most of those who participated were members of the Church, but in only a few instances did members of the clergy actively participate. The brother of Bishop Mitzenheim of Thuringia, for example, was given a six-year sentence by a court in Erfurt, for having assembled an "illegal meeting" of the directing board of a local "Farmers' Mutual Aid Society" and for having read a resolution urging the retirement of the Grotewohl government. This resolution had been adopted, and a delegation had gone to East Berlin on June 16th to present this resolution to the Deputy Minister for Agriculture. The same delegation had also gone to a West Berlin refugee camp and told some of their fellow farmers who had fled that a new day was coming for them and that they might feel quite safe in returning to their farms in the East.

The Church leaders, however, made no secret of the fact that their sympathies were with the striking laborers, and Bishop Dibelius himself spent the 17th of June in a Church office in the East Sector of the city. Immediately after the revolt was over, he and Dr. Krummacher, the general superintendent for East Berlin, got in touch with the Soviets by telephone and telegraph, urging conciliatory action and advising against harsh reprisals. A few days later the bishops of all the East German Churches sent a letter to Soviet High Commissioner Semjonow, expressing deep concern over the wave of arrests which had followed nevertheless, and which they felt would lead only to new enmity and bitterness rather than to the internal and external peace everyone desired.

Never before in German history had the Church aligned itself so boldly on the side of the laboring man in a common struggle for humanity and for right in society and economy. "We are not hiding the fact," declared the Churches, "that as evangelical Christians we have a deep human understanding for the requests of the laboring men as they were brought to light on June 17th, and therefore we do not believe that any real satisfaction can be achieved merely with soothing explanations and halfway measures."

It is difficult to ascertain whether the Church's appeals and warnings had any direct effect on the course of the government in carrying out its reprisals against alleged "conspirators" of the 17th of June. The new course had already been announced before the uprising took place, and inasmuch as it had an international counterpart in a much more conciliatory emphasis in Soviet policy in general, a much greater degree of leniency was probably to be expected in any case in the government's handling of those held responsible for the violence.

This also explains why the uprising had little noticeable effect on the implementation of the government's promises to the Church given on June 10th. A failure to fulfill these promises might also have been interpreted as an evidence of the weakness of the government's position, and in the embarrassment surrounding the 17th of June, Grotewohl's regime could not afford that.

Consequently, after June 10th the press was filled with notices of the release of pastors who had been arrested during the *Kirchenkampf*. Pastor Johannes Hamel, for whose release so many pleas had been made, was released on July 14th. His arrest had never been officially admitted by government authorities, although he had been in prison for five months. Student Pastor George was released on September 5th after a six-month imprisonment. Pastor Schumann and all of the eighteen pastors from Saxony who had been arrested during the persecutions were released early in July. By the end of the year about forty pastors and Church workers had been restored to freedom, but almost as many still remained in prison, mostly on political charges.

Welfare institutions of both the Protestant and Roman Catholic Churches were actually returned as promised, and young people who had been expelled from schools were readmitted. Those who had been deprived of taking their certificate examination were now offered the opportunity to do so. Such sweeping concessions caused serious embarrassment to many local school authorities who had been very outspoken in their denunciation of certain youth as "unfit for education in the public schools." These men had certainly not been consulted about the new course, and were as surprised as anyone when it was announced. For them to display any sincerity or enthusiasm in inviting the same youth whom they had publicly denounced to return and take their examinations was more than could be reasonably expected. The result was that many of the young people were grudgingly reinstated, and many who had already fled to West Berlin or to West

Germany preferred not to return at all on the promises of such a capricious regime.

Following June 10th, the State also resumed payment of its financial obligations to the Church, though it insisted upon a 30 per cent reduction. Street collections by the Church remained restricted in number. House collections were not permitted at all. State officials continued to show an unwillingness to place tax information at the disposal of the Church which would facilitate the Church's task of levying its own assessments on its members. There was no great improvement in the financial situation of the Churches because of the new course.

It was, therefore, of special significance that just at this time, on the suggestion of the Evangelical Hilfswerk, plans were worked out by the EKD looking toward the equalization of the salaries of pastors in the East with those of the West. Under the proposed plan, West German pastors would voluntarily contribute a portion of their salaries. These gifts would be channeled through the Hilfswerk to the appropriate Church headquarters in East Germany and distributed as salary supplements. This program, appropriately named the "Brothers' Aid," brought about three million marks in voluntary gifts from West German pastors during the first two years of its operation. It was continued every year thereafter, with increasing response from West German pastors and Church workers, some of whom contributed as much as 25 per cent of their salaries to the aid of their eastern brethren.

One of the most welcome indications of the new course was the opening of the Iron Curtain between the two parts of Germany. Travel documents were still needed, but they were now freely issued for almost any reason, either personal or professional. Family visits multiplied, and Church conferences were attended in both East and West. Ten thousand interzonal passes for the Evangelical Kirchentag at Hamburg in July were authorized by the government. Within the sponsorship system inaugurated by the Hilfswerk, exchange visits of pastors and people from sister congregations in East and West Germany were carried out. In November 140 pastors and church elders from the Province of Saxony spent a week visiting the Evangelical congregations of the Rhineland, and the entire Preachers' Seminary of the Westphalian Church in Brackwede made a visitation trip into the East Zone.

It was even possible to secure permanent residence permits for some of the young vicars and pastors of the East German Churches who had gone to West Germany for a portion of their theological study and had not been allowed to return to their home Churches to accept parishes. The Church of Berlin-Brandenburg was able to bring back forty-four young men, though even this number failed to fill all the vacancies that existed. There were a few instances of native West German pastors who voluntarily left their Churches and by sheer determination won the right to serve in the East. One young pastor who had tried to enter in 1951 but had been expelled, returned in 1953 during the new course, and managed to secure the residence permit which enabled him to become a permanent pastor in the Church of Berlin-Brandenburg.

Although there were many evidences of improved relations between Church and State during 1953 and 1954, the new course never embodied any fundamental change of attitude toward religion and the Church on the part of the Communists. Leaders of the Church were fully aware of this fact and were consequently not surprised by recurring signs of hostility and by failures on the part of the government to abide consistently by its promises of June 10th. For the Church the importance of the new course was that it brought to an end a period of excessively bitter persecution. The State had given no assurance that it would assist or promote the work of the Church, and in local situations the agreements of June 10th were sometimes virtually ignored by lesser party functionaries.

Restrictions on worship services continued in many communities where the congregations had no church buildings of their own and were dependent upon the use of the schoolrooms. In the five-hundred-meter border security zone, worship services continued to be banned, although dances, movies, and sport activities were allowed. Several instances of the abuse of church buildings by the military border guards were reported to the Church authorities.

Walter Ulbricht had once been asked whether there would be any towers in the new industrial city of Stalinstadt which was being built as a model of the Socialist society. He had replied that there would be a tower for the city hall and a tower for the house of culture.

But, said Ulbricht, "we will not need other towers in this socialistic city." Even after the coming of the new course, there were not only no church towers, but for eleven months it was impossible for the Church even to buy land on which to erect a barrack church or to secure the necessary permit to rent a dwelling for the pastor.

When Bishop Dibelius came to Stalinstadt to preach on Christmas Eve in 1953, it was impossible to rent a hall in the city. Worshipers who wanted to hear the bishop had to gather in two empty restaurants in a neighboring village.

In addressing a meeting of the Central Committee of the SED only six weeks after the sweeping promises of June 10th had been given to the Church, Ulbricht assailed the presence of reactionary elements in the Church and among the clergy, and claimed that the "provocations" of June 17th, were especially noticeable in those cities where subversive activity had been carried on under the cover of the youth congregations. When Bishop Dibelius called public attention to this renewed attack on the youth congregations in direct contradiction of the agreements of June 10th, the Communist press in East Berlin accused him of misusing his pulpit in the service of those western agents who had instigated the uprising of June 17th.

In spite of such inconsistencies and breaches of faith by the government, there was nothing which was even remotely comparable to the persecutions of the previous year. And when permission was granted by the government early in 1954 to hold the sixth Evangelical Kirchentag in Leipzig in July, a wave of rejoicing and gratitude spread throughout the congregations of the entire East. Leaders of the great Protestant rally selected as a theme the phrase from the letter to the Romans, "Rejoicing in Hope." In just such a spirit the twelve thousand participants from West Germany came to Leipzig to join hands freely for the first time in many years with the fifty thousand who swarmed in upon Leipzig from all parts of East Germany. Special trains from West Germany were greeted at the border crossings by delegations from the local congregations singing their welcome to the travelers piercing the erstwhile forbidding Iron Curtain.

The Church literally "took over" the city of Leipzig for five days. Christian flags were suspended on every main street. Bells pealed forth every hour from churches and street corners. Special trains arrived several times an hour and disgorged singing, rejoicing people into the growing throngs. In spite of a drizzling rain that fell almost steadily for four days, this spontaneous spirit prevailed in the crowded streetcars, on the public streets, and most of all in the great exhibition halls of the Leipzig Fair, where every morning five simultaneous Bible studies were held in order to accommodate the masses of people.

Part of the program was a huge youth rally, held in the Soviet Exhibition Pavilion, which had also been turned over to the Kirchentag. Twenty thousand young Christians swarmed through the rotunda of this huge building with its tall golden steeple crowned by a red star, past the heroic statue of Joseph Stalin, and into the vast exhibition area. Against the background of the skyline of Moscow etched on the huge glass wall which formed one entire end of the hall had been erected a great cross, beneath which the Christian youth of Germany were assembled. The roll of every German Church in East and West was called aloud, and selected representatives from each Church joined hands with the guests from foreign lands in a living chain that extended around the entire hall and came together beneath the thirty-foot cross on the platform. This kind of unity was the answer of the Christian youth of Germany in both East and West to the persistent political appeals that promised brotherhood but often ended in calls to hatred and to violence.

Throughout the week a contagious spirit of good will seemed to infect the entire city of Leipzig. The People's Police were universally courteous and helpful. Government officials attended sessions of the Kirchentag. On Sunday afternoon, when the vast meadow which had been intended as the gathering place for the closing rally was under several inches of water because of the incessant rains, a cabinet official of the East German government undertook extraordinary measures to drain the water into a nearby excavation in order to permit the rally to take place.

As the closing rally was about to begin, the rain ceased, and during the service the sun even shone occasionally. A crowd of 650,000 people sang chorales to the accompaniment of a massed brass choir, listened to the addresses of leaders from East and West, and bore their witness to the Hope that could bring joy to the heart even in the midst of discouragement and disappointment. As the service ended, the rain began once more, but with umbrellas raised the crowd pressed forward about the speakers' rostrum, waving handkerchiefs and singing, unwilling to have this great experience of Christian fellowship come to an end. For most of these people who shared this experience in Leipzig in 1954, there was no certainty whatever that such an opportunity would ever come again to demonstrate so openly for the Christian faith.

Beginning in July, 1953, the new course was also reflected in a more generally conciliatory spirit in Soviet diplomacy, but there was clearly no intention of making any concrete concessions in Germany. Following an extended exchange of notes with the western powers, the Russians proposed the calling of an international conference of "all interested States," including the German Democratic Republic, to discuss the draft of an all-German peace treaty. Since this proposal again sought to by-pass free elections, the Allies refused to accept it, but countered with the suggestion that the foreign ministers of the four powers, who had not convened since the Paris Conference of 1949, should meet to discuss the German question. The Russians at first rejected this proposal unless China were included in the conference, and the agenda broadened to include a general discussion of European security. If West Germany should be incorporated into NATO, the Soviets indicated that reunification would become virtually impossible. Eventually, the Allied invitation was accepted, and the conference was scheduled for January 25, 1954, in Berlin.

In spite of Russian efforts to deter them, the Allies moved steadily forward with their plans for the inclusion of West Germany in the European Defense System, making it clear that under no circumstances would they sacrifice the principle of free elections as a basis for German reunification. The Berlin Conference, therefore, offered little hope of an immediate solution of the problem of a divided Germany.

Nevertheless, the Churches took the conference seriously, and the EKD urged all congregations in Germany to hold special intercessory prayer services for its success. A telegram was sent to the four foreign ministers appealing for reunification and for the release of additional political prisoners. But the conference concluded on February 18th without any visible results, except to underline the determination of the Soviets to force the recognition of East Germany by the western powers and the equal determination of the West that free elections should be the basis for reunification.

The failure of the Berlin Conference was a severe blow to the people of East Germany. From the pulpit of St. Mary's Church on the Sunday following the close of the conference, Bishop Dibelius expressed some of the disappointment felt by his countrymen. The concluding statement of the foreign ministers, he said, had simply announced in blunt language that questions which dealt with the very life of Germany and Austria had been discussed but that no agreement had been reached. "Nothing further!" exclaimed the bishop. "No word of hope that perhaps in future discussions unity might be achieved. No word suggesting a will to bring relief in some other way to these two bitterly disappointed peoples. There it stands in all its harsh clarity: No agreement could be reached!"

With human agencies bringing only bitter disappointment, Dibelius summoned the people of East Germany to a renewed trust in God. "If He is not ready to release us yet from the school of distress and disunion, then He wants to ripen us for some very special purpose! Of this we are confident!" Cautioning against resignation and bitterness, which certainly were the temptations of the moment, Dibelius reminded Germans in both East and West that the Church did not operate with political means but with those provided by God Himself. "God's hand lies heavily upon our shoulder," he concluded. "We make no secret of our deep disappointment and our real anxiety! But here is the patience and the faith of the saints! We thank God for all of it!"

In East Germany, following the failure of Berlin, the theme of the National Front for peace and unity was resumed. In preparation for the coming parliamentary elections, a public referendum was conducted in June. Voters were confronted with the question: "Are you in favor of a peace treaty and the withdrawal of all occupation troops, or the European Defense Community and the retention of occupation troops for fifty years?"

As it had done in almost every election and referendum since 1946, the Provincial Church of Saxony sent a letter to the government protesting that the form of this question constituted a violation of the consciences of many people. Everyone, said Bishop Mueller, is in favor of peace, especially the Christians. But when people are asked to vote Yes or No on a peace treaty, the content of which they do not know, and which the powers have not even discussed, this raises the question whether a conscientious Christian can properly participate in the referendum at all.

Moreover, in the administration of the referendum no rules had been established to determine what constituted a valid ballot. The election board could even count blank or spoiled ballots as valid if it wished. The Church requested that a clear statement be made defining a valid ballot and requiring the use of voting booths by all voters, so that those who did use them would not be looked upon with suspicion by party officials. The complaints and requests, however, were ignored as usual, and the referendum produced the expected result. The voters favored the peace treaty by 93.5 per cent, the European Defense Community by 6.5 per cent.

The parliamentary elections in October again presented single lists of candidates sponsored by the National Front, and outdid the referendum by returning a majority of 99.46 per cent. During the campaign the CDU again directed a special appeal to Christian people, and produced a campaign pamphlet entitled "God's Law and State Law." The aim of this pamphlet was to interpret the Bible and the Ten Commandments in the interests of the National Front. One of the stories it contained was that of King Zedekiah of Judah who had made a pact with King Nebuchadnezzar of Chaldea. Zedekiah wanted to break this agreement and enter into a secret treaty with other kings to make war against his Chaldean partner. Jeremiah, the prophet, warned against such deceit, but Zedekiah proceeded with his underhanded plans. Nebuchadnezzar discovered the treachery and prepared to destroy Judah completely. When Zedekiah then turned to Jeremiah, asking him to call upon God for help against the godless Chaldeans, the prophet replied: "I have placed before thee a way of life and a way of death. If the people do not want to be destroyed by the sword, by hunger, and pestilence, they must give up their deceitful plans and fulfill their agreement with the Chaldeans. Then there will be life for them."

The moral of the story followed. "Are you thinking, dear reader, as I am, of the secret military alliance between West Germany and the American imperialists? Are you thinking about the similarity between the position of Zedekiah and the men in Bonn? If so, you can certainly relate the words of Jeremiah to our situation. We, too, have been presented with a way to life and a way to death, and we have to decide which way we shall go—either the way into war, or the way of understanding with the Chaldeans."

The campaign of the National Front for peace and unity extended beyond the October elections into 1955, stressing the Soviet proposal of a peace treaty and the withdrawal of all occupation troops as an alternative to the impending West German alliance with NATO. Even after the London and Paris conferences in September and October, 1954, at which the occupation statute was terminated and West Germany was admitted to NATO, the National Front continued to work, hoping to prevent the final ratification of the agreement by the Bonn Parliament.

Vigorous support for this effort came from certain West German groups. The Socialist opposition to Adenauer, which took a neutralist position, bitterly opposed rearmament. In Church circles Martin Niemoeller, Dr. Gustav Heinemann, lay president of the Synod of EKD, and the Brotherhoods of the Confessing Church, held public discussions and rallies and wrote open letters urging young men to refuse military service. Together with Socialist opposition leaders these churchmen participated in a great rally in St. Paul's Church in Frankfurt, from which emerged the German Manifesto, denouncing the venture into NATO as a fatal recourse to militarism that would close the door to reunification.

One of the most rabid of the agitators was a student pastor named Mochalski who, after the Bonn Parliament had finally ratified the NATO pact, declared publicly, "In 1945 Germany capitulated; in 1955 she prostituted herself." In his official yearly report at the Synod of EKD in Espelkamp in March, 1955, Bishop Dibelius took occasion to denounce such a statement within the Church as "intolerable" and "unworthy of an evangelical pastor."

The Espelkamp Synod was also marked by the election of a new president of the EKD to replace Dr. Heinemann, and by the reorganization of the EKD foreign office to replace Niemoeller as its president. Both of these actions were prompted in part by the fear that the strongly partisan political activities of Heinemann and Niemoeller might identify the Evangelical Church too closely with one side in a national political controversy.

Neutralists in the West German Church were given great encouragement by the new and friendly countenance being exhibited by

Walter Ulbricht, Communist Party Leader in East Germany,
Delivering Youth Dedication Address in Dessau (1957)

...rch Bulletin Board in Falkenhagen Defaced by Communists (April, 1958)

Propaganda Billboard in East Germany

Propaganda Parade for Youth Dedication in East Berlin (1958)

the Soviets in world affairs. Their peace offensive, begun shortly after Stalin's death, had been treated at first with understandable skepticism by western nations, and especially by the United States, which suspected that Russia's real aim was the defeat of NATO and the European Defense Community and the eventual exclusion of the United States from European affairs.

By mid-1954 both Churchill and Eisenhower conceded that the West must at least examine the intentions of the Russians to see if their desires for peaceful coexistence were sincere. When in April, 1955, the Russians suddenly declared their readiness to sign an Austrian peace treaty, largely along the lines advocated by the West, it seemed that the spirit of East-West relations had really entered a new era. It was in this optimistic atmosphere that a "meeting at the summit" was proposed for July, 1955, in Geneva.

These developments also encouraged the National Front in East Germany, which had long extolled the peaceful intentions of the Soviet Union. As long as the Paris Pact was still being debated in West Germany, the National Front assailed it as an aggressive move endangering the peace and unity of Germany. Premier Grotewohl appealed directly to his "dear countrymen in West Germany" not to yield to the militarists in their midst. To you, he said, "we extend the hand of a brother, and appeal to you under no circumstances to permit the ratification of the Paris Pact. . . . We appeal to the laboring men of West Germany to unite in common actions, protests, demonstrations, and strikes to avert this great danger which threatens Germany." The CDU in East Germany added the ominous threat that if the pact were ratified by the Bonn Parliament, not only would reunification be prevented, but a division would take place between the Churches of East and West.

In spite of all efforts to prevent it, the Bonn Parliament voted on February 27, 1955, to approve the Paris Pact, whereby the Federal Republic of Germany was granted its independence and at the same time became a member of the North Atlantic Treaty Organization.

With West Germany committed to rearmament, anti-NATO activity by the National Front in East Germany took a new direction. On April 24th the presidium of the Communist-controlled German Peace Council began a vigorous campaign to gather signatures to the Vienna Peace Appeal against preparations for atomic war, and to urge attendance at the World Congress for Peace in Helsinki in June, 1955.

The CDU in East Germany directed an appeal to all "Christian men in Germany" to join the "great front of humanistic, peace-loving forces of the entire world." Pastors were especially urged to sign peace petitions, and all of the great national synods were urged to endorse the "peace front" and denounce West German remilitarization.

Early in October the Central Committee of the CDU met, and Nuschke spoke on "The Church and the German Peace Movement," urging once more a deeper sense of national responsibility on the part of the Church. "One often has the impression," complained Nuschke, "that a social resentment against our government policies hinders the Church leaders from recognizing and supporting our national interests."

Attempts to align the Church with the political "peace front" of the Soviet Union found no response in official Church circles in East Germany. One of the clearest statements came from the Provincial Church of Saxony pointing out to the District Peace Committee that the Evangelical Church had frequently expressed itself on the subject of peace but that the Communist press had given little or no attention to these statements. In fact, the Weissensee Declaration of the EKD had actually been suppressed in many parts of the German Democratic Republic, simply because it had not embraced a political formula for peace but had directed people instead to righteousness as the only true basis for peace.

It also observed that the Church had long ago spoken out against all atomic weapons and in favor of general disarmament. The Evanston Assembly of the World Council of Churches had adopted a statement on peace, and the Church of Saxony believed this statement to be adequate. Unless the conditions embodied in the Evanston statement were substantially incorporated, the Churches of East Germany would refuse to subscribe to any peace appeal.

This official coolness of the Churches in East Germany toward the Soviet-sponsored peace efforts was not shared by Dr. Heinrich Grueber, who represented the Church as liaison with the East German government. He had always taken his role as mediator and "bridgebuilder" seriously, and during 1954 and 1955, while the "Spirit of Geneva" prevailed, he devoted his energies as never before to the task of building bridges of peace between East and West.

With the dark shadows of atomic rearmament lowering over the whole world and threatening to envelop both East and West Germany, coexistence did not appear to him as "a Communist discovery, but as an absolute necessity" for survival in the atomic age.

Of Grueber's deep sincerity and of his loyalty to the Christian faith there was no doubt. But he yearned so desperately for peace and for unity that he overlooked or discounted the simplest and clearest premises of dialectic materialism which recognized no binding divine moral law. He shared with Otto Nuschke, also well intentioned but wishfully optimistic, the belief that Germans were far too prone to discuss such questions academically. In the world of coexistence, Nuschke told members of the CDU, every man should live his own world view, and things would somehow work out for the best. "The better Christian a Christian is, and the better Marxist a Marxist is, the better will be the cooperation among all humanitarian forces for the well-being of our people and for peace."

During the Week of German-Soviet Friendship, Grueber described to an East Berlin audience his impressions of a recent visit in the Soviet Union. Wherever he had gone in Russia, declared Grueber, he had found the spirit of peace. In churches, in stores, on the streets, the people reached out their hands and repeated the word "Peace." As visiting Germans, he and his colleagues had found a more sympathetic spirit in Russia than in any other country they had visited. He found it hard to understand why there were still people in Germany who pharisaically refused to grasp this outstretched hand of friendship. Coexistence, he declared, must be more than a "cool living beside each other." It must be a "conscious, responsible living together!"

On the other hand Grueber viewed the western democracies and their affirmations of peace and freedom with suspicion and even cynicism. "The silliest slogan of the moment," he proclaimed, "is that of free elections. The more it is used, the less it means. If the masses of voters should be deluded by the dollars of foreign masters, would such elections be free?"

Actually, if peaceful coexistence really meant a "conscious responsible living together" with respect for one another's views, a more concrete means of giving it expression could scarcely be devised than free elections. For more than five years, this had been the constant plea of the western Allies, but not even neutral control and supervision of the process by the United Nations had been able to win Soviet approval. Free elections would unquestionably mean a rejection of the Communist regime in East Germany, and this, despite all its friendly gestures in Austria or in Geneva, the Kremlin did not intend to risk.

A summit conference, however, carried with it no such risks. With the "spirit of Geneva" running high, the chiefs of state from the four great powers arrived in Switzerland for their first top-level meeting since Potsdam in 1945. Seldom have such high hopes surrounded an international conference as this one, ten years after the war had ended. Telegrams and letters were sent to the statesmen pleading for an end to the painful separation of East and West Germany. In Germany, prayer services were held for its success on the evening of the first day of the conference. Bishop Dibelius conducted a service of intercession in St. Mary's Church in East Berlin. At the same time services held in the Luther Church in Bonn were attended by President Heuss and several members of the cabinet and the West German Parliament.

But the "spirit of Geneva" was not strong enough to brush aside the fundamental fears and differences of the great powers. The Russians insisted upon the dissolution of NATO and the erection of a new all-European security system before Germany could be reunified. The Allies insisted upon reunification first, based upon free elections. The only area in which agreement finally seemed possible was the improving of cultural and economic relations between East and West. But even on this subject no specific decisions were made.

Despite the fact that the Geneva discussions were to be continued in October by the foreign ministers of the great powers, there was little prospect of substantial progress in the matter of German reunification. On their way back to the Soviet Union, Nikita Khrushchev and Premier Bulganin paused in Berlin to announce that the German question could never be solved until it was recognized that two sovereign States now existed on German territory, each with its own economic and social order. No method of reunification would be acceptable which would jeopardize the political and social achievements of the workers in the German Democratic Republic.

To demonstrate that these were serious intentions on its part, the Soviet Union invited Chancellor Adenauer to visit Moscow in September to establish diplomatic, trade, and cultural relations between the Soviet Union and the German Federal Republic. At this meeting Adenauer secured the promise that prisoners of war still in Russian hands would be returned, a promise that was subsequently fulfilled in part by the return of 9,626 persons. But neither this achievement nor diplomatic recognition by the Soviet Union could obscure the ominous warning that West Germany's adherence to NATO prevented German reunification.

Shortly thereafter, the Soviet Union concluded a treaty with the German Democratic Republic, confirming its sovereignty and assuring it of the continued cooperation of the Soviet Union in economic, scientific, and cultural affairs. The control of all border traffic was turned over to the East Germans, with the exception of the personnel and matériel belonging to the Allied military forces stationed in West Berlin.

The second Geneva Conference took place in late October and early November, but there was little expectation of any substantial achievement. As the season of Advent moved into Germany in 1955, with wreaths and candles and songs of welcome to the Prince of Peace, the lines of the cold war seemed once again to have stiffened across the frozen fields from the Baltic to Bohemia. The dream of Geneva was past, and East Germans, more discouraged than they had been at any time since the grim days of the war's end, turned once more to face the depressing reality of single-list elections, ration cards, and closed borders. The new course had brought no lasting relief to Moscow's unwilling satellite on the Elbe.

TEN

THE PLEDGE OF ALLEGIANCE

In July, 1954, the Synod of Brandenburg observed that the new course had come to an end. A whole series of external interferences from which the Church had been relatively free since June 10, 1953, were recurring with ominous regularity. Pastors were being spied upon by agents of SSD. Youth meetings involving more than a single congregation were being prohibited. Unfriendly State officials were again refusing to cooperate in giving necessary tax information to the Church.

More significant than these recurrences of old problems during the summer of 1954 was the appearance of an organization known as the Society for the Promotion of Scientific Knowledge. Founded under the direction of Johannes Becher, the new Minister of Culture, the purpose of this new organization was the popularization of the scientific approach to nature and society through lectures and publications. The corresponding Soviet organization, the Union Society for the Promotion of Political and Scientific Knowledge, was the direct successor of the League of Militant Atheists, dissolved by the Soviets in 1945.

The new assault upon the Church did not stress the direct methods of prohibitions, disturbances, and even open violence which had characterized the dark months of 1952 and 1953. A much more subtle approach was contemplated, using the ideas of dialectic materialism as weapons and carrying the campaign for the minds of the younger generation into every possible phase of life: educational, economic, cultural, and social. While claiming to guarantee freedom of conscience and of religious belief, the State encouraged an atheistic philosophy, and extended special privileges to those who acknowledged it.

The keynote of this new program was sounded by an article which appeared in *Pravda*, official Communist Party newspaper in Moscow, on July 24, 1954, under the title "Broader Development of Scientific-Atheistic Propaganda." An important part of this tremendous task of the party in overcoming the remnant of middle-class ideology, declared *Pravda*, was popular education in natural science and a fight against all kinds of prejudice and superstition. Dedicated members of the party, according to Lenin's essay on "Socialism and Religion," could never take a neutral position toward ignorance and the "devilish darkness which appears in the form of religious beliefs."

The entire process of instruction and of education in the schools, particularly in such subjects as history, literature, and the natural sciences, must be carried out in the spirit of militant materialism. Every possible measure must be taken for the strengthening of propaganda for the materialistic world view in the institutions of higher learning.

Scientific atheistic propaganda in the Soviet press, according to *Pravda*, had been completely inadequate. Books and pamphlets on scientific atheistic themes had been scarce, and those which had been published had apparently overlooked their most important task, namely, the communistic education of the worker. Too many of them had been written in an "unpopular style, and in difficult and un-understandable language."

All this must be changed in the future, concluded *Pravda*. "In our socialistic society, all the objective conditions are at hand for the complete elimination of the remnants of capitalistic thinking, including religious prejudices and superstitions, from the minds of our people. It is therefore absolutely essential that the scientific atheistic propaganda be carried forward on a broad front and that the content of this propaganda be decisively improved."

The genealogy of this new program can be traced one step further to the Central Committee of the Communist Party of the Soviet Union. On November 11, 1954, there appeared over the signature of Nikita Khrushchev, secretary of the committee, a document entitled "Mistakes in the Conduct of Scientific Atheistic Propaganda Among the People."

Although the aim of the party was to free the working masses from religious prejudice, the Central Committee noted with great concern that the methods being employed in certain areas were crude and offensive. Local party organizations were using people who were ignorant in science and in the techniques of propaganda. Occasionally, even "hacks," whose knowledge was limited to "anecdotes and stories about ministers of religion," had been permitted to write for the press and to deliver lectures. "Such an irresponsible approach" to Communist propaganda, the committee declared, was "stupid and harmful." "Profound, patient, and well-organized scientific atheistic propaganda among believers will help them in the long run to free themselves from religious errors. On the contrary, offensive attacks and stringent administrative measures against believers and ministers of religion can only lead to the strengthening of religious prejudices among them."

The Central Committee left no doubt concerning its fundamental attitude toward religion. The aim of the Communist Party, it declared, was to educate the Soviet people to a scientific outlook, and to wean them away from the superstitions of a religious ideology. Science was based upon facts which were meticulously tested, while religion was based solely on Biblical and other traditions or fantastic inventions. Science could not reconcile itself to religious conceptions of life and of man, and for this reason was entirely incompatible with religion.

With this statement the Central Committee gave its blessing to a program of "systematic and thorough atheistic propaganda" to be carried on throughout the Soviet sphere of influence under the direction of carefully selected and scientifically qualified experts only.

The advance agent of this new program in Germany was a small pamphlet entitled "Communistic and Religious Morals," written by a Russian, P. F. Kolonizki, and translated into German late in the summer of 1953. Its thesis was the classic Marxian contention that religion was simply the product of man's helplessness in his struggle against nature and the ruling classes. Not only did Kolonizki deny that religion was ever the foundation of morality but he asserted also that it was actually immoral. "Religion," he declared, "is the fountain-head of hypocrisy and lies. Everything which religion preaches is consciously false, and contains not even a small kernel of truth." The "so-called holy Gospel" is simply a mass of falsehoods and fairy tales invented to divert the thoughts of the workers from the realities of this world to a "fantastic heavenly salvation with a mythical life after death."

Such superstitions, declared Kolonizki, the Communist Party could not tolerate, because they were completely unscientific. Communistic morality, however, was founded on the constructive principle as stated by Lenin, that "whatever helps to destroy the old society of exploitation and to erect the new communistic society of the proletariat is moral." This principle had created the new Soviet man, the conscious builder of the new society and the free master of his fate.

Not only was this booklet placed on the newsstands and distributed from house to house, but it was sold to high-school students, and teachers in current-events courses were urged to use it as a part of their instructional material.

Thoroughly shocked by the flagrancy of the entire episode, Dr. Erich Andler, chairman of the Youth Department of the Protestant Churches in East Germany, wrote a letter to Erich Honecker, chairman of the Central Committee of the FDJ, protesting this pamphlet as the "most monstrous broadside attack on the Church and its teachings yet published in the German Democratic Republic." "The descriptions of the Christian Church and its message which are contained in this pamphlet," he said, "are so thoroughly false and so biased and unobjective that they scarcely merit attention. There is every indication that the author was not motivated by a desire to encourage intellectual discussion but was driven by burning hatred." Dr. Andler doubted that such rabid and irrational polemics as this would shake the faith of Christian people, but would rather make it very clear that between the Christian faith and Marxism-Leninism there could be no bridge of understanding.

For this reason the Church might not have raised such a protest against this pamphlet as it did, had not the publication been sponsored by the Free German Youth. This was the organization that had filled the columns of its newspaper, *Junge Welt*, with such scurrilous attacks upon the youth congregations that Bishop Dibelius had sought to bring legal action against it for libel and slander. This was the organization that had led the drive to oust young people from the high schools because they remained loyal to the "illegal" youth congregations of the church.

It was in large measure these activities of the Free German Youth which the government had publicly confessed to be a mistake in the agreements of June 10th. Faithful promises had been given that no further interference with the recognized functions of the Church would be permitted, and the government had agreed to make this position clear to the FDJ. Yet less than two months later, the FDJ sponsored the publication of Kolonizki's rabid pamphlet and even distributed it in the schools and homes of East Germany. Andler was certainly entitled to the doubts he expressed to Honecker that the FDJ was taking its promises seriously.

A similar letter to the District Council of Erfurt written by Bishop Moritz Mitzenheim of Thuringia followed largely the same line as that of Dr. Andler, though its main purpose was to protest the use of the pamphlet as instructional material in the high schools of the area. It seemed extremely strange to the bishop that such a direct affront should be permitted just at a time when in practically every issue of the newspapers efforts were being made by party and State to win the support of the Church for a government-sponsored program of peace and good will.

Apparently in its eagerness to reinstate itself in the good graces of the SED as an effective and energetic instrument for the promotion of Communist doctrine, the FDJ had once again overstepped itself. Early in December, Prime Minister Grotewohl intervened to suspend the mass distribution of the Kolonizki pamphlet. No comment was made on the content, though the pamphlet seemed to be a perfect illustration of the "offensive" type of propaganda Khrushchev and the Moscow Central Committee had denounced. Only the timing was wrong. As soon as the situation seemed more favorable, Kolonizki's gospel would once more be made available to the youth of East Germany.

By the spring of 1954 the time was apparently ripe. In May the Politburo of the SED established the main lines of the new party study course for 1954–1955. The influence of the Soviet Central Committee was clearly present in the recognition that previous courses had not given adequate emphasis to ideological questions. This was to be remedied in the future, and in accordance with the Moscow directive party leaders were to exercise the closest possible supervision over their propaganda corps. As the study year opened, the Central Committee of the SED, the new Society for the Promotion of Scientific Knowledge, the FDJ, and the schools all prepared to carry a vigorous campaign of scientific atheism into every community in East Germany.

Walter Ulbricht himself announced the new emphasis in the schools. He told the fourth party rally of the SED in April that the scientific level of instruction must be raised during the coming year. The party organizations within the schools, he said, had not assumed sufficient responsibility for the political-ideological position of the teaching staff or for the quality of instruction. There had not been enough aggressive discussions of Marxism-Leninism in the teachers' councils. All of these things had long been expected of the schools, but there had been a dangerous tendency to hold back. This must now be changed, and the schools must become real ideological centers.

The Ministry of Education had already issued a series of regulations requiring every teacher to be a functionary of the "Workers' and Farmers' State" and a loyal supporter of the political program of the SED. According to these regulations, all major examinations should seek to test the political attitudes of the pupils and their qualifications as potential "activists." The brief life history required of every applicant for admission to these examinations must include a description of the applicant's "socialistic activity" and of his political development.

The Synod of Brandenburg lost no time in raising official objections to these new developments in the schools. When their complaints were ignored by the Ministry of Education, the entire East Conference of the EKD addressed the government, protesting both the increasing political emphasis in the schools and the refusal of the government to acknowledge the letters of concern written by the Churches.

Dialectical materialism, declared the East Conference, laid claim to being the only true science, and rejected all religious notions of reality, including a belief in God. By making dialectic and historical materialism the only admissible basis for the training of teachers and for teaching in the classrooms, the State had made of the public schools an instrument for the promotion of atheism and materialism. The selection of teaching materials and the content of school text-books confirmed this as a fact.

Yet Prime Minister Grotewohl had solemnly assured Church leaders at the June 10th conference of the previous year that the objective character of the schools in East Germany was guaranteed by the constitution. "Plain instructions were given at that time," declared the East Conference, "that Marxism was not to be forced upon anyone, and that neither teachers nor pupils were to be evaluated on the basis of their attitudes toward Marxism."

In direct violation of their promises, many highly qualified children from Christian homes had been prevented from entering high school because they refused to make the materialistic-atheistic confession of faith required for admission. Children who were already attending these schools were being thrust into the midst of a contradictory struggle between Christianity and materialism that undermined them spiritually, psychologically, and even physically. Such a situation was an open violation of the constitution, which guaranteed to every citizen complete freedom of conscience, and expressly forbade any discriminatory treatment of a citizen because of his belief.

To these earnest protests of the Church, directed both to the prime minister and to the Parliament, there was no response whatever. Four additional letters on the same subject, signed by the most representative leaders of the Protestant Churches, were sent to the East German government in the next ten months without receiving even the courtesy of an acknowledgment. Confronted by this stone wall of silence, the Church turned in desperation to the parents, hoping through them to strengthen the resistance of the children against the anti-Christian influence of the schools.

The new ideological attack, however, did not leave the bastion of family authority unscathed. New elections for the Parents' Councils were ordered for October, 1955, under conditions which made it impossible for Christian parents ever to secure a local majority. All nominations for membership on the councils were made by committees controlled by the SED. Secret elections were eliminated, and all members elected to the councils were required to assist in the formation of groups of "activists" among the parents to support the ideological program of the school. Representatives of the Communist youth and women's groups and other party-affiliated organizations were included as voting members on the councils.

Some Churches still encouraged parents to take part in these elections in the forlorn hope of maintaining some influence. But when the Ministry of Education declared that the right of the State to determine the content of their children's education took precedence over that of the parents, the Provincial Church of Saxony publicly urged its members to protest by refusing to take part in the elections.

The entire Christian concept of the family was challenged in the draft of a new family law proposed in June, 1955, by Dr. Hilde Benjamin, Minister of Justice. Before the draft law was turned over to the Parliament for final revision and enactment, the government encouraged several months of public discussion. The Church made full use of this opportunity. Special lectures were arranged to give Christian answers to questions raised by Church members. Interest was so great that halls were filled to overflowing even before the lectures began. One general superintendent had to start speaking fifty minutes before the appointed time because no more people could be crowded into the church. He repeated the same lecture later in the evening to a second audience. Many non-Church people also attended, and young people turned out in large numbers. In one town lecturers were applauded so enthusiastically that they had to stop speaking several times, although applause in the church sanctuary was a most unusual occurrence. The Evangelical Academy of Berlin-Brandenburg conducted a one-day conference in East Berlin, with lectures and discussions on the subject "The New Laws Relating to the Family and What the Bible Says About Marriage." Six hundred applications were received, two hundred of which had to be rejected because of lack of space.

The position of the Evangelical Church on the proposed law was best expressed in a memorandum issued by the East Conference. Many parts of the law were entirely acceptable, but the State was exceeding its proper limitations when it sought to impose specific political purposes upon the family life of its citizens. Terms such as "democracy," "socialism," and "patriotism" were out of place in a family law.

The question of the equality of the sexes, which was the basic issue motivating the new law, was not dealt with according to the understanding of the Christian Church. There was no disagreement concerning the equal worth and value of men and women, but the church objected to claiming for men and women the same functions in society. The occupational activity of a woman should not be regarded as self-evident. Her first task should be the fulfillment of responsibilities within the home. The abdication of this position could only lead to the complete breakdown of the family as the basic unity of society.

Another paragraph of the draft law placed the Socialist youth organizations on an equal footing with the schools in their responsibility for the education of the children. The record of the Free German Youth in the youth persecutions of 1952 and 1953 and the more recent sponsoring of the atheistic Kolonizki pamphlet scarcely recommended such an organization to Christian parents as an agency responsible for their children's education.

The Church's basic criticism of the draft law was its tendency to place marriage and the family under political control. In view of this tendency even the paragraph allowing an agency of the government to step in to protect a child in the event of a dereliction of parental responsibility became questionable. According to the law, parents were obliged to educate each child as "a responsible citizen of the democratic state, who loves his country and fights for peace." If the parents failed in this or in any other legal parental duty to their child, "or if the welfare or the economic interests of the child should be endangered for other reasons," he district council was given legal authority to remove the child from the custody of the parents. A State so capricious as to oust three thousand young people from high school as saboteurs and agents of western imperialists, and at the behest of party politicians to restore them to full privileges on the day following, might easily employ such a weapon as the family law for arbitrary political purposes.

The public discussion came to an end in December as announced by the Ministry of Justice. With the assurance that all opinions would be carefully considered, the draft law was turned over to the Parliament. It was enacted into law without substantial change, and stands at present on the statute books as one of the innumerable "hidden" legal instruments whereby the State could, if the occasion seemed auspicious, prohibit even the private teaching of the Christian religion to the children of East Germany.

The increase of atheistic propaganda in East Germany was accompanied by a stringent limitation upon the Church's freedom of expression. Detailed licensing regulations affected the smallest of Church publications. Monthly announcement leaflets, corresponding to the Sunday bulletin of an American congregation, could not be printed without an individual permit. A special regulation issued by the Office for Literature and Publication even specified the content of such bulletins. Two Bible verses, a hymn stanza, a list of worship services and other Church meetings, and a list of Church baptisms, marriages, and burials, though without addresses, were permitted! A brief devotional message by the pastor or a commentary on a text of Scripture, even if it were only one sentence long, was sufficient ground for the denial of a permit to print! The proper place for such editorial expression, said the State, was in the regularly licensed periodicals and Church papers, of which there were less than a dozen in the entire German Democratic Republic.

Church papers were limited not only in number but also in circulation, presumably because of serious paper shortages. Curiously, however, just at this moment of particular tension the first issue of a very attractive new religious monthly magazine appeared entitled *Glaube und Gewissen* (Faith and Conscience), luxuriously printed on expensive heavy paper. For the small circle of "progressive pastors" who were willing to support the National Front and who sponsored the new publication, no paper shortage existed.

Because of the limited size of the issues, the Churches had long followed the practice of sending their Church papers to pastors through the mails in bulk and asking the pastors to distribute them so as to cover the parish most effectively. This also saved a considerable amount of postage, which, in view of their very limited budgets, was an important item. Even here the long arm of regulation reached out to hinder the spread of religious ideas. Bulk shipment of newspapers was prohibited, and publishers were ordered to send subscriptions individually through the post office to each subscriber's home address. Pastors suspected that the purpose behind this regulation as this particular time was to secure for government use lists of the most loyal supporters of the Church in each parish.

Individual issues of Church weeklies were placed under strict censorship, and on several occasions an entire edition was confiscated because of some article or statement which appeared too critical of the government or of its policies. The November 30th issue of the Saxon Church paper *Der Sonntag*, for example, was seized because of an article which contained the statement: "If one no longer believes in God, a substitute must be provided, because it is necessary to have some ruling power to prevent complete chaos. Such a substitute may be found in ideologies, in propaganda devices, and finally, in force." The censor claimed that this sentence was directed at the German Democratic Republic, and sought to disparage its government by implying that it was based upon arbitrary force.

The Berlin weekly *Die Kirche* had an especially sensitive and nervous censor, and its issues were confiscated on several occasions. On December 11, 1955, it carried an article appropriate to the Advent season on the subject of the Last Judgment. The author called attention to the unusually lively interest being displayed by the people in court trials and judgments of all kinds. Whatever might be the outcome of these trials, he observed, whether just or unjust, it would be well to remember that God Himself would give the final verdict in the Last Judgment. The entire issue of the paper was confiscated on the ground that this article was "discriminatory," that it implied a reproach against the administration of justice in the German Democratic Republic, and that it attributed to the people of East Germany an improper appetite for trial publicity.

The most spectacular phase of the ideological campaign in East Germany in 1954 was the launching of the first Youth Dedication. This was a ceremony, climaxing a series of instructional periods over the course of several weeks, in which boys and girls were asked to pledge their lives and energies to the building of a socialistic order in Germany. The Communists apparently recognized that the formal Marxist-Leninist presentation of history, biology, and literature in the public schools was not sufficient. They were eager for some personal commitment from the young people, and they therefore resorted to the use of liturgical ceremonies and a public profession of faith.

The Youth Dedication was not a new idea. It had first been used in Germany by groups of rationalists in the mid-nineteenth century who had been ousted from both the Protestant and Roman Catholic Churches. Crusading against supernaturalism, these so-called "free congregations" had rejected some of the Church festivals and changed the content of others. Christmas, for example, was celebrated as the birth feast of all great fighters for freedom and truth. The liturgical services of the Church were gradually replaced with moral-religious lectures by preachers or other speakers, and the sacraments were eliminated. Confirmation was renamed the Youth Dedication, and served merely as the occasion on which young people were received into the fellowship of a congregation.

About 1875, the Socialist Labor Party in Germany accepted the ideas of Karl Marx and the class struggle in its efforts to change the social order. Finding little sympathy within the established Church for their aspirations for social improvement, increasing numbers of laborers began to renounce their Church membership at about the turn of the century. To provide a ceremonial substitute for these people whose children were therefore not eligible for Confirmation, the Socialist Labor Party and the Proletarian Freethinker Societies took over the Youth Dedication, using it for the first time in 1905. They made of it a festival to commemorate the end of school and the "entry into life." The preparatory instruction and the ceremony itself were based solely on the naturalistic world view, the materialistic view of history, and the Marxian program. The Youth Dedication continued in use throughout Germany until 1933, though participation in it was never very widespread. The National Socialists developed a similar ceremony, but in no sense did the Youth Dedication ever challenge the preeminent position of the Confirmation in the average German Protestant family and community life.

Nevertheless, historical traditions were present when the SED began to build its own Youth Dedication in East Germany. When the program was first introduced in November, 1954, every effort was made to convey the impression that it was a completely spontaneous development. A Central Committee for the Youth Dedication purporting to be an independent citizens' group was organized, appealing to all young people both in East and West Germany without regard to their political views. The occasion for the Youth Dedication was to be the completion of elementary-school training and the entry into a new and significant period of life. On the Day of Dedication, parents and children together would have the opportunity to look back upon the years of training and childhood and to face together the great challenge of a new and responsible life in a People's Democracy. The ceremony would be a festive family experience, but beyond that, an opportunity for the maturing young person to sense his own role among his colleagues in the building of the new Germany.

The structural organization of the program was carefully planned. Volunteer district and local committees made up of parents, teachers, artists, laborers and leaders in public life were formed throughout East Germany. These committees publicized the Youth Dedication through conversations with young people, meetings of parents and youth, and through press, radio, posters, and handbills.

Beginning in January, 1955, a series of ten two-hour periods of instruction was scheduled, under the leadership of outstanding personalities from the various fields of community and professional life, who were to speak to the young people on questions relating to science and society. These classes were not regarded as formal instruction, but as inspirational meetings to open the eyes of the youth to the accomplishments of science and technology and the opportunities which the Socialist society offered them. Lectures were made as attractive as possible, and additional interest was created through field trips into factories, theaters, laboratories, and museums. All community resources were mobilized in order to make participation attractive and to give it a broad cultural appeal.

The ceremony itself was also planned and carried out by the local committee as an impressive and colorful public event. April was selected as the month for the great event because of the symbolism of awakening nature. The months of May and June were avoided because at that time the eighth-graders would be burdened with final examinations and with preparations for promotion into high school.

Leaders claimed that the Youth Dedication was conceived in a spirit of broad tolerance and that no religious sensitivities could possibly be injured through participation in it. The Churches noted with alarm, however, that the dates for the ceremony itself had been selected to coincide as closely as possible with the traditional season of Protestant Confirmation services.

Moreover, the entire program reached its climax in the administration of a pledge which even followed the liturgical pattern of the Christian Confirmation. Words and ideas out of churchly and religious experience were borrowed and given a political turn. The Youth Dedication was described, for example, as a deep experience for all youth, which would root them firmly within a great fellowship. Through such an experience the young people would not only learn about the achievements of the new society but would also be placed in touch with a great source of strength that would be valid for all their lives.

"Dear friends," began the ceremonial address to the assembled parents and candidates, "these young people are now about to declare their solemn vows. With all their knowledge and the abilities which they have acquired and shall continue to acquire with the help and protection of the entire community, they are to serve the unity of our fatherland and the building of Socialism."

Then followed a series of questions addressed to the young people:

"Dear young friends, are you prepared to devote all your strength together with peace-loving people everywhere in fighting for peace and defending it to the utmost?"

The youth were expected to reply, "Yes, we promise."

"Are you prepared to devote all your strength together with all true patriots in fighting for a united, peaceful, democratic, and independent Germany?"

"Yes, we promise."

"Are you prepared to devote all your strength to the building of a happy life, to progress in business, science, and art?"

"Yes, we promise."

"We have heard your vows. Receive in exchange the promise of the fellowship of all working people to protect, encourage, and help you, so that you may reach the high goals you have set for yourselves."

The response of the Churches to the Youth Dedication was prompt and unequivocal. Protestants and Roman Catholics agreed that the Youth Dedication could not be judged simply on the basis of its own profession of tolerance and nonpartisanship, nor upon the seemingly noncommittal words of the pledge. It must be judged on the basis of its connection with the ideological aims and objectives of the Socialist Party and the Socialist State. On November 30th, therefore, the Church of Berlin-Brandenburg sent a message to its congregations, advising parents and children that the confessions of the Evangelical faith could not be harmonized with the Youth Dedication. Roman Catholic Bishop Wilhelm Weskamm sent a letter to Catholic parents and youth on December 26th, also declaring the incompatibility of the Youth Dedication and a Christian profession of faith.

The claims of the Churches were vindicated when the Youth Dedication Committee decided to present as a gift to each child taking part in the ceremony a book entitled *Weltall, Erde, Mensch* (The Universe, the World, and Man). Sumptuously illustrated and prefaced with a glowing recommendation by Walter Ulbricht, this book was intended as an inducement to the children and as a guide to their future thinking. According to the essayists of this book, the Christian faith was sheer superstition and mysticism, the conquest of which was one of the most important tasks of progressive thought. Ludwig Einicke, vice director of the Marx-Lenin-Stalin Institutes and a member of the Central Committee of the Youth Dedication, wrote in one of the essays, "In the capitalistic countries the leading reactionary powers have always used mysticism, superstition, and religion for the purpose of holding down the masses and oppressing them."

On the other hand, declared Einicke, the nature of dialectical materialism, which is the only true basis of reality, "permits no fairy tales about a creator, a world spirit, or a director of the world. It operates on the theory that the world has developed out of material which is governed by eternal laws of movement and change."

The community appeal of the Youth Dedication Committees naturally produced conflicts in many homes between alert Christian parents and children who were attracted by the glamour of a group experience. In most congregations, however, the outspoken disapproval of the two large Churches was sufficient to reduce participation to a minimum, particularly since the Youth Dedication Committees themselves had laid great stress upon the nonofficial and voluntary character of the program. The Central Committee claimed that between 60,000 and 83,000 young people took part in the ceremonies in April, 1955, but Church records indicated that less than 4 per cent of the children eligible for Confirmation had chosen the Youth Dedication.

In the autumn of 1955, a new campaign was launched. Local committees were reorganized with a view to intensifying the approach to parents and children. The program of instruction was scheduled from October to March, and the number and length of the meetings were increased. Direction remained under the Central Committee for the Youth Dedication, but this group now established its headquarters in the building of the Ministry of Education where its operation could be supervised by party and government officials.

A new booklet was published by the Central Committee containing testimonials from parents, teachers, and pupils, and also from four pastors later exposed by the Church as frauds. The strict "either-or" position of the Church was assailed as a violation of the citizen's constitutional guarantee of freedom of conscience. Parents, it was alleged, were being forced by the Church to make decisions limiting the freedom of their children. Young people were being deprived of opportunities to participate in a program designed to open up new fields of scientific knowledge and experience.

The support of State-owned shops and stores throughout East Germany was also enlisted for the new campaign. Pictures and posters appeared in store windows, and advertisements in the newspapers described how the well-dressed candidate should appear at the ceremony. Boys and girls were advised to wear the dark-blue suits and the white dresses that for many years had been associated with the Church ceremony of Confirmation.

Bishop Dibelius described the typical experience of a family that had decided to send its child to Confirmation instead of to the Youth Dedication. "First of all," he said, "either the father or the mother is summoned before the labor-union leader in the factory. The mother is visited by the Communist Women's Organization. A representative of the Free German Youth goes to work on the young person and the parents. The school principal and the teacher add their bit. The family is caught in a pinch from every side. Threats are employed. Children who refuse to take part will not be permitted to enter high school or to secure an apprenticeship to learn a trade. The father will lose his job, and the mother her position as a teacher. Afterward it will be denied that these threats were used. But the decisive thing is not what may be said afterward, but these facts, that everywhere threats such as these are being used. The Minister of Education has declared that the government must make certain that the Youth Dedication achieves its objectives. The State gives its support to this program."

The wording of the pledge was altered slightly from the previous year. Its actual phraseology remained innocuous enough, but participation in the ceremony itself bore the unmistakable character of a confessional act. A child who had publicly promised to dedicate all his strength to "a joyful life for the workingman and for progress in science, art, and economy" could be claimed by the FDJ and by the Communist State as a loyal supporter and friend. These confessional implications of the Youth Dedication led both Churches to announce with even greater vigor the second year their uncompromising refusal to sanction the Confirmation of any child who took part in this rival ceremony.

As the new program developed, it became increasingly clear that the Youth Dedication was not privately sponsored, but was a studied part of the long-range program of materialistic-atheistic propaganda. Occasional expressions from party leaders confirmed these indications. A Magdeburg official, for example, commented approvingly upon the "either-or" position taken by the Church, and urged the same clarity on the part of the Communists. "Because of the incompatibility of religion and science," he declared, "no Marxist-Leninist can ride on two horses at the some time. It is impossible for him to propagate a materialistic world view and pay homage to religion at the same time."

Teachers in the schools were subjected to pressures to enlist the participation of their pupils in the Youth Dedication. Goals were established by school principals, and teachers who failed to cooperate in reaching these goals were singled out as reactionary and unpatriotic, threatened with removal, and in some instances actually fired.

A mother, for example, whose husband had disappeared in 1945 finally got a job as a teacher. She was supporting her old parents and had no other source of income except her teacher's salary. When asked to solicit her pupils for the Youth Dedication, she refused. Ordered to visit the parents of her pupils for the same purpose, she refused again. Finally, she was told that she must either sign a statement that she was prepared to encourage parents to have their children join the Youth Dedication or resign her position.

What counsel should a pastor give to a teacher in such a position? The teacher's Christian conscience would not permit her to urge children to join an atheistic course of instruction climaxed by a pledge of allegiance. She also felt a Christian responsibility to her aged parents, whose 75-mark monthly pension was inadequate for their support. Should she flee to the West? If so, could she take her parents with her? How would they live as aged people among the masses of refugees? Which Christian duty was greater, the honoring of father and mother or the maintaining of personal integrity as a Christian teacher? This teacher quit her job and her profession rather than betray the children placed under her care, and accepted menial employment in order to fulfill her obligations to her aged parents.

The multiplication of such instances, together with the recognition that the State had at its disposal almost unlimited propaganda resources, made some direct move by the Church imperative before the enlistment campaign reached its climax. The East Conference of the EKD requested a meeting of Church and government leaders for the purpose of halting the use of high-pressure measures upon parents, teachers, and children. The only reply the Church leaders received was an increase in the vigor of the campaign and a series of newspaper attacks upon bishops and pastors for their "obstinate" stand on the Youth Dedication. At its meeting in Leipzig in December, the Block of Antifascistic Parties and Mass Organizations announced that whoever was opposed to the Youth Dedication was opposed to progress. Dibelius was characterized as a reactionary churchman dominated by medieval intolerance, a man whose leadership ought no longer to be endured.

The Church tried in every possible way to show both children and parents that the Youth Dedication was not merely a political decision but a decision of faith, to which only an "either-or" position could be taken. With the columns of the secular press completely closed to them, however, and with every medium of mass communication under the control of the State, such opportunities of interpretation were extremely limited. In this situation the synods and the bishops became the key interpreters of the Church's position. Their statements were passed on from the local pulpits and through the restricted medium of the Church press.

As the year 1956 opened, the Central Committee noted that registrations for the Youth Dedication were lagging seriously. All possible "progressive strength" was therefore mobilized during the first three months of 1956 to secure more general participation. The official organ of the Free German Youth urged its members, "Don't fall back!" "We need men for the building up of Socialism who have the truth and a scientifically correct world view, free of mysticism and dogma."

To swell the ranks for the spring festivities youth who had not attended the preparatory course were also permitted to participate in the ceremonies. Others who had finished the elementary school in previous years were invited to join the "graduates" of 1956. Announcement was made that participation in the Youth Dedication would be entered in the family record books, thus giving it a kind of official status, together with births, marriages, and deaths. Party agencies in the factories joined in the campaign, and in Stalinstadt workers were denounced by name for not sending their children to the Youth Dedication.

By the end of March the legend of the compatibility of the Youth Dedication with Confirmation had been completely scrapped by official party sources. Paul Froelich, one of the leading SED secretaries in Leipzig, declared at the third party conference of the SED in East Berlin, "Our world view is incompatible with religion, and coexistence in the question of world views is impossible."

Despite initial professions of liberality and tolerance by the sponsors of the Youth Dedication, it was now clear that the pledge involved commitments far more serious than its innocuous phraseology might seem to imply. The young person who accepted that pledge was taking the first entangling step into the mesh of Communist commitments intended to lead eventually to a full commitment to atheistic materialism. The strong resistance of the Churches forced the party to declare its open sanction and official support of the Youth Dedication sooner than had been intended. But even this endorsement and the deployment of the propaganda forces of the party failed at first to produce any impressive successes. Of 54,000 children of confirmation age in 1956 in the Lutheran Church of

Saxony 2,000, or 3.8 per cent were denied Confirmation because they took part in the Youth Dedication. Church authorities estimated that another 3,500 did not report for Confirmation instruction at all because of their intention to join the Youth Dedication. The Communists had therefore been able to secure at least the tacit cooperation of 9.9 per cent of the young people of Confirmation age in this industrial area of East Germany. Participation in the predominantly rural areas was smaller.

Nevertheless the pattern had been established. The massive propaganda resources of party and State had been brought to bear upon the youth for only a short time. Yet ominous gains had been registered in the face of unyielding opposition from the Church. A third and a fourth campaign might be expected to produce greater increases.

It seemed doubtful that the Church would be able to rally its members effectively for any length of time around the rite of Confirmation as a symbol of their loyalty to God and to the Christian faith. The compulsion of social custom and institutional loyalty might hold the youth for a year or two or three. But when the full force of the State propaganda machine was brought to bear, there would have to be something much stronger than an institutional loyalty to the Church to engender resistance to the Socialist ceremonies. The door to educational and economic preferment would eventually be opened to those willing to pay the price of a pledge of allegiance to the Socialist State.

The real pledge of Christian allegiance was the one that was made within the person himself to serve no other master but Jesus Christ. As the assault of materialistic atheism continued from one year to the next, it would be such pledges of allegiance that would display the true inner strength or weakness of the Christian community in East Germany.

ELEVEN

ROOM FOR THE GOSPEL?

The European winter of 1955–1956 was one of the bitterest of the century. During January and February the temperatures dropped below zero, and snowdrifts blocked highways and village streets. The blasts that roared out of the East and gripped Germany in their clutches seemed symbolic of the icy despair that had seeped into the hearts of people following the failures of Geneva.

Ominous signs appeared in January when, in spite of the bitter temperatures, the refugee stream increased again to an average of five hundred per day. The unusual number of public officials among them reflected the rumored approach of a new Communist purge and the tightening of party lines. Disturbed by its failure to forestall the incorporation of West Germany into the NATO defense system, the East German government formally unveiled its own new 110,000-man army which had already been several years in training as part of the People's Police. Nattily togged out in new gray-blue uniforms patterned after the Nazi Wehrmacht, both boys and girls shouldered rifles, according to the Communist press, to safeguard the people of East Germany against the aggression of NATO and to "guarantee all nations a quiet and peaceful development."

Even more sharply indicative of the new trend was the sudden and completely unexpected arrest of fourteen workers of the Railway Mission, the Church-sponsored travelers' aid, which for nearly a century had offered its human and spiritual services in practically every sizable railway station in Germany. Press releases from the government indicated that the arrests were based on espionage activities by the mission, the alleged channeling of information to western military officials on train and troop movements in East Germany. Coupled with the arrests was the order to evacuate the rooms occupied by the mission in the big Frederick Street railway station in East Berlin and in two other large cities. All further contacts of the Railway Mission with West Berlin and West Germany were forbidden.

The Council of the EKD immediately issued a public repudiation of the charges of espionage. Bishop Dibelius announced his profound regret that he must leave Berlin on a world-circling tour to Australia as one of the presidents of the World Council of Churches, carrying with him the unpleasant impression of this unwarranted attack upon an agency of the Church which for decades had been known and respected for its service to men and women in need.

East German authorities, however, were not so easily forced into retreat. They carried forward their action against both Protestant and Roman Catholic missions in East Germany, until virtually all of the one hundred centers had been closed. A "guilt confession" from one of the women workers was published shortly after her release, in which the familiar formula of "self-criticism" employed by the Communists was clearly evident. "Through my oral and written reports," she declared obediently, "I have contributed to the illegal activity of the Railway Mission within the German Democratic Republic. I will now try to atone to some extent for my guilt by devoting myself to a new area of service through public welfare work among the citizens of the city of Potsdam."

Neues Deutschland, Communist newspaper in East Berlin, described in detail subversive activities of the mission that it claimed to have uncovered in West Berlin, even to a formal espionage course lasting several weeks, in which former Nazis supervised the instruction. Even the fact that the two women who headed the mission work in East and West Germany stemmed from families of the old German nobility was cited as evidence of the "reactionary" affiliations of the missions. Several other "confessions" were also published, quoting workers whose arrest had allegedly brought them to realize the error of their ways. These "confessions" confirmed the Communist claims that the mission had sheltered criminals wanted by the police, violated currency regulations, gathered military statistics, and operated centers to encourage and facilitate the flight of refugees.

Government officials insisted that arrests and charges were being carried out against individuals who had misused their Church offices for subversive purposes, but that the Church itself was not being assailed. Nevertheless, staff members of the Railway Mission who themselves were not under arrest were deprived of the passes admitting them to the railway platforms where they normally performed their services, and subjected to the obligation of purchasing a ticket for each entry to the platform. Others were forbidden to enter the property belonging to the railway station or even to appear in the vicinity of the station. Mission barracks located on railroad property in many cities were ordered immediately removed in spite of the prevailing extremely cold weather.

If only a fraction of the charges brought against the mission workers had been true or even plausible, the persons charged with such crimes would have been quickly brought to trial and given severe prison sentences. However, by the end of April the last of the mission workers were quietly released from jail and the entire subject was allowed to drop without a single person ever having been brought to trial.

The real purposes of the government, however, had by that time been accomplished. As Bishop Mitzenheim protested in a letter to Karl Maron, Minister of the Interior, "a work of the Church, which was forbidden by the Nazis in 1938, and since 1945 has sought in all simplicity to do nothing else than to serve without respect of persons with a good word, some counsel, a cup of coffee, a bowl of soup, or a warm bed, has been brutally liquidated in just a few days through local measures which are in contradiction to official explanations."

The Church leadership of the Evangelical Church, declared Mitzenheim, "will thus be compelled to inform these willing workers, most of whom have been serving voluntarily without pay, and the congregations which are affected that the work of the Railway Mission in East Germany is suspended—that this selfless work has been rendered impossible through encroachments and interferences against which no legal recourse is available."

Still another ominous sign of the sharper course being taken toward the Church in East Germany following the Geneva conferences appeared in the schools of East Berlin. On February 15th the City Council issued a set of regulations affecting religious instruction. According to these new regulations, known as the Fechner Decree, the school director was required to supervise the form and content of all activities before and after school hours and designate the place where such activities might be arranged. In order to protect the health of the children and to be sure that they were as alert as possible when the day's lessons in the school began, no religious instruction was to be permitted before the regular school hours. As a further health measure, at least a two-hour pause must intervene after the close of the school day before any religious instruction might be given by the Church.

Since fourteen-year-old children were said to be capable of making their own religious decisions, no more religious instruction was to be permitted in the high schools even when given on a voluntary basis by pastors or catechists.

All persons who wished to give any kind of instruction to the children outside school hours were required to secure an identification card authorizing such activity. These cards were to be issued by the school director and were renewable every three months. This meant that not only catechists but even pastors who gave religious instruction of any kind to school children might be required to apply for such permission from the director of the local public school. Fortunately, no attempt was made to carry out the full implications of the Fechner Decree, but it remained in force nevertheless, ready for use whenever the city officials might be so inclined.

Accompanying the Fechner Decree was a general press attack in the East Berlin newspapers directed against the Church schools of West Berlin. These schools were declared to be "hideouts for Nazi teachers" and centers of propaganda seeking to lure young people out of the East Berlin schools and to bring them under the dubious "blessing" of the West Berlin educational system. The EKD Department of Christian Education in West Berlin was likewise accused of fostering a spirit opposed to the education of good citizens, and one speaker at a district teachers' conference in East Berlin called upon his colleagues not to tolerate catechists any longer who had been trained in West Berlin to agitate against the Socialist State.

On Sunday, March 5th, an official Church protest was read from every pulpit in East Berlin, demanding the immediate withdrawal of the Fechner Decree which the Church declared to be a violation both of the East German Constitution and the Berlin School Law of 1948. "Jesus Christ has charged His Church with the duty of proclaiming the Gospel to all people," it read. "Therefore the Church cannot recognize any control by outside authorities in activities which concern the teaching of God's Word. Fellow Christians, a struggle is being forced upon us here which we have not sought. The Word of God calls us to stand firm in this matter. Insist therefore that your children receive Christian instruction, be prepared for Confirmation, and attend the children's worship services."

Bishop Dibelius himself read this proclamation from the pulpit after he had preached to an overflow congregation of three thousand persons in East Berlin's St. Mary's Church. Standing room only was available in this huge cathedral twenty minutes before the services began. The text of the bishop's sermon was the theme of the 1954 Kirchentag in Leipzig, "Cast not away your confidence."

Quite as characteristic as the clarity of the bishop's proclamation and protest was the lack of response by the East Berlin government. There was certainly no withdrawal of the regulations. Nor was there even a comment on the Church statement, but merely another sharp personal attack on the bishop as a representative of the West German NATO politicians.

Even more sobering than these straws in the wind were the indications that the Communist government was preparing a full-scale attack upon the economic foundations of the Church. All three of its major sources of income seemed to be under threat. The Church tax, which for several years had been levied and collected by the Church itself and not by the State, was being rendered more difficult by the refusal of the State to permit Church finance officials to examine the State tax lists on which the levies had always been based. Free-will offerings and street collections, which under these circumstances would be the supplementary or even the substitute source of Church income, were also rigidly restricted in number. Finally, the gradually disappearing direct subsidies from the State, based upon historic Church-State property settlements, were arbitrarily reduced by a million marks in 1956. Whereas in 1955 the East Zone Churches were themselves able to raise 75 per cent of the 100,000,000 marks necessary to carry on their total program, indications were that in 1956 they would be able to raise less than 70 per cent.

The most far-reaching of all the financial measures of the government was actually the so-called Benjamin Decree. Issued on February 10, 1956, by Dr. Hilde Benjamin, Minister of Justice, this decree declared flatly that in the future the payment of all Church taxes would be a voluntary matter. The enforcement machinery of the State would no longer be available for assistance in collecting the tax.

Thus was destroyed in a single stroke the most significant remnant of the old State Church system. Though for a time the compulsion of custom and tradition might support the old system, the Church was being rudely but unmistakably thrust into a new era. This was not an easy prospect for a Church which for centuries had depended upon fixed and stable sources of income. Yet the older system was clearly out of step with the times and certainly with the political situation in which the Church of East Germany was living.

Whatever the motivations of the Communist government may have been, the Benjamin Decree was also forcing the Church into a long-overdue inner financial reform which in the long run could strengthen the Church as a congregation-based structure. Unfortunately, however, the Church in East Germany was not prepared to accept this challenge. Instead, it complained of the State's injustice and ill will and then turned to its own membership, half in panic and half in threat, and declared it to be the obligation of every Christian to continue paying his Church tax even without the compulsion of the law.

With only a brief gesture toward the principles of Christian stewardship which interpret the financial support of the Church as a part of the Christian's service to God and an expression of his faith, the Lutheran Church of Saxony bluntly announced the penalties for Church members who refused to pay the Church tax after receiving the proper reminders. Delinquents might be deprived of their right to vote in Church elections, the right to be a Church officer or a sponsor, or the right to Christian marriage or burial. Such an approach to Church members may have assured a continued conformity for the time being; it could scarcely win the warm and devoted personal loyalty of large numbers whose relation to the Church was merely a formal one. The Church was evidently not prepared to yield its privileged position and to appeal to its membership for support on the basis of loyalty to the faith.

Even more disturbing was the increasing intensity of the open and public attack upon the Church in the early months of 1956. The arrest of the Railway Mission workers for alleged espionage activities touched off a wave of general accusations directed against the loyalty of the Church. The Communist press led the attack, claiming that the Church was receiving money from Bonn and orders from West Germany, that it was carrying on the cold war on behalf of the western powers, and that it was hindering Christians from carrying out their loyal duties to the republic.

Alarmed by this new wave of abuse, the East Conference of the EKD sent a letter to Prime Minister Otto Grotewohl requesting a conference with him. Instead, the official Church delegation was received on February 10th by Karl Maron, the Minister of the Interior, who used the occasion to read a lengthy formal complaint against the Churches in which the main theme was that of alleged disloyalty. Maron listed a long series of incidents which he declared showed the tendency of the East German Churches to become the instruments of NATO policy.

During a centennial celebration of the Evangelical Young Men's Work, for example, East Zone youth had been invited to attend a rally in the Schoeneberg Sport Arena in West Berlin. The East German government raised strenuous objection on the ground that the exposure of East German youth to the West Berlin atmosphere of gangster films and trash literature and subversive espionage would undermine the morality of the youth. The invitation was therefore regarded as an unfriendly act toward the East German government and its people.

Mothers Leaving "House of Culture" in Luebbenau After Communist
Name-Giving Ceremony (May 5, 1958)

Communist Marriage Ceremony in a Factory Clubhouse (1958)

Furthermore, declared Maron, a series of Church rallies had recently been staged in Saxony for the purpose of stirring up dissension against the government. In one of these rallies, Dr. Kreyssig, lay president of the Provincial Synod of Saxony, had declared that there could be no peace or coexistence with the godless. In another, Dr. Fraenkel of Goerlitz had described the Evangelical Church in East Germany as "a place of freedom in a very unfree world." These and other quotations from the addresses of leading speakers were taken out of their contexts and interpreted as if the Church were attacking the government and advocating its overthrow.

A questionnaire prepared by the Social Research Office of the Church of Westphalia in West Germany had also been sent to pastors in East Germany, requesting information which Maron regarded as espionage. Pastors were asked concerning the attitude of workers toward the system of State-owned factories and toward their jobs within these factories. Did the worker regard himself as a co-owner of the "People's Own Factories"? If reunification should come, would the worker wish to retain this system or would he prefer private ownership? How was the morale of the laboring man? Did he do shoddy work with a good conscience? Questions of this kind, observed Maron, certainly reflected a reactionary orientation, and he found it difficult to see what connection they had to the task of the Church. Religious liberty, he said, was guaranteed by the constitution, and the government was desirous of maintaining peaceful relations with the Church. But if the Church did not cease mixing into political, economic, and educational questions and misusing its organization for the furthering of NATO policies and antipeace activities, it could expect severe reprisals from the government.

Astonished as they were to have an expected conference turned into a classroom session in which Maron was the lecturer and they were the listeners, the leaders of the Church did not accept the accusations passively. On March 3rd they returned with a statement denying the charges of NATO-subservience, but agreeing to investigate the detailed charges made by Maron and to rectify any irregularities which might be found. The second part of the Church statement listed nineteen specific complaints regarding the official treatment of religion and the Church. Following Maron's lead, the Church gave this document as wide publicity as it was able.

The major complaints centered around the new set of regulations interfering with the handling of religious instruction, especially in East Berlin, and the increasing attempts to force the materialistic world view upon the children in the schools. Not only were children being discriminated against for not accepting this view, but the prime minister himself no longer even acknowledged the letters of protest written by the leading officials of the Church.

The extent to which the materialistic campaign was being carried was given shocking expression in the excesses that took place in the city of Brandenburg just at the time that these documents were being exchanged by Church and State leaders. In the midst of the secularized version of a Catholic pre-Lenten carnival encouraged by Communist youth leaders as a kind of "folk festival," one blasphemous reveler appeared in the parade masquerading as Jesus Christ Himself. A local Communist newspaper reported the incident approvingly.

Completely horror-stricken, the Church of Brandenburg issued a public denunciation of the blasphemy. Realizing that the bounds of propriety had been sadly overstepped, the Communist mayor of the city apologized to the Church superintendent for the incident and assured him that party authorities had had nothing to do with the demonstration. The Church itself announced a public service of penitence and prayer for God's forgiveness upon a city in which such a heathen demonstration could take place. All church bells in the city were ordered to remain silent for a period of three weeks.

The Church also complained that the Youth Dedication had been changed into an official State function and that guarantees which had been given to the youth and student congregations in June, 1953, were no longer being observed. Moreover, pastors were being denied the right to hold services, devotions, or Holy Communion in old people's homes and convalescent homes operated by the State. Similar limitations were being applied to many hospitals, and even Christmas services were denied, sometimes over the strenuous objections of the doctors in charge. In regular prisons pastoral conversations were permitted only in the presence of a member of the People's Police, and general services of worship were declared to be impossible because of lack of room. No pastoral ministry at all was permitted in youth prisons and detention prisons.

Of more general effect upon the congregations was the failure of the government to protect the observance of Sunday and the high religious holidays. Seven-day work weeks were employed in State-owned factories and shops. Residence permits for pastors and Church workers from western Germany remained impossible to secure, and even travel permits were denied more often than they were granted.

In spite of the widely publicized government aid, the program of church reconstruction had been restricted and hindered. Sometimes this was due to a general shortage of key building materials in East Germany, such as nails or zinc fixtures for a roof, but frequently, the government simply refused to grant building permits even when materials were available. In one case a village church was in need of a new door and window frames but was repeatedly told that materials were not available. One day a windstorm blew down several trees on the church property, and the Church authorities requested permission to have the wood from these trees cut properly and used for the needed frames. The request was rejected because this lumber had not been calculated in the planned quotas for that area. The church building consequently remained unrepaired while the fallen trees rotted where they fell.

Another case in point was a church in East Berlin that was returned to the Germans by the Russians in the summer months of 1955. Since this church was located in a settlement of Russian-occupied houses, a steel fence had been built around the church, with only a narrow roadway allowing access to the building. Not damaged at all during the bombing of Berlin, this relatively new church had been allowed to weather and decay until the roof literally fell in. Every stick of wood furniture had been used for firewood, and eventually the building was converted to a stable and a warehouse. Finally, in 1955, with great festivity, the church had been returned, bearing, it was admitted, a few marks of the occupation, but nevertheless a sign of the government's "abiding friendliness toward the Church." Early in 1956 the church still stood desolate, with only the most elementary reconstruction having been undertaken and with great holes still gaping in the roof. Money was available, but neither the metal building materials nor the permit to import them from West Berlin could be secured from the government.

Aside from the promise given by Karl Maron to investigate the complaints raised by the Church and to confer again with its representatives at a later date, nothing came of the March 3rd meeting. Ever since the arrest of the Railway Mission workers, leaders of the Church had sought a conference with the prime minister, but it was apparently not the wish of the government to discuss relations with the Church. Even after March 3rd, week after week passed without a reply to their request for a top-level meeting.

The strategy of the government at this time was rather to publicize its charges that the Church was serving as a tool of NATO in East Germany, while asserting its own desire to honor the constitutional guarantees of religious freedom for the Church. While Mr. Maron lectured the Church leaders on their alleged servility to NATO, the elusive prime minister mounted the podium of the third party congress of the SED in Berlin late in March to appeal for the rightful allocation to both Church and State of the loyalties and duties which rightfully belonged to each.

To such a fundamental principle as this no Christian could take exception, even in the German Democratic Republic. But as Bishop Krummacher of Pomerania pointed out, some very difficult problems arose when a professedly materialistic State assumed the right to decide what those things were which rightfully belonged to the Church and to the State. When the government raised the question of loyalty, it was touching the fundamental Church-State issue upon which either some working agreement must be found or upon which open warfare must sooner or later break out.

Such loyalty to the State could exist on several levels. The first level, that of tacit recognition, merely drew the line at open resistance and gave the necessary tribute of obedience to laws governing public order and behavior. Such a relationship could scarcely be described as a positive loyalty at all, but simply as conformity under compulsion.

The State was eager that the Church should make a more positive official declaration of loyalty than this. Such a declaration, according to Deputy Prime Minister Otto Nuschke, would not commit the Church to any particular political and economic system, but would only guarantee the obedience of the Church and its organs to the laws of the State. It would also reassure the government that the all-German unity of the Evangelical Church was not being used as a cloak for hidden power politics, Nuschke saw such a loyalty statement as a means of achieving honest and genuine cooperation between Christians and Marxists, between Church and State.

"In the light of the two-State division of Germany," declared the CDU newspaper *Neue Zeit,* "it is unendurable that the loyalty of the Church in the German Democratic Republic remains constantly under a shadow. It would be in order for Church leaders to declare that they respect our laws and that they separate themselves from the NATO policies which seek to involve the EKD in the cold war."

While the bishops of East Germany consistently expressed their readiness to seek ways of easing Church-State tensions through discussion and agreement, they refused to make any pledge that would compromise the conscience of the Church and its witness to God's truth. They also vigorously rejected the implication that their unwillingness to make such a pledge in any sense suggested that they were endorsing the political views of the West German government. Neither in East or West, declared Bishop Beste of Mecklenburg, is the task of the Church to give its official support to any political position or policy. The Church must seek to exercise the office of a watchman, and on the basis of God's Word alone speak its words of admonition and warning to the people and, when necessary, to the State.

Quite in this spirit of independence was the forthright declaration of the synod of the Lutheran Church of Saxony, early in April, that the Church can never become the tool of any political power or system. To make a general pledge of loyalty to a government which has, for example, "forcibly halted the work of almost one hundred Railway Missions of the Church in East Germany, and still holds about thirty pastors and Church workers in prisons would be impossible. Moreover, that a high official of this government, namely, the Minister of the Interior, speaking in his official capacity, should have described the Christian faith as "superstition," the Saxon synod declared to be "monstrous."

The third possible level of Church-State relationships would be that of active cooperation by the Church in various programs of the State such as the Peace Front and possibly even the Youth Dedication. On this level, only a handful of so-called "progressive" pastors and professors were cooperating, and very few of these were willing to give their public approval to the Youth Dedication. A larger number, however, led by Dr. Heinrich Grueber and encouraged by such West German churchmen as Martin Niemoeller and Swiss theologian Karl Barth, lent their support to the Peace Front and participated regularly in the international peace conferences such as that held in Stockholm, Sweden, in April, 1956. However, at a local meeting of the Berlin Peace Society Grueber told the "Marxian friends of peace" that if they expected to count on his "confident cooperation," they must not speak presumptuously of the Christian faith as "superstition." In fact, insisted Grueber, a "change of climate" must take place in the East if these relationships were to continue at all.

Such a plea from Grueber might have struck a responsive chord among the politicians of the East CDU whose characteristic approach to the Church was always one of friendly appeal. The CDU, under Otto Nuschke's leadership, was sponsoring the campaign to win a pledge of loyalty from the Church, and Nuschke seems to have understood the misgivings of the Church on this matter much better than did the Communists of the SED. Not only did he plead with the Church leaders to give the desired statement, assuring them that it need not imply an endorsement of specific political policies of the government, but he also chided the SED officials for their increasingly doctrinaire statements concerning the incompatibility of their views and those of the Christians. Paul Froelich, the Leipzig District party secretary, for example, had stated flatly at the third party congress in Berlin in March that "the ideology of superstition" was hindering progress, even within the SED. "Coexistence in questions of world view," he declared, "is not possible."

Nuschke took sharp issue with Froelich's statement, in an article in *Neue Zeit*, calling them a "tactical blunder" and an "offense to all Christian circles." Anyone who spoke in such a vein, declared Nuschke, was weakening the strength of peace "against the dark powers" of reaction and war which presumably both the SED and the CDU wanted to fight. Even Premier Otto Grotewohl supported Nuschke on this.

Froelich was apparently expressing the emphasis of the Ulbricht group in East Germany, which represented the old-line Communist position and tended to be less sympathetic toward the Church. The repercussions of the twentieth party congress of the Communist

Party in Moscow, held in February, 1956, were beginning to be felt in East Germany, and these may have emboldened Nuschke and Grotewohl to speak as critically of Froelich as they did.

The twentieth party congress had been the occasion of Nikita Khrushchev's astonishing address denouncing the dead hero Stalin as the archbetrayer of Leninist principles and as a power-hungry despot and murderer. This complete reversal of official opinion concerning Stalin was immediately reflected throughout the Communist world, and politicians who had lauded the great leader to the skies one day denounced him as a traitor and a scoundrel the next. This was true even in East Germany, although Walter Ulbricht was known to be a follower of the old Stalinist line. The third party congress of the SED obediently accepted the new revelation from Moscow, and irrepressible Berlin humor suggested that the flamboyant Stalin Boulevard in the East Sector of the city be renamed the Boulevard of the Great Mistake. In the rotunda of the great Soviet Exhibition Hall on the Leipzig Fairgrounds, the monumental statue of Joseph Stalin yielded silently to a brotherly duo of Lenin and Stalin.

There was actually some question whether the Moscow shift might bring new leadership to the fore in East Germany more in keeping with the "new look" of Soviet diplomacy. But Ulbricht and the old regime remained in power, shrewdly paying the necessary tribute to the new line, but never altering its basic policies in any appreciable way. Froehlich's statements doubtless represented the unvarnished party conviction concerning religion and the Church somewhat impatiently voiced by an eager functionary, but Ulbricht was willing to give way temporarily to the Grotewohl-Nuschke program of "coexistence" with the Church, since it was tactically more in spirit with the new diplomatic line from Moscow.

The discussion of this proposal of "coexistence based on loyalty," conducted largely by the CDU, dragged on through April and May while the frustration of Church leaders increased. The personal meeting with the prime minister for which they had vainly petitioned month in and month out still failed to materialize. Accusations of NATO subservience were regularly mixed in the party press with demands for loyalty declarations from the Church, but any discussion of basic relationships of Church and State at a responsible level was consistently avoided.

Church authorities finally agreed among themselves to force a discussion of the issues. Although a regular synod of the Evangelical Church in Germany was scheduled for the fall of 1956, it was decided that in view of the continuing tensions between Church and State to summon a special synod to meet in June to discuss the very suggestive theme: "Room for the Gospel in East and West."

Delegates from Churches in East and West Germany gathered accordingly on June 27th for their opening service in East Berlin's big St. Mary's Church. After listening to a moving sermon on the unity of the Body of Christ by Professor Helmut Gollwitzer of Bonn, the synod went directly to work on its main theme. Fiery General Superintendent Guenter Jacob from Cottbus in East Germany and quiet, studious Bishop Hermann Dietzfelbinger of Bavaria delivered the keynote addresses and left no doubt of the Church's determination to fulfill its divine responsibility of declaring the Gospel both in private and in public.

Dr. Jacob made it clear that while the Church was scripturally bound to recognize government as a safeguard against public chaos, the State would await in vain any special loyalty declaration from the Church which might soothe the State's bad conscience. Moreover, the character of the Gospel as "the good news of the incarnation, crucifixion and resurrection of Jesus Christ" would never permit its limitation either as a "cult" or as a purely personal and private matter separated from public responsibility. In humility and in obedience to God, the Church must regard the whole world as its working room, in which it worships, witnesses, and serves.

Dr. Jacob's address also provided food for thought for those who looked back with nostalgia upon the old days of the privileged institutional Church. The present situation of Christian Europe, declared Dr. Jacob, was distinguished by the fact that it stood at the end of the Constantinian Era. This era had been characterized by a close relationship between State and Church, throne and altar, and the identification of the entire population with the Christian congregation. In these past centuries the life of the Church had been formed on the assumption that Christianity was a privileged religion which formed the foundation of the State and shaped the general character of the world view of that State.

However, observed Dr. Jacob, since the termination of the imposing medieval structure of society, two very powerful historical movements had tended to break down this Constantinian picture. The first was the secular force of the Enlightenment which drew so many intellectuals away from the Church. The other was the defection of the working classes in the middle of the nineteenth century. Both of these forces had worked to undermine the privileged position of the Church in European society. The Church, however, clung tenaciously to its past, and managed to preserve its dignity and standing, though it had lost its prophetic voice. Instead of being the clear unmuted voice of Christ speaking to all men and all situations, the Church had become largely the voice of an obsolete social and ecclesiastical structure.

Against this background, said the General Superintendent from Cottbus, the attitude of Marxism toward religion and the Church was to a certain extent understandable. The Marxist and the workingman had looked upon the Church as a fortress of privilege, erected to defend an obsolete way of living and thinking and to discourage the reshaping of society to fit the very practical and material goals which underprivileged people had set for themselves.

Whether the Marxists were right or not in their radical rejection of the whole of the Christian Gospel together with the ecclesiastical and social structure of the Church, Christians in the twentieth century, said Jacob, must themselves rediscover the mission of the Christian witness. The Constantinian Era, with all of its artificial protections and safeguards for the institution of the Church, was gone. As in the primitive Christian Era when the dominant social and political order was openly anti-Christian, the Church must depend solely upon the witness of the individual Christian and the congregation. Naturally every Christian would be expected to respect the political power under which he lived, whether in East Germany or in the Rome of St. Paul, but his first obedience is to the Law of God. To this Law he must adhere, even in case the State should violate it and demand that he do likewise.

This, said Dr. Jacob, was the problem of finding room for the Gospel in East and West. The same responsibility rested upon Christians whether in one power area or another. For room to exercise this witness the Church had every right to plead with the State not to advocate one political system or another, not to support one social

structure or another as the final hope of humanity, not to become a
tool for the furtherance of human causes, not to seek special privileges for itself as an institution—but only for the freedom to preach
the Gospel and to measure all men and their conduct against the
living standards of God's Word and Law.

The preceding ten years, however, had left considerable question as
to the willingness of the East German Communist State to grant
freedom of this kind to the Gospel. Guarantees in the constitution
were clear, but practice was frequently contradictory, and leaders of
the State had even refused to discuss these issues with the Church
leaders. It was because of doubts concerning the intentions of the
State at this very point that the special synod of the Church had
been called.

A committee headed by Dr. Kurt Gruenbaum of Magdeburg prepared a dramatic report to the synod on the "Present Situation of the
Church in East Germany." The committee proposed to speak "on
behalf of the distressed consciences of all those who have had to live
for years in a growing conflict between those things that God's Word
tells them and things that are expected of them as citizens."

Even after the most solemn guarantees given by responsible leaders
of the State on June 10, 1953, the report continued, the Church had
been harassed constantly by forces within the State "to whom the
Christian faith means nothing more than a religious superstition"
and to whom constitutional guarantees provided no restraint. Repeated attempts by Church officials to discuss these grievances with
State leaders had been repeatedly ignored. The catalogue of protests
presented to Karl Maron in March, 1956, but never answered, was
therefore presented again in overwhelming detail. The report concluded with a warning and a plea directed to the government, reflecting the profound urgency of the question for which the synod had
been called: "Is there room for the Gospel?"

The impression of a planned repression and undermining of the Church
is becoming more and more intense. Fundamental questions have arisen
concerning the relations of the State and the Church, which should be
discussed for the sake of justice and freedom. If this is not permitted to
take place, the press, film, and the apparatus of the State and of its related
organizations will be devoted to a one-sided proclamation of materialistic

and atheistic ideology, and an honest understanding will no longer be possible. Fear and mistrust are being sown, and thereby the confidence of broad masses of Christian population in the government is being destroyed.

In an hour in which the world powers are seeking some form of co-existence of nations in freedom and peace to prevent another world-wide catastrophe of blood and tears, the Synod of the Evangelical Church in Germany earnestly pleads that the Evangelical Christians in the German Democratic Republic also be granted freedom and peace for their service.

Some of the potency of this dramatic statement was drained away by the fact that the synod simply "took cognizance" of it instead of endorsing it. No one questioned its accuracy, but the counsel of caution was followed lest such an outspoken declaration destroy the possibility of reopening conversations with the government.

The question of a loyalty declaration to the State was frankly and thoroughly discussed. The synod finally adopted a theological declaration based on the principle of Romans 13, recognizing the State as a part of the order of God in this world, regardless of the manner in which it came to power or the form of its political structure. This was the traditional position of the Church, and the restatement of it could not be interpreted by Communist authorities as an endorsement of their policies.

Otto Nuschke was disappointed. He understood that the Church could not sanction any particular political or social order, but he felt that the statement of the synod had too carefully avoided disassociating itself from western propaganda and politics. Such a disassociation had been suggested by Dr. Jacob's address, but Nuschke felt the synod had failed to pick it up, and had taken a course instead which indicated that the EKD preferred a role as "the last resistance center to the new social order."

Unsatisfactory though the theological declaration of the special synod of Berlin was to the government, the policy of "peaceful co-existence" was still maintained between Church and State during the remaining months of 1956. Charges of disloyalty against the Church still stood, but the government continued its profession of readiness to live on friendly terms with the Church if only it would renounce NATO leadership and proclaim its patriotic loyalty to the German Democratic Republic.

Under the banner of this coexistence, the seventh Evangelical Kirchentag was held in Frankfurt am Main in West Germany. As living symbols of the readiness of the East German State to cooperate with a loyal Church, Deputy Prime Minister Otto Nuschke and Parliament President Johannes Dieckmann headed a delegation of several thousand visitors from East Germany who were given exit permits to attend this great Church rally.

Although claiming that his mission to the Kirchentag was entirely nonpolitical, Nuschke used the opportunity to address a discussion session on "People and Politics." It was absurd, he declared, to assert that the East German government was unfriendly to the Church. On the contrary it was furthering Church life by maintaining the theological faculties at the universities, paying the salaries of professors, and granting scholarships to theological students. More than 100 million marks, he declared, had been given by the government in the past ten years to restore war-damaged churches and to build new ones in East Germany. Nuschke's remarks, however, were rather rudely cut short by the chairman of the discussion group, who insisted that he confine himself to the three-minute time limit accorded all participants in the discussion.

When West German President Theodor Heuss visited the Kirchentag, stringent precautions were taken by Kirchentag authorities to prevent any meeting between him and the two governmental dignitaries from the East. Reacting sharply to such maneuvers Johannes Dieckmann left Frankfurt after two days, expressing his deep regret that this Kirchentag, in contrast to the one held in Leipzig in 1954, was achieving nothing in terms of progress toward the reunification of Germany. The Frankfurt meeting, he declared, was obviously under the influence of government circles in Bonn which were unfriendly toward a policy of "peaceful coexistence."

Nuschke, too, turned down a breakfast invitation from Kirchentag President Dr. von Thadden-Trieglaff, and refused to attend the final meeting of the Kirchentag as a protest against the allegedly discourteous treatment he and Dieckmann had been accorded.

A few weeks later, back in East Germany, Nuschke mounted the platform of the CDU party rally in Weimar to reaffirm his desire, and presumably that of his government, to maintain a friendly relationship with the Church. He repeated the things he had said in

Frankfurt concerning the many financial aids given by the government to the Church, and expressed his conviction that in the great quest for peace, Christians and Marxists could work together.

The unpleasant experiences he and Dieckmann had had in Frankfurt, declared Nuschke, could not destroy the spirit of good will which existed both in the Church and in the government of East Germany. They merely indicated that there were some elements in the Church and in the West German State that were determined to sabotage this spirit of unity and of peace. Letters of regret over these incidents, however, had been received from both Bishop Dibelius and Professor Thielecke of Hamburg, and these emboldened Nuschke to continue his efforts and those of his party for better understanding. Such understanding could very easily be secured, he said, if the Church would simply, once for all, announce its loyalty to the existing State in East Germany. The responsibility for the burdened consciences concerning which the Church complained did not rest with the State at all, but with those elements in the Church which constantly encouraged their people in the illusion that someday there would be another kind of State in East Germany to which they might conscientiously pledge their loyalty. By refusing to declare its own loyalty to the State, the Church was depriving its members of the peace of conscience to which every loyal Christian citizen was entitled.

Under Nuschke's leadership a resolution was adopted, spelling out the role the CDU expected to play in bringing about an atmosphere of understanding between Church and State. The special task of the CDU, it declared, was "to win the cooperation of all Christians for democratization and economic reconstruction. The CDU bears witness that the peaceful work of the German Democratic Republic is in keeping with the will to peace proclaimed in Christian teaching. It recognizes that Socialism offers far better possibilities than earlier economic systems for the fulfillment of many Christian concerns. It declares that the Christian confessions enjoy complete freedom of faith and conscience in East Germany and that our State is concerned about protecting all of the rightful interests of religious organizations."

A much more accurate measure of long-range prospects for cordial relations between the Church and the Socialist State was the official principle announced almost simultaneously for the seventh annual study course of the SED. In all future party instruction, Marxist-Leninist dogmas were to be carefully safeguarded against any possible modification through "ideological coexistence" with the West. "The politics of coexistence," declared the party authority, "may be applied only in economic and purely political areas, but never in the field of ideology." Translated into practical terms, this meant that although the politicians of Moscow or East Berlin might for tactical reasons at a given time display a friendly smile toward those who stood opposed to their policies, the basic objectives of the Communists remained unchanged. This would be true whether the tactical "coexistence" was being applied in international politics or in the relations between Church and State in East Germany.

In spite of the dogmatic emphasis of the party study program, however, the tactic of peaceful coexistence toward the Church continued throughout the remainder of 1956. Several West German Church leaders were granted entry permits to East Germany for the purpose of visitation and preaching. Not only Martin Niemoeller and President Wilm of the Church of Westphalia, both of whom tended to be critical of West German governmental policies, but also Pastor Heinrich Giesen, general secretary of the Kirchentag, was permitted to visit the city of Goerlitz in Silesia and there to deliver addresses on the themes of the Frankfurt Kirchentag. Thirty-six pastors and laymen from Westphalia were granted permission for a one-week visitation in the parishes of the Church Province of Saxony in late November. On December 3rd even the long-postponed conference between Prime Minister Otto Grotewohl and the bishops of the East German Churches took place, and the government reiterated its shopworn promise to examine carefully the individual complaints presented by the Church.

Part of this apparent desire to avoid any frontal conflict with the Church can be explained by the conditions of political unrest in neighboring East European satellites, which rose to a climax in October in the violent revolution in Hungary and in the triumph of the Gomulka regime in Poland. As soon as these crises were over, however, and order had been restored, evidences of a sharper and more aggressive tactic toward the Church began to appear. A new campaign for the Youth Dedication was launched in the schools. More atheistic literature appeared. Walter Ulbricht used Hungary as an object lesson for the need of a more thoroughly grounded support of Socialism, and called for the opening of a "great new ideological offensive" in East Germany.

For a Church which had thus far refused to yield either to blandishments or threats and to declare its loyalty to the socialistic state and its program, such an announcement by the first secretary of the party sounded an ominous note. If "room for the Gospel" meant freedom for the Church to carry on its normal ministry of teaching, preaching, and works of mercy, and for the individual Christian to profess his faith in God without fear of discrimination, it seemed likely by the end of 1956 that the question of the special synod of the EKD would have to be answered in the negative. In the Marxist-oriented pattern of society, there would eventually be no room for the Gospel of Jesus Christ.

TWELVE

THE ATTEMPT TO SPLIT THE CHURCH

In addition to the inner unity of spirit in its confrontation with the Communist State, one of the great strengths of the Evangelical Church in Germany has been an organizational structure bridging the Iron Curtain. The Church structure had been achieved during the years from 1945 to 1948 when Communist leaders, still hoping to secure the reunification of Germany on terms satisfactory to them, were encouraging relationships between East and West Germany. When the political division became fixed in 1949, with the organizing of two separate governments, the structure of the Evangelical Church in Germany was still maintained. Its annual synod and its executive council contained representatives from all parts of Germany, and the president of the council was Bishop Otto Dibelius, whose own Church territory of Berlin-Brandenburg was partially under eastern and partially under western jurisdiction. Such a situation actually made Dibelius the ideal symbol of the unity of the EKD, since his own diocese transcended the political divisions and he himself could travel quite freely in either area. Although he maintained his residence and his main offices in West Berlin, his official pulpit, from which he preached regularly on the first Sunday of every month, was in St. Mary's Church in East Berlin.

As the political tensions between East and West and also between Church and State in East Germany increased after 1949, Dibelius came frequently under attack because of allegedly pro-western attachments or expressions. These attacks reached periodic climaxes corresponding to the trends of broader Soviet policy, and subsided when that policy altered its direction. The first climax came in 1950 when Dibelius was accused of acting as a front agent for western espionage, and the government tried to force the Church to move its offices from West Berlin into the province of Brandenburg within the political jurisdiction of the Communists.

The second crisis occurred during the so-called "build-up of Socialism" proclaimed by the Soviets in 1952–1953 when the Church was again subjected to severe persecution, but immediately upon the announcement of the new course in 1953 the tensions were relaxed. The granting of permission to hold the 1954 Kirchentag in Leipzig reflected this new trend and was as much a tactical maneuver as the new course itself. The "smile" as well as the "frown" could be useful in promoting long-range Soviet aims. Likewise, the theme of "peaceful coexistence," which expressed itself in Soviet policy during the Berlin and Geneva conferences in 1954 and 1955, had its counterpart in the friendly attempts of the East German government to draw the Church into the so-called Peace Front.

Early in 1957, however, evidences of a new and sharper course began to appear, partly because of the Hungarian crisis, and partly because of the failure of the government to win either a loyalty pledge from the Church or any substantial support for its programs of peace and the National Front. The third major crisis in Church-State relations in East Germany was precipitated by the announcement of the agenda for the Synod of the EKD scheduled to be held March 3–8 in Halle in East Germany. The main theme of this synod was actually to be the merging of the two great Church welfare organizations, the Inner Mission and the Evangelical Hilfswerk, and for this reason the historic city of Halle was chosen, where August Hermann Francke did his pioneer work in the field of Christian service. But before the synod met, another, more controversial, theme had been added; namely, the proposed agreement between the Church and the West German government to establish a military chaplaincy service for the West German army.

The discussion of such a theme at a Church meeting within the territory of the German Democratic Republic, declared government officials, was simply unthinkable. The signing of a military chaplaincy agreement would be regarded as clear evidence that the EKD had become a collaborator with the NATO politicians of West Germany. Unless the Church dropped this discussion from its agenda no delegates to the synod would be permitted to enter the German Democratic Republic. Unwilling to be intimidated by the government, and refusing to admit that the signing of an agreement to provide a spiritual ministry for members of the armed forces implied either approval or disapproval of western military policies, the EKD announced that its synod would be held in Berlin rather than in Halle.

The signing of the agreement on February 22nd by Dibelius and Adenauer, preliminary to its discussion and ratification by the synod, touched off one of the most violent attacks upon Bishop Dibelius ever to appear in the East German press.

The bishop was accused of being tied to America. It was alleged that he had given his blessing to the pact between Adolf Hitler and President von Hindenburg when he had preached in the church at Potsdam in 1933. Now for the second time, declared the Communist press, Dibelius had announced his support of a revived German militarism.

When the synod convened on March 3rd, the chaplaincy agreement was ratified by a vote of 90 to 18, well above the necessary two-thirds majority. A few dissenting voices were raised, such as that of Martin Niemoeller, who felt that an open discussion of the matter in the synod should have preceded the actual signing of the agreement by Dibelius and Adenauer. Most of the members of the synod, however, looked upon the agreement simply as a confirmation of the right of the Church to carry on a spiritual ministry among those of its members whose special service to the government happened to take them away from their home congregations. Synodical delegates from the Churches within the German Democratic Republic, although not directly affected by this agreement, voted in favor of it without exception.

To demonstrate that the proposed agreement with the West Ger-

man government was not a political move, Bishop Dibelius had written to the Minister of Defense of the German Democratic Republic
on February 8, 1957, indicating the desire of the Church to establish
a similar understanding with the East German government. Defense
Minister Willi Stoph's reply made it clear that the East German
government had no intention of even discussing this subject with the
Church. He also informed the bishop that so far as he knew no wish
had ever been expressed by any member of the National People's
Army for the spiritual counsel of a military chaplain.

On March 7th, immediately after the ratification of the chaplaincy
agreement, the German Democratic Republic announced the creation of a State Secretariat for Church Affairs in the East German
government. Werner Eggerath, former East German Minister to
Rumania, and a thoroughgoing Communist, was appointed to fill
the position. The erection of this new office indicated a significant
shift in government policy. Relations with the Church had previously been handled by Deputy Prime Minister Otto Nuschke, Chairman of the Christian Democratic Union and himself a member of
the Evangelical Church. The Office of Church Relations, which had
been under Nuschke's supervision, was now eliminated, and its responsibilities were handed over to Eggerath.

This organizational change brought the machinery of the East
German government for dealing with the Church more closely into
harmony with other Communist-bloc States of eastern Europe. This
implied that it was the ultimate intention of the SED and of the
government to bring the Church under the control of the State, as
in Hungary and Czechoslovakia.

As the first step in the process, the government announced that it
would have no further dealings with any representative of the Church
who was not a resident of the German Democratic Republic. It took
the position that by adopting the chaplaincy agreement the leadership of the EKD had chosen to line up with NATO, and thereby
had disqualified itself as a spokesman for Churches located within
the jurisdiction of the German Democratic Republic.

Shortly after his appointment to office, Werner Eggerath extended
an invitation to all of the bishops of the German Democratic Republic calling for an open and friendly conference "without fronts
and without demands." Neither Dibelius nor Grueber received in-

vitations, since both of them were residents of West Berlin. Because these two men were left out, the other bishops also refused to accept the invitation, but suggested instead that Eggerath receive a Church delegation to discuss the question of a more inclusive consultation. The State secretary, however, refused the suggestion and expressed his regrets that the intended "new beginning" had been frustrated. He described the attitude of the bishops as a disavowal of the government which might have serious negative implications.

The new policy was further reflected in the fact that Bishop Dibelius was denied permission to enter the German Democratic Republic even for the purpose of conducting Church functions in his capacity as Bishop of Berlin-Brandenburg. At no time since then has the bishop been permitted to visit any part of his diocese lying outside Berlin.

Dr. Heinrich Grueber, official representative of the EKD to the East German government, was also made to feel the force of the new policy. When he tried to approach Eggerath personally to facilitate a conference of the East German bishops, his efforts were rejected, and he was given to understand that as a representative of the NATO-dominated EKD, he himself would no longer be welcome in the new government office for Church affairs. Considering the ready reception that Grueber had always found in dealing with the officials of the East German government, this brusque rejection at the hands of Werner Eggerath must be understood as marking a distinctly new era in Church-State relationships in East Germany.

The intentions of the new Church secretariat were made clear in the first letter which went out to all of the bishops in the German Democratic Republic. The bishops were requested to recommend to the pastors of their respective Churches that their Easter sermons encourage the rejection of the atomic bomb and advocate the peaceful use of atomic energy. Each of the bishops was asked to respond to Eggerath's letter.

There then followed an exchange of correspondence between Eggerath and Bishop Moritz Mitzenheim of Thuringia, senior Evangelical bishop resident in the German Democratic Republic. It seemed strange, Mitzenheim pointed out, that such a request should be made, because the synod of the EKD had long ago made clear the Church's official rejection of the use of atomic weapons. He warned Eggerath against any attempt to split the Evangelical Church by discrediting its leadership. Eggerath insisted that this was in no sense the intention of the East German government, but reminded Mitzenheim that it was now the official policy of the East German government not to permit any person who favored NATO politics to enter the territory of the East German Republic. This policy, he said, applied to Bishop Dibelius and other members of the Evangelical Church as well.

Mitzenheim replied that he did not understand how it would be possible to clarify the many pending problems between Church and State when the East German government refused to confer as long as Bishop Dibelius was present. Dibelius, Mitzenheim pointed out, was not only head of one of the Churches in East Germany but also Chairman of the Council of the EKD, to which all German Churches belonged. Discussions with only a part of the Church would not be fruitful in solving the general issues dividing Church and State.

Eggerath's reply indicated clearly the desire of the East German government to drive a wedge into the united front of the Evangelical Church in Germany. It was his understanding, he declared, that any bishop in the German Democratic Republic ought to be able to speak with authority on behalf of his particular Church and that further authority was unnecessary in dealings with the East German government. Obviously, the new Church secretariat would much prefer to deal individually with bishops and with Churches, and even with individual pastors, rather than with a united Church organization. "If the bishops in our republic who are citizens of the German Democratic Republic stand solidly with Bishop Dibelius and his political activity," Eggerath observed, "that is extremely regrettable." However, he added, presuming that his invitation to the bishops had probably been rejected under pressure, he would still be happy if it were possible for them to follow his original suggestion.

Mitzenheim's reply made it clear that this rejection represented the thoroughly discussed and united free opinion of all the bishops of East Germany, and reminded Eggerath that the Church had been waiting for fourteen months for an answer to a series of formal complaints it had prepared for the prime minister. Eggerath terminated the correspondence with a curt reply, four lines in length, the essence of which was contained in one sentence: "An answer to this letter does not appear to me to be, at this moment, necessary."

Additional evidences of the new government policy continued to appear in the weeks following the Synod of Berlin. Although invitations had been extended and the government of East Germany had agreed to the holding of the 1957 Kirchentag at Erfurt in Thuringia, certain conditions were now attached which made this impossible.

Karl Maron informed Dr. von Thadden-Trieglaff, Kirchentag president, that recent developments such as the Kirchentag in Frankfurt, the agenda of the General Synod, and the signing of the military chaplaincy agreement, indicated that West German militarists and imperialists were working in close connection with some of the leaders of the Church and were attempting to misuse Church agencies in the interests of NATO politics. For this reason, he said, any general all-German mass meeting to be held in the East German Republic must give assurance that no such misuse of its facilities would take place.

Only if the leadership of the Kirchentag could guarantee that everything would be excluded from the program of the Kirchentag that might strengthen NATO could permission be granted for the Erfurt meetings. The Kirchentag leadership must obligate itself not to sponsor the appearance of any individual on its program who was a NATO supporter. Guarantees must be given that there would be no repetition of the indignities suffered by East German political leaders at the Frankfurt Kirchentag in 1956. Finally, there must be opportunity for representatives of the East German government to appear on the platform at the Kirchentag in the interests of government-sponsored peace policies.

Although Dr. von Thadden attempted to reassure Mr. Maron of the nonpolitical character of the Kirchentag, no discussion could induce the East German government to alter its stated conditions. The result was that in mid-April, 1957, Dr. von Thadden announced that the plans for the Erfurt rally had been canceled.

Elections in the German Democratic Republic in June afforded another opportunity for identifying the church with the NATO politics of the West. As usual, a single list of candidates was prepared, and as the election approached, members of the Church feared recrimination if they did not participate. The EKD therefore authorized Dr. Grueber and Dr. Heinemann, former lay president of EKD, to visit Prime Minister Grotewohl and express this concern of the Church. It was, however, not possible to arrange a conference either with the prime minister or with State Secretary Eggerath; Grueber therefore directed a letter to Grotewohl in which he asked assurance that those who could not participate on conscientious grounds would suffer no reprisals from the State. And when three-fourths of the Protestant pastors in East Germany refused to vote in the election, it was interpreted as another evidence of the Church's subservience to the spirit of NATO politics.

During the campaign itself, Bishop Dibelius was subjected to renewed vilification. A preelection poster depicting Dibelius with wings but carrying an atomic bomb bore the caption, "Von Himmler hoch, da komm ich her." This was a word play on the familiar German Christmas carol "From Heaven above to earth I come," but the name of Hitler's notorious anti-Jewish lieutenant Heinrich Himmler had been inserted in place of the word for heaven. When Bishop Dibelius went to East Berlin to consecrate a new church, local parishioners hurriedly removed a wall slogan bracketing Dibelius' name with that of a convicted sex criminal named Balluseck as one of the great despoilers of German youth.

The bishop struck back at his critics both in letters to his own pastors in Berlin-Brandenburg and from his pulpit in East Berlin. In his pastoral letter he called attention to the fact that he had been prevented from making official visitations within his Church, and observed that during the Nazi times the State had interfered in a similar fashion. But, he said, in case of such interference the final result had usually been that the inner strength of the Church had been deepened. In a sermon delivered in St. Mary's Church, he made it clear that it was the task of the Church to stand firmly for truth and truthfulness in public affairs even when it became necessary to criticize the official social and political system.

Hopes of the SED that a wedge might be driven between Dibelius and the Churches of East Germany by such frontal attacks upon the bishop were doomed to disappointment. Dibelius' own Church of Berlin-Brandenburg declared on May 8th: "The synod refuses to separate itself from the bishop who has been called to be its spiritual leader. The synod expects that the responsible organs of the state will also reject attacks of this kind against the bishop and the Church." Similar sentiments were echoed by the Council of the EKD, the Conference of Bishops of the East German Churches, the General Synod of the United Lutheran Church, the Council of the

Evangelical Church of the Union, and by individual Church synods throughout East Germany.

Much less spectacular but potentially more effective than simple name calling and ridicule of the bishop was the technique of singling out individual pastors or groups of pastors either for especially favorable treatment or for attack. Following his failure to secure a conference of East German bishops on his own terms, Werner Eggerath launched a series of conversations between Church and State officials on the district level. Parish members, pastors, and superintendents were urged to separate themselves from "reactionary Church leaderships" and to seize the initiative in improving relationships between the Church and the State in their communities. Beginning July 1, 1957, it was announced that the financial payments which had previously been channeled through central offices in Berlin would in the future be paid through the district councils. Local authorities would thus have greater opportunity to reward cooperative pastors and Church administrations and to penalize the uncooperative. Among those so encouraged was the small group of so-called "progressive pastors" whose monthly publication, *Glaube und Gewissen*, openly advocated the support of the National Front.

On the negative side many attempts were made to discredit pastors and Church leaders. Pastors who had been especially successful in conducting Christian youth programs in their parishes or who had been able to prevent a large participation in the Communist Youth Dedication were attacked on trumped-up charges in the local press. Children from the Confirmation classes were questioned under pressure for bits of information that could be exaggerated into monstrous tales. Following an instruction hour in one church, for example, a group of fun-loving boys went out the main church door and held it shut after they were out. The pastor tried to open it from the inside, but the boys, not realizing it was the pastor inside, held the door shut. Finally the pastor got his foot through the crack and in so doing bruised the shin of one of the boys. The local Communist press seized upon this insignificant incident and prepared a front-page feature article to the effect that the pastor had kicked one of his confirmands and badly abused him. A public rally was called in the community, and party members were given the privilege of the platform to denounce the pastor and to testify that he was unfit to deal with youth.

Minor disciplinary actions in confirmation classes were likewise exaggerated. A pastor who had boxed the ears of a recalcitrant four-teen-year-old was publicly humiliated and sentenced to ten weeks in jail for abusing the youth. Another pastor who had objected to the staging of a practice session of the local volunteer fire department at the same time as Church services were being held on Sunday was scored mercilessly by the local newspaper as an enemy of the people. Any loyal and cooperative citizen should know that a volunteer fire department that was risking life and health in a self-sacrificing way to protect the community had to have practice in order to be ready for emergencies.

One of the most common grounds of accusation against pastors was that they had denied Christian burial services to families who had either resigned their membership or were under Church discipline. Actions of this kind, which were in accord with regulations long fol-lowed by the Church, were interpreted as evidence of the pastor's in-humanity and lack of sympathy and understanding for people in distress.

In this organized campaign to discredit individual pastors the services of the secret police were widely and effectively employed. One pastor was summoned twice for interviews by the secret police in the fall of 1957 and accused of having spoken against Sunday work by the farmers in his parish. Although no action was taken against him, he was warned that the police were not through gathering material about him. A few months later, in a funeral sermon, the same pastor contrasted the resurrection hope of the Christian with the materialist's lack of hope for the life hereafter. A leading party functionary who attended the service remarked, "With this sermon the pastor has dug his own grave, for this was agitation against the German Democratic Republic and the Soviet Union."

Not long thereafter secret police agents came to the pastor and accused him of preventing the children in his parish from attending the Socialist Youth Dedication and of influencing his young people by giving them gifts of chocolate from packages he received from West Germany. A few days later the local newspaper carried a head-line article entitled "Pastor Works Against Free German Youth with Chocolate," describing the pastor as a subversive western agent in the community.

From an East German pastor who was eventually forced to flee for his life came an astonishing report of threatenings and intimidations from the secret police which extended over a period of three years. In the summer of 1955 the pastor was visited by two men who requested him to report on political conditions in his village. When he refused to do so, suggesting that there were plenty of party men in the village better qualified for such service, the agents told him they trusted his honesty more than theirs. An offer to pay for the motorcycle which the pastor had recently purchased failed to change his mind, and the agents left him. A few weeks later one of them returned and demanded political reports on the activities of pastors in the district and copies of the pastoral letters written by the superintendent and the bishop.

When the pastor refused again, an article appeared in the local newspaper accusing him of heading reactionary forces at work in the community.

Several times during the succeeding months he was visited by members of the secret police who alternately made promises and issued threats as they sought to enlist his services. More articles appeared in the newspapers, accusing him of abusing the children in his Confirmation class and of working subversively against the government. Visits of the secret police continued. The pastor was requested to submit reports on the synodical meetings of his Church, and in the summer of 1958, when he applied for permission to visit West Germany, the secret police appeared in his home and gave orders that during his visit he should observe western military installations and troop movements and also get in touch with pastors who might be open to propaganda material. Any funds he might need to carry out the assignments would be provided for him. Once again he refused to comply.

Although he returned to East Germany following his summer vacation, the pressures became so great upon him as the autumn progressed that he was no longer able to continue his work. He and his wife, therefore, found an occasion to visit West Berlin, and while there they joined the ranks of political refugees.

In addition to threats, rumors, public denunciation meetings, and newspaper attacks, arrests were also employed to discredit the pastors in the eyes of the community. At the beginning of January, 1957, the official prayer list of the EKD in Berlin contained only seven names, but by the end of the year the number had reached twenty-two. The arrest and imprisonment of Dr. Siegfried Schmutzler, pastor for students at the University of Leipzig, illustrated one of the most dramatic of the Communist techniques, namely, the "show trial."

Dr. Schmutzler, whose sermons, Bible studies, and personal counseling among university students had made him an extremely popular figure, was arrested in his home in Leipzig on April 5, 1957. Shortly thereafter his office and his library were searched and certain books and files confiscated which became the basis for a long investigation culminating in a trial in the district court of Leipzig late in November. During this extended period of detention Dr. Schmutzler was permitted to confer with no one, and the haggard and exhausted appearance which he presented at the trial suggested very strongly that his plea of guilty to the State's charge of "agitation to boycott the republic" came as a result of severe mental and physical fatigue.

Dr. Schmutzler was sentenced to five years' imprisonment, and every effort up to the present time to secure a shortening of his term has proved fruitless.

The immediate cause of Schmutzler's arrest was an evangelization tour during which he visited several congregations in the industrial area of Boehlen. In the course of his lectures and discussions Dr. Schmutzler declared that the Christian was obligated to love all men, even war criminals. He also spoke critically of the common practice of requiring factory work on Sundays, to the detriment of the worship of God. Finally, he expressed concern that the problems of the aged and invalid workers were not being adequately met. On the grounds of these statements Dr. Schmutzler was accused of sowing dissension among the workers and undermining the Five-Year Plan.

West German books, allegedly filled with hatred and with slander concerning the Communist regime, were found in Dr. Schmutzler's library, and he was accused of using them to mislead the students in his discussion groups. The three books specifically mentioned were George Orwell's *1984*, Wolfgang Leonhart's *Child of the Revolution*, and Eric Wendland's *The Church in Modern Society*.

In the course of the trial a witness was produced who accused Schmutzler of saying that all who sought to enlist young people for the Socialist Youth Dedication should have a millstone placed about their necks and be drowned in the depth of the sea. On the basis of this inaccurately quoted statement, taken entirely out of the context in which it had been spoken, the State officially accused Dr. Schmutzler of "inciting to murder."

The pastor was further accused of having established illegal cell groups among his students for the purpose of stimulating unrest and dissatisfaction in the university and distributing information which Schmutzler allegedly was receiving from NATO agencies in West Germany and in foreign countries. He was also accused of expressing sympathy with the Hungarian revolt and of favoring the military chaplaincy agreement approved by the Synod of EKD in Berlin.

As the trial opened the East German press emphasized the fact that Schmutzler was not being tried for ideological differences with the government but for violations of the law. As if to demonstrate its good will, the State permitted a whole series of character witnesses to speak on behalf of Schmutzler. Although the trial was announced as open to the public, only 150 tickets were distributed, and most of them went to workers' groups, the Free German Youth, and representatives of the East press. Correspondents from western newspapers were not admitted, and Schmutzler's own Lutheran Church of Saxony was assigned only three tickets, one of which was used by the bishop, Dr. Noth. Representatives of the Church were not permitted to take any notes during the trial.

Because Dr. Schmutzler was kept under careful surveillance from the time of his arrest, it was impossible to ascertain whether his confession of guilt was the result of physical and mental pressure. In any event, his statements to the effect that he had learned a great deal and that he believed the Church must finally reconstruct its thinking in the matter of social relationships was seized upon by the East press as conclusive evidence that Schmutzler had no claim to the role of martyr.

When the trial was over and Schmutzler had been sentenced to a five-year prison term, the Lutheran Church of Saxony issued an official statement in which it indicated that it was not particularly interested in creating the role of a martyr for one of its pastors but that it was very eager to keep the factual record straight. If Dr. Schmutzler had not handled himself properly in all political matters, this was a matter of deep regret. However, it was perfectly clear that he had on many occasions also pointed out publicly the responsibility of obedience which the Christ must bear toward existing governmental powers.

The student congregations, however, with which Dr. Schmutzler had worked, were in no sense illegal organizations but were a regular part of the life of the Church. Nor were the Evangelical academies, either in West or in East Germany, in any sense agencies of NATO. Their purpose was to promote vigorous exchanges of opinion and mutual understanding between people. Anyone who was honestly seeking for peace and understanding and for reunification, it seemed to the Saxon Church, ought to welcome and further such contacts instead of misinterpreting their intentions.

But the East press and the East government were not eager to have the record set straight. The purpose of the Schmutzler trial and of the entire current series of attacks upon pastors was to discredit the Church and the ministry in the eyes of the public as unpatriotic and even subversive. The substance of the comment which appeared in *Der Morgen* on November 30, 1957, appeared in practically every newspaper throughout the German Democratic Republic: "The trial is a clear warning to those circles within the Church which maintain close connections with the Adenauer regime, and which seek to carry out their NATO politics to the detriment of our republic. At the same time it is an admonition to loyalty for the Church circles within the German Democratic Republic. Enemies of our State will be met with the full force of the law. Schmutzlers will always suffer shipwreck here."

Not long after the close of the Schmutzler trial, two leading laymen from the Church administration of Madgeburg were brought to trial for alleged illegal currency transactions. Ever since the currency reform in 1948, East and West Germany had used different currencies. Since the West mark was always four to seven times as valuable as the East mark, the East German government felt it necessary to place rigid regulations upon the export and import of its own and all foreign currencies. This created a special problem for Berlin, since many residents of East Berlin were employed in West Berlin, and vice versa. Such people ordinarily received a portion of their wages in East marks and a portion in West marks with the tacit approval of both governments, and this led inevitably to at least a limited transfer of East and West marks across the sector lines.

The Church became involved in problems of currency exchange when West Berliners who worked in the East Sector paid their Church taxes in West Berlin with East marks. Sunday offering plates in West Berlin churches always included some East marks. Since the Church carried on its work in both sectors, it was very simple to carry the East marks across the line and deposit them in an East Berlin bank.

Strictly speaking, such transfers were not authorized by the law, but the East German government was fully informed of them and legal negotiations had been under way for many months to modify the currency regulations to conform to the practice. The government was actually very eager to secure the return of its controlled currency, large amounts of which tended to leave the republic illegally, either in the pockets of the refugees who fled each month to West Germany, or in the pockets of East German citizens who purchased goods in the more attractively stocked shops of West Berlin. In the latter case, the East Germans had to smuggle their East marks across the border and exchange them at the rate of four or five to one in West Berlin currency-exchange booths.

One day in October, when the volume of illegal currency transactions had reached a dangerously high point, the East German government suddenly replaced its entire supply of currency with a new issue, and gave its citizens twenty-four hours in which to make the exchange. On hand at the time in the Church headquarters in West Berlin were 400,000 East marks. In order to avoid losing this amount, Dr. Kurt Scharf personally carried the money to the city of Magdeburg and turned it over to the president of the Church consistory, Dr. Kurt Gruenbaum. When Dr. Gruenbaum and his colleague Dr. Siegfried Klewitz presented this money for exchange in Magdeburg, both were arrested for the illegal transfer of currency from West Berlin.

In the hearings which followed, the Church and its officials were accused of smuggling money into the East German Republic for speculative purposes and to finance subversive activity against the government. In its diligence to unearth evidence in support of its charges, the People's Court in Magdeburg subjected one leading member of the Church administration to such strenuous questioning, in spite of a well-known heart ailment, that he died of the effects. Two other staff members, threatened with arrest if they refused to serve as spies for the secret police, took refuge in flight to West Germany.

In an effort to clarify its position, the Church issued a complete statement explaining the source of the money and the purpose for which it was to be used. Dr. Kurt Scharf went voluntarily to the secret police to explain that he had personally carried the money to Magdeburg, and during the trial in Magdeburg again appeared as a witness in defense of Gruenbaum and Klewitz. Nevertheless, on January 24, 1958, both men were given prison sentences for violation of the currency laws of the East German Republic. However, since the main political purposes had already been achieved through the publicity of the proceedings, the actual prison sentences were suspended.

Along with the attempt to drive a wedge between the pastors and the Church membership went an accelerated ideological program. As early as 1956 a new emphasis upon the conflict between scientific materialism and religion had appeared in publications of the Ministry of National Defense. Two pamphlets entitled "Faith or Knowledge," by Herbert Gute and Hans Ritter, and "Scientific Knowledge and Religious Prejudice," by G. A. Gurgow, appeared during the course of the year.

Following the thirtieth Conference of the Central Committee of the SED in January, 1957, an article by Hermann Matern in the periodical *Neuer Weg* reported a special emphasis upon party ideology and a summons to all party members to lead an offensive against the politics of revisionism. Marxism-Leninism, he said, recognized that it might be necessary to accept coexistence in world politics but could never recognize coexistence in questions of ideology. Religions and Church organizations could only be looked upon as organs of middle-class reaction that helped to promote the exploitation of the working classes.

The attack against the Church and religion in both schools and factories must therefore be carried forward. Even when atheistic intentions were concealed through the use of such slogans as "Education for Socialism" and the "Building of the Socialistic Conscience," it should be understood that the basic principle was still that of dialectic and historical materialism.

In line with the new ideological emphasis, the task of distributing atheistic propaganda was transferred from the Ministry of Culture to the Society for the Furtherance of Scientific Knowledge, an organization so outspokenly atheistic that even the East CDU had criticized its propaganda methods as offensive to people with Christian convictions. By the fall of 1957 the new program was well organized and prepared to move forward in coordination with the defamatory attacks upon pastors and Church leaders.

The launching of the campaign for the fourth Youth Dedication late in September, 1957, offered an excellent opportunity. Two events reflected the special significance the party placed upon this particular campaign. During the course of the third Youth Dedication, which was carried through in the atmosphere of coexistence, the textbook for the Youth Dedication, *Weltall, Erde, Mensch*, had actually been withdrawn and replaced by another gift book called *Unser Deutschland*. This book laid primary stress upon the national culture and was by no means as sharply ideological as the standard text had been. Dr. Paul Wandel, Secretary for Culture and Education in the Central Committee in the SED, had introduced this change without the knowledge of Party Secretary Walter Ulbricht. When Ulbricht discovered it, he immediately restored *Weltall, Erde, Mensch* to its official status as the textbook for the Youth Dedication, and fired Wandel from his post on the Central Committee. "When I have time," declared Ulbricht, "I also enjoy walking in the woods, but I do not approve treating education and the Youth Dedication as a lark through forest and meadow."

The second significant sign was the fact that Walter Ulbricht himself opened the campaign for the fourth Youth Dedication with a public address delivered in Sonneberg on September 29th. Three points made by the party secretary in his speech indicated the new importance that was being attached to the Youth Dedication. First, he established a direct connection with the old ceremony of the Freethinkers, pointing out that he himself had participated in such a rite at Eastertime in 1907. The anti-Church character of the Youth Dedication was thereby made clear. In the second place, Ulbricht called for the participation of all children in the Youth Dedication, "regardless of what world view their parents may have, or in what world view they have thus far been brought up." This made it clear that a strenuous enlistment campaign was impending in which religious objections would be treated as unimportant. Finally, Ulbricht outlined the obligation of all organizations, including the official educational agencies of the State, to cooperate in carrying out such a program. All pretensions of the Youth Dedication as a privately sponsored function were thus thrown overboard.

To such a clear statement by the first secretary of the SED the Churches could not remain silent. The East Conference of Evangelical Bishops immediately dispatched a letter to Prime Minister Grotewohl protesting against the statements of Ulbricht as contradictions of previous assurances by the State. Both Evangelical and Roman Catholic bishops prepared pulpit proclamations, to be read in all congregations in East Germany, declaring that participation in the Youth Dedication and in the Christian Confirmation were incompatible.

On October 19th, even before the pulpit declaration of the Evangelical bishops was scheduled to be read, Karl Maron, Minister of the Interior, published a reply accusing the Church of seeking to control the thinking of its members and thereby violating the freedom of conscience of citizens in the German Democratic Republic.

More significant was the note of assurance and triumph in his letter, born of the successful launching of Sputnik by the Soviet Union in the first days of October. Triumphs of technology such as this, thought Maron, ought to make it clear that the future belonged to science and not to religion. Other Communist leaders joined Ulbricht in proclaiming the obsolescence of faith. "Man," he exulted, "is already in a position to remove mountains." Gerhard Grueneberg, first party secretary of the District of Frankfurt, told the opening session of the Youth Dedication course that man and science would soon be regarded as the final authority for all questions of life: "Man is the most powerful of all creatures, and there is no one higher than he." Poems and songs such as that by Elsa Czech-Kuckhof put the same ideas in more popular form: "My heart is filled with pride, with reverence and with love for the scientific giants who are opening the door to the universe for all mankind. And together with me, millions of others are hoping that this sublime new star may finally bring to pass that which the Star of Bethlehem promised in vain: peace on earth."

The highest point of the new doxology to science was reached by the East Berlin *Freie Welt*, which glowingly asserted that Communism had now been able "to continue the creative work of God and to outdo Him. With Sputnik," it boasted, "the eighth day of creation has begun. The Bible tells about the seven others, and what is said is but a dream of fantasy. But the eighth day of creation, which has given to the earth its second moon, is a reality, a true act of socialistic creativity. With such the Bible cannot compete."

The new and accelerated campaign for the Youth Dedication launched under the rising star of Sputnik aimed to discredit the Church just as did the open defamations and show trials of pastors which were going on at the same time. By taking the position that a child might participate in both Confirmation and Youth Dedication, Communist leaders sought to stigmatize the Church as the agency which was restricting free choice of the youth. When the Church cited documented instances in which children who had refused to take part in the Youth Dedications were discriminated against in schools, the Communists simply countered by holding before the young people the wealth of opportunities that would come to those who joined in the victory march of Socialism.

It was on the parish levels that the real decisions had to be made. The Communist newspaper *Freie Erde*, in Griefswald, made the implications for a young person very clear. "A public confession in support of the objectives of our State can only be helpful in promoting the further development of the children," it declared. If such a profession is not made, there is serious question "whether such children should continue in the high schools or whether they should be permitted to enter the profession of teaching." In one community in North Germany nine parents of children who had refused to join the Youth Dedication directed a letter of protest to their Church superintendent requesting help because their children had been denied entrance to high school. In another community on the Baltic Sea three families, after having resisted all kinds of pressures both within and outside school for several weeks, were presented with a written ultimatum by a member of the Parents' Council, stating that participation in the Youth Dedication had officially been made a condition for admission to high school in their community.

In another community parents who registered their children as beginners in school were asked to sign a certificate on which was written, "I declare that after my child has completed his elementary school training, I will send him to the Youth Dedication."

In Karl Marx Stadt lists of factory employees whose children were completing the elementary school were distributed to members of the party organization in the factories with instructions to see that everyone participated in the Youth Dedication.

Bishop Dibelius described a typical example of the pressures for participation. "There is a visit from the schoolteacher hammering into the family what he has been saying in the classroom repeatedly: 'No promotion for those who stay away from the Youth Dedication.' The visit to the family is followed by similar pressure on the child's father from a selected party functionary, while the mother is taken in hand by an activist of the Women's Democratic League. If this has not been sufficient, the appointed chief of the Socialist House Community has the next turn, possibly to be supplemented by the Communist block captain. All of them find their objectives underlined by radio and press, and the child himself is already expected to know the right answer to this question: 'Are you going to ruin not only your own life but also the work and the living of your father and mother?'"

Under pressures such as these, said the bishop, it is a miracle that there are families that still stand up. Declarations of the Church could only serve to encourage and to strengthen the conviction of such people in the moment of decision. This was the intent of the pulpit proclamation read from the pulpit of every church in East Germany late in October, 1957. "As your bishops, we warn that the decision between Youth Dedication and Confirmation affects the souls of your children and your own soul's salvation. Our answer to the new propaganda must be that we take Confirmation instruction much more seriously than ever and that together with our children we remain unyieldingly faithful to God and to the Church of Jesus Christ.

"Threats should not frighten us. In the years of the great Church struggles we have constantly experienced that God supports His own through all sorts of tribulations. He will not leave us without His help.

"It is written, 'You should obey God rather than man.' And our

Saviour Jesus Christ says, 'Whoever confesses me before men, him will I also confess before my Father which is in heaven.' "

As the campaign for the Youth Dedication developed, the official Communist spokesmen left no doubt about the atheistic emphasis it was now seeking to promote. Professor Hermann Duncker told a workshop of the Central Committee for the Youth Dedication that "every materialism which desires to be honest and logical must be atheistic. However, we ought to remember that the word 'atheistic' is a purely negative word. It declares that we reject the idea of God. But it does not indicate that which we offer in its place. I believe that one can speak wonderfully about atheism without mentioning that word at all. It is possible to make it clear to the young people that we believe in humanity . . . and that mankind can achieve everything that is necessary for the development of society. This faith in man is the thing that we offer in place of faith in God."

Ulbricht himself urged all youth to attend in order that they might discover "that man is able to change the world" and that their lives were in no sense dependent "upon any supernatural powers." Karl Namokel, first secretary of the Central Council for the Free German Youth, also added his confirmation: "We desire that every young person shall have a clear understanding for what is new. We desire that he shall recognize that the earth was not created by a higher being but that it came into existence by entirely natural processes."

The new form of the pledge adopted for the fourth Youth Dedication also indicated a clearer intention to make of the Youth Dedication an ideological confession of faith. No longer were the young people called upon merely to work for "progress in economy, science, and art," but to dedicate their "entire strength for the great and noble cause of Socialism." If the interpretations of Ulbricht, Duncker, and Namokel were to be taken seriously, the Youth Dedication and its pledge did represent a commitment to an anti-Christian creed and program.

As the year 1957 drew to a close, the Communist leadership in East Germany was following two distinct lines in its effort to split the Evangelical Church. On the negative side, attempts to link the Church and its leadership with the policies of NATO and West German militarism continued in the Communist press. Arrests of pastors and Church workers also continued, in an effort to discredit the clergy in the eyes of the people. The new ideological emphasis, sparked by the recent Soviet achievements in the field of science, represented the positive phase of the program. Thrusting all previous pretense aside, the Socialist State declared its open sponsorship of the Youth Dedication and other ceremonials through which it proposed to wean away the loyalty of the people from the Church and attach it instead to the State. The large increase of participation in the fourth Youth Dedication in the spring of 1958 showed alarming progress toward the achievement of communistic goals.

THIRTEEN

A TRUCE OF UNCERTAINTY

One of the most striking characteristics of the ideological crusade in East Germany during 1958 was the introduction of a series of pseudoreligious ceremonies to compete with the Christian rites of baptism, marriage, and burial. The Communists recognized in these crucial human experiences an educational opportunity which they could ill afford to ignore. The elaborate procedures were so obviously patterned after the Christian ceremonies as to raise serious question concerning Communist originality. But they explained such similarity as only a temporary concession to the personal orientation of the people during the transition period from capitalism to Socialism. Later on, the preeminence of the group orientation would render such concessions unnecessary.

One of the first name-giving ceremonies was held in Altenburg, in Thuringia, on Christmas Day, 1957. Every effort was expended to make it appear as a reasonably acceptable substitute for the Christian sacrament of baptism, as universally practiced by the Churches in East Germany. A special room was fitted out in City Hall, and equipped with an organ and with lighted candles. The table used by the presiding official was festively decked with flowers, and in the background stood a flag-draped bust of President Wilhelm Pieck.

In keeping with the dignity of the occasion, an organist played Handel's "Largo" as parents and sponsors assembled in the pseudo-chapel. The speaker of the City Council, a specially selected orator, delivered the festival address, reminding the parents that the socialistic name-giving was a confession of allegiance to the Workers' and Peasants' State and that the infant in arms was being initiated into the ranks of fighters for peace, Socialism, and progress.

"You should take care, dear parents and relatives," intoned the orator, "that from earliest childhood on, this child is trained as an enthusiastic, socially conscious individual. He is destined to experience not only the socialistic but also the communistic social order. To this end you must be his conscious guide and director. All who are gathered here I admonish to devote their strength to the building of Socialism and the maintenance of peace."

After the parents had pledged themselves to bring their child up as a true Socialist, a savings book valued at 100 marks was given to them, accompanied by the good wishes of the mayor of the city and the text of the festival address. The district leadership of the SED provided an appropriate certificate, and the sponsors were invited to sign it, just as they might have signed a baptismal certificate. The ceremony was also entered in the family record book. As the music resumed and the parents and their well-wishers left the office, they were greeted by a delegation of Young Pioneers, who filled their arms with bouquets of festive flowers.

The intention to make of this ceremony a Communist confessional was clearly evident in a subsequent news report. "Many people are probably wondering why this name-giving ceremony is being carried through, and who may take part. Increasing numbers of our citizenry, especially members of the SED, are expressing the wish to have their children educated atheistically. Consequently, ceremonies of this kind are becoming a social necessity. This begins with our small children, continues through their entry into the schools and through the Youth Dedication, and finds its climax in the festival marriage ceremony at the State offices."

In Stalinstadt, the model city of Socialism, a remarkable document appeared, spelling out detailed procedures, not only for the name-giving ceremony, but for socialistic marriages and burials as well. In its basic statement of principle this document announced that these great life experiences were finally to be freed from the yoke of exploitation imposed upon them by the Church, and assume their proper role as aspects of the developing socialistic community. Their content was to be a "socialistic humanism, atheistic in character, which recognizes no higher reality than mankind, working and fighting for peace, democracy, and Socialism."

Before each ceremony, whether name-giving, marriage, or burial, thorough and careful preparatory conversations were to be conducted by a State official, in order to make it clear to the principals that the vows and pledges undertaken involved a personal commitment to Socialism. Any unclarity at this point, however, would vanish for the young bridal couple, when they finally confronted the State official and recited their marriage vow: "Being responsible to all working people, to ourselves and to each other, we pledge to regard our marriage contracted this day in mutual love as a community founded for life. We vow to strengthen by concerted efforts the Socialist achievements, and the power of the workers and peasants. . . ." Should it be thought necessary, a warning word might be spoken to the young people lest they tend to view their marriage in any sense as bearing religious implications. "Religion is rejected as a safeguard of marriage," declared the manual of practices, "because of the impotence of the Church, the non-existence of God, and the immorality of Church leaders who approve war as a means of governing, and who place woman in a position subordinate to man."

Nowhere was the irreligious character of these ceremonies more painfully apparent than in the prescribed burial rites. Instead of a solemn service of worship bringing the comfort of the Gospel to the bereaved and giving expression to the hope of eternal life and resurrection, the Socialist funeral was presided over by a paid orator who reminded the sorrowing that their loss was also a loss to the labor movement. The achievements of the deceased were to be honored as a symbol of the struggle of all workingmen against exploitation, militarism, and fascism. And finally, those who were left behind were exhorted to close the ranks, and move forward according to the example established by the fallen hero, to the ennobling of life and the perfecting of the only true reality, the Socialist society on earth.

The introduction of these ceremonies in every community in East Germany was accompanied by a vigorous publicity campaign carried on through the press, radio, and mass organizations. The chords of sentiment were played upon through pictures and articles emphasizing the festive character of the socialist name-giving and the marriage ceremony. Statistics were published, conveying the impression that practically everyone in the community was taking part. Financial contributions were solicited from factory unions so that generous gifts could be given to all parents and children who took part in the name-giving. In some communities parents received a congratulatory card from the mayor of the city at the birth of a child, accompanied by an invitation to present the child at city hall for the festive name-giving ceremony. Particularly energetic party members circulated through maternity wards in the hospitals, soliciting participation from new mothers. But not all of the appeals were straightforward. Factory workers or public employees were given to understand that failure to present a child for the name-giving ceremony might prevent promotion on the job, or even cost the job itself. This led to a large number of requests by young parents that pastors baptize their children secretly, sometimes in towns or communities where they were not known.

Similar pressures were exerted on behalf of the socialistic burial ceremony. Bishop Dibelius reported visiting a community of seven thousand people which was normally ministered to by two pastors. He discovered that these two pastors were confronted by the competition of five secular orators, whose services were being constantly urged upon the people by the local newspapers. Widows whose husbands had been employed in factories found it extremely difficult to insist upon a Christian burial service which might jeopardize the payment of the small widow's pension they were entitled to receive from the State.

Together with the Youth Dedication, all of these ceremonies represented the efforts of the Socialist State to wean away the loyalty of the masses of the laity from their Churches. Communists were aware that in the folk Church of East Germany, the ties of large numbers of the people were often formal ones, based upon traditional respect for the institution of the Church and the pastor, and symbolized in the great ceremonial rites of baptism, confirmation, marriage, and burial. If therefore, the pastors could be discredited as unpatriotic or as out-moded, and if acceptable ceremonies with a socialistic content could be imposed upon the people to replace the religious ones, Communist aims might be realized without a direct assault upon the Church itself. Obviously, this would take time, but with the State in com-plete control of all mass media of communication, of all educational opportunities and, increasingly, of all economic opportunities, the Communists could afford to work patiently and consistently toward their professed objectives. If a child refused the socialistic pledge of the Youth Dedication, he would be faced again and again with the same harrowing decision, whether he sought to further his education, to learn a trade, to work in a factory, and inevitably when he sought to establish a home of his own and rear his own family of children in a Socialist State.

It was against this kind of environmental coercion that leaders of the Church protested on behalf of the embattled laity in their con-gregations. The constitutional guarantees of freedom of conscience, and the safeguards against discrimination because of religious beliefs, had become illusions when a totalitarian State put all of its facilities at the disposal of the ideology which openly professed its intention to eliminate religion as a vestige of decadent medieval superstition.

With these concerns uppermost in their minds, leaders of the Church proposed to devote the agenda of the impending Synod of the EKD in April to a discussion of the problems faced by parents and children from Christian homes, who were obligated to attend schools in which educational benefits and advantages were made de-pendent upon the pupil's acceptance of atheism. The church noted with alarm the announcement of the so-called Lange Decree on Febru-ary 12, 1958, placing new restrictions upon the giving of religious instruction. No classes in religion could be held before the regular opening of school in the morning, lest the children not be at their best for the regular classes of the day. Nor might such instruction be given until at least two hours had elapsed following the close of the regular school day. Moreover, any person instructing pupils outside school, in whatever program, was required to demonstrate a positive attitude toward the Workers' and Farmers' State. The director of the public school should have the final decision as to the qualifications of such persons, and he would issue appropriate certificates, renewable every three months and revocable at any time. The responsibility for licensing both catechists and pastors as instructors in religion was thereby placed in the hands of secular school officials, although this was in direct contradiction to the East German Constitution. If the State at some future time should wish to enforce the Lange Decree stringently, it had at hand the instrument for halting religious instruction entirely.

At a conference of village schoolteachers, Fritz Lange, the Minister of Education, also made it clear that teachers in East Germany could not "serve two masters." They were all expected to give positive support to Marxist ideologies, and especially to promote the Youth Dedication among their pupils. Coexistence, Lange observed ominously, was not permissible; no teacher could expect to play the organ or serve the Church in some capacity, and at the same time satisfactorily instruct the children and the youth in the spirit of scientific Socialism.

As soon as the theme was announced for the forthcoming synod, an organized campaign was set in motion by members of the SED in East Germany to force a change in the agenda. Education, it was asserted, was a monopoly of the State, and was therefore beyond the competence of the Church to discuss. Much more appropriate would be a discussion of the issue of atomic rearmament in West Germany and the military chaplaincy agreement which the preceding synod had made with the West German government. The question of atomic rearmament in West Germany became an extremely current subject in the early months of 1958, as the Federal Parliament debated the question of permitting NATO atomic installations within its territory. Very articulate groups within the West German Church bitterly opposed such a step, and they provided strong support for the SED demands that the coming synod place the question of atomic rearmament on its agenda. Walter Ulbricht added the oft-voiced demand that the EKD demonstrate its independence of NATO control by renouncing the military chaplaincy agreement of the previous year.

In an unprecedented campaign, more than five thousand petitions were directed to the synod, demanding an alteration of the agenda.

Most of them came from East German schools, listing the names of teachers, pupils, and school officials. Village councils, trade unions, political and cultural oganizations flooded the Church headquarters with such a volume of petitions that a special three-man committee had to be appointed to read and evaluate them. From Church groups in East Germany, however, the number of requests was very small, though the pacifist-minded *Bruederschaften,* or Brotherhoods, from West Germany, under the leadership of Niemoeller and Heinemann, prepared ten articles they wished the synod to adopt.

Immediately preceding the opening of the synod, the East German press launched massive attacks against the synod and its leading officials. The SED organ *Neues Deutschland* asserted that the "NATO wing," represented by Dibelius, Lilje, and Bishop Bender of Baden, had forced the education theme and had thereby committed a clear provocation against the educational program of the German Democratic Republic. Any member of the synod who accepted this provocation in silence would have to assume serious responsibility as a NATO supporter.

The opening service of the synod was conducted in St. Mary's Church on April 26th, by Bishop Krummacher of Greifswald. Following the service the 120 delegates returned to the Adolf Stoecker Foundation, also in East Berlin, where the first session was to take place. They were greeted upon arrival by a crowd of about two hundred disturbers, who warned them not to take their seats in the convention hall until they had forced the synod's presiding officers to change the agenda of the forthcoming session. Chanting a chorus, interspersed with occasional threats to knock the delegates' brains out, the demonstrators marched around the hall and through the corridors, creating such an uproar that the synod was unable to convene in an orderly fashion. Not until the spokesman of the mob, an elementary-school teacher named Preckel, was allowed to present their demands for a change in the agenda of the synod was it possible for normal parliamentary procedures to be resumed. The synod received Preckel's remarks as information, and then turned to its official agenda as planned.

In the midst of the confusion attending the opening of the synod, Bishop Dibelius delivered his official report as chairman of the Council of EKD. Although he discussed at length the issues of atomic rearmament, and left no doubt that the Evangelical Church in Germany heartily endorsed the outlawing of all atomic weapons by all nations, he strongly opposed the use of a Church synod as a platform for political debate. The issue of a government-sponsored atheistic ideology in education, he declared, was the crying spiritual problem of the Church in East Germany. As high an authority as the Politburo of the Central Committee of the SED had only recently issued a resolution announcing that the foundations of a Communist pattern of life in East Germany had now been well established. The future task of the party must therefore be the application of principles of Communist education to the masses, and not merely to the members of the party. The educational process was to be focused on "an early inculcation of atheism," because belief in a supernatural being "prevents people from putting all their strength into the building of a Communist world society." In all general instruction outlines, priority was to be given to subject Number One: "Atheism, the determining factor in dialectical materialism."

These things, declared the bishop, were no surprise to the Church. It had long been clear that there could be no compromise between the Christian religion and Communism. But never before had such a high party organ as the Central Committee asserted it in such bold language.

In keeping with this new ideological emphasis unlimited propaganda had been directed toward the annulment of Church membership. It had become compulsory for party functionaries to leave the Church. Army officers likewise were required to do so, and common soldiers were occasionally deprived of Bibles discovered in their possession during barracks inspections. Teacher-candidates were being expelled from school for refusal to separate themselves from the Church and from the Christian faith. And within the schools themselves, children were being required to pledge their loyalty to the world concept of materialism. The bishop granted that it was not the task of the Church to write the curriculum for the schools, but it was under obligation to demand that Christian faith and conscience be given proper freedom, and that it not be infringed by acts of violence or intimidation. "It is here," declared the bishop, "that the poisoning of our young people's souls is beginning to bear its bitter fruits. We will not tolerate, however, that the public standard school should continue to mutilate the integrity of the young by adjusting their receptive minds to untruth and dishonesty. It is an unbearable state of affairs that parents should reply to the reports their children bring home from school: 'What the teacher has said is all wrong, but you had better agree with what he says, or you will get neither an apprenticeship nor a transcript for higher education.'"

Just a few weeks previous to the synod, the East Conference of the EKD had submitted a complete memorandum to the government, containing documentation of specific instances cited by the bishop. No reply had been received. At the end of that document, the question had been raised: "Is it possible for those who reject the atheistic world concept to live any longer as citizens of the German Democratic Republic without forfeiting the essential rights of citizenship?" Dibelius raised this question once more, on behalf of more than ten million Protestant Christians living in East Germany, and announced dramatically that he waited for the government's answer.

With the distinct implication that he already knew what the answer would be, Dibelius then directed to the Churches of East Germany a series of suggestions growing out of the prevailing relations between Church and State. It would be necessary, he observed, to make a fresh start in the realm of Christian education, with a much greater stress upon the Christian guidance of the children. Confirmation would have to be reexamined, for it could no longer be regarded as the traditional family ceremony marking the end of a formal course of religious instruction. Its confessional significance must be rediscovered and reemphasized, even though the number of confirmands should drastically decline. The confessional character of Church membership itself would eventually find its expression through a smaller nucleus of people who were Christian by conviction rather than by tradition and who were willing to undertake the high cost of discipleship in a Marxist land.

After the stormy opening sessions, the synod settled down to a careful consideration of its agenda. Two major committees were appointed, one to deal with the education question and one with the question of atomic rearmament. Both issues were thus given consideration on the floor of the synod, and Professor Heinrich Vogel in particular raised an earnestly warning voice against all atomic armaments. Opinions within the synod varied from those of Professor Vogel, who viewed even atomic preparedness as a national sin, to those who could justify before God the possession of equal weapons as a deterrent to the outbreak of war. Common ground of agreement was found in a reaffirmation of the World Council resolutions against atomic warfare and a plea to all the great powers to undertake programs of disarmament, both in atomic and in conventional weapons.

The synod sought to alleviate the fears of the East German government concerning the military chaplaincy agreement of 1957 by reemphasizing the purely spiritual character of the ministry to be carried out among the soldiers of the West German army. Moreover, the synod declared that the agreement had no validity for the Churches in the German Democratic Republic, nor for its members.

In keeping with the recommendations of Bishop Dibelius, the synod urged its member Churches to give special emphasis to the First Article of the Apostles' Creed in their programs of Christian instruction. Forms and methods of religious instruction, and especially of Confirmation practices in all the Churches, were to be given particular attention, in view of the growing successes of the Communist Youth Dedication.

The committee on educational questions decided not to issue a public statement, but rather to seek once more an opportunity to discuss with the government the matters already clearly publicized in the bishop's report. The synod agreed to this procedure, and appointed a committee of five men to seek a conference with State authorities in hopes of securing some modification of the stringent new ideological course.

The synod concluded as dramatically as it had opened. On the closing day Dr. Heinrich Grueber, always a controversial figure, called for the floor and announced his intention of answering the scurrilous attacks which had been made upon Bishop Dibelius, both before and after his report to the synod. It was well known, declared Grueber, that he and Dibelius were not always in agreement on important issues, but for the sake of truth he could not stand by in silence while ill-informed and malicious people deliberately misquoted the bishop and presented a distorted picture of him.

Most of those, said Grueber, who had accused Dibelius of giving his blessing to the regime of Hitler had themselves not even been on hand to witness the courageous resistance which Dibelius had actually shown to the Nazis. Through his active participation in the Confessing Church movement in Berlin, Dibelius had distinguished himself far more than the so-called *Remigranten,* who had fled Berlin during the Nazi times and then had returned with the Russians, well nourished and rested, and established themselves in leading positions at the expense of the leaders of the real resistance movement. The most prominent of the *Remigranten,* though Grueber did not name him, was Communist Party boss Walter Ulbricht, who had spent the war years in the safety of the Soviet Union.

Having spoken courageously in defense of Bishop Dibelius, Grueber sat down, knowing perfectly well that his usefulness as an official Church representative to the East German government was at an end. For the brutal exposure of such a very sensitive matter, Walter Ulbricht could not possibly forgive Grueber.

In one sense this was a very fitting and characteristic conclusion of a stormy career. Always the dramatist, Grueber had chosen this as the final act. Knowing on the basis of Church-State developments of the preceding year that the "point of no return" had been passed, Grueber used this highlighted stage from which to fire his farewell blast against the party leadership in the East. Grueber's influence with the government had been based upon his own praiseworthy record of anti-Nazism and upon his many personal relationships with Communists who had shared with him the suffering of Hitler's concentration camps. Little by little, however, these men disappeared from government positions in East Germany and were replaced by more cynical, doctrinaire Communists to whom personal ties meant nothing.

With the replacement of Otto Nuschke by Werner Eggerath, as the government official responsible for Church affairs, followed by the death of Nuschke in December, 1957, the machinery was ready for the attempt to integrate the Church into the new order. In this machinery there was no place for Grueber, and he could see that his usefulness was past.

Moreover, in all the years of Grueber's mediating service between Church and State, he had never been able to win a response from Walter Ulbricht. Only on one or two occasions had he even spoken with him. This, too, helped to determine the character of Grueber's valedictory address before the synod.

But when other theories have been presented, Grueber's own explanation must also be considered. His long and distinguished record of unselfish service to friendless people and friendless causes lends an undeniable note of sincerity to his straightforward assertion that such falsehood and slander against the bishop he simply could not tolerate, "for the sake of the truth!"

After the conclusion of the synod several weeks went by without any answer by the government to the letter requesting a conference relative to educational questions. Instead, the climate of Church-State relations became progressively worse. Renewed attacks on Bishop Dibelius appeared in the party press. Several members of the synod, particularly Dr. Fraenkel of Goerlitz, were assailed for having characterized the demonstration at the Stoecker Foundation as "organized terrorism." Characterizing themselves as "Spokesmen of the Christian Population," units of the CDU in Thuringia and Mecklenburg launched a flood of telegrams and letters upon the provincial synods which met shortly after the EKD Synod, urging them to denounce atomic rearmament and to annul the military chaplaincy pact. An open letter to all members of the Saxon Synod in Leipzig protested against the decisions of the Berlin Synod. When the Synod of Mecklenburg convened in Schwerin, so many Communist groups demanded a hearing that the regular day's session had to be broken off because of the tumult and the demonstrations. The People's Police were notified of the disturbances and were requested to step in to restore order, but delayed their appearance for more than an hour. The General Synod of the United Evangelical Lutheran Church, which had scheduled its tenth anniversary meeting in Eisenach in June, was forced to move its sessions to Berlin when West German leaders were denied entry permits because of their alleged subservience to NATO.

A new wave of arrests among the clergy, both Protestant and Roman Catholic, broke out. The Evangelical prayer list, including pastors and Church workers in prison, rose to twenty-four by May 6th, and a few weeks later a mass rally of both Protestants and Catholics assembled in the great cathedral of Naumburg to protest the arrest of Catholic clergy and the confiscation of books in Church

and private libraries. A window display of "filthy and trashy" literature gathered from these libraries in Naumburg included copies of
a West German translation of the Old Testament, and writings of
West Berlin and West German theologians Vogel and Iwand.

Following the pattern of 1953, several institutions of the Church
were seized. A house mother in a Greifswald children's home was
sentenced to one and one-half years in prison for having rapped the
knuckles of a rambunctious child with a ruler. A Catholic home in
Stralsund was arbitrarily closed for alleged "sadistic" treatment of
the children, and the thirty-six residents were transferred to a State-
owned home.

During the month of June the Church of Anhalt scheduled a provincial Kirchentag, or Church rally, in the city of Koethen. Newspaper announcements of this function were not permitted, nor was
it possible to secure permission to print the programs. As soon as the
plans of the Church had been fixed, a Festival of Young Pioneers, a
special observance for Fire Prevention Week, and a rally of railroad
employees were suddenly transferred to Koethen. Public concerts
were arranged everywhere, often in the vicinity of the Christian assemblies, so that speakers could scarcely be heard or understood.

On the morning of the Kirchentag, busses and trucks which had
been ordered weeks in advance to bring the participants to Koethen
were canceled without explanation. In a few cases where congregations were still able to find a truck, these vehicles were stopped on
the highways a few miles from Koethen and sent back because of
"impassable highways." Participants were able to reach the town only
by foot or on bicycles. In spite of this flagrant planned interference
by SED agencies, a congregation of more than three thousand people
assembled in Koethen and carried through their Kirchentag under
the theme "Serve the Lord with Gladness."

Efforts of this kind to disrupt the life of the Church indicated the
determination of the Communists not only to discredit and defame
the Church leaders but also to intimidate the laity. The same intent
lay behind the organized efforts to establish the "Socialist Sunday" in
the cities and the "Land Sunday" in the rural areas, with special
work projects calculated to deprive Sunday of its character as a day
of rest and a day of worship.

Newspapers and factory publications stressed the renunciation of

Church membership as a sign of true devotion to the cause of Socialism, and published specific directions concerning the necessary procedures. Booths were frequently set up in factories or in public assemblies, with officials on hand to receive declarations of withdrawal.
Although SED members were not yet required to withdraw from the
Church, less and less patience was being shown toward those who
sought to reap the benefits of party membership but avoid the ideological commitments. An article published in the *Leipziger Volks-
zeitung* on May 20, 1958, not only illustrated the pressures exerted
upon factory workers but also provided an extremely enlightening
view of the nature of the Communist commitment. The article was
entitled "The Robes of Comrade Lommatzsch," and began as a
monologue by a party member who sought to maintain his respect-
ability in both Communist and Christian camps:

". . . now, Comrades, as we come to the conclusion of the study course
set up by our party, let me summarize briefly: The future belongs to
Socialism. Through the study of Marxism-Leninism, we know the laws
of development in nature and in society. And on the basis of these we
conclude that Socialism also gives the proper perspective for Germany!
   "Are there any further questions?"
   No one had anything else on his heart. So Group Leader Comrade
Lommatzsch arose from his chair, proud that he had once more rendered
a service for his party. That was on Monday.

". . . now, Colleagues, as we come to the conclusion of today's session
of our shop management committee, let me summarize briefly: Our
plant may well be called the 'black sheep,' but what more can we
possibly do to expand production? I am of the opinion that under
present circumstances we are producing at top level.
   "Does everyone agree? Are there any further questions?"
   No one raised any objections. So Shop Manager Comrade Lommatzsch
arose from his chair, satisfied and proud that he had once more rendered
a service for the plant. That was on Thursday.

". . . now, Frieda, let's be done with breakfast! Are you or are you not
going with me to church? Usually you're there every Sunday, but for
some reason, today you insist on working in the garden. . . . Oh, well, give
me the hymnbook, then. . . ."
   And Private Citizen Lommatzsch arose from the table, proud that he

had once more been able to do something for his soul's salvation. And that was on Sunday.

". . . now, Comrades, this is my position: In the shop I'm a Marxist and at home I'm a Christian. That's all I have to say about the matter!"

And since no one else had anything further to add, Party Member Comrade Lommatzsch arose from his chair, satisfied that he had been able to put another party assembly behind him.

Comrades and readers are going to ask whether such a thing is actually possible. Yes, it is possible, and it actually happened in the Dimitroff Power Plant in Leipzig. In just this way, or at least very similarly, Comrade Lommatzsch, plant manager, propagandist for the party study course (recently relieved of this function), and zealous churchgoer, conducted himself. For a long time this Comrade has practiced an ideological coexistence. He supposed that he could speak at the same time about the unconquerable power of dialectical materialism, *and* about the omnipotence of God. . . .

Let us be clear about this. This is a serious situation which faces us in the Dimitroff Power Plant. If this plant has been properly named the "black sheep," the reason is that until recently there was no real party activity there. Halfhearted efforts toward collective work by the plant management and party membership were tolerated, and the voice of the workingman was accorded little or no attention. . . .

Comrade Lommatzsch is to blame for this. And he will bear this guilt just as long as he believes it is possible to wear different robes to fit each different situation.

On May 6th, just before the opening of the party assembly, Comrade Lommatzsch handed to Party Secretary Comrade Benndorf his declaration of resignation from the Church. However, in the assembly itself, in spite of all urging, Comrade Lommatzsch refused to express himself as to which teachings he had thus far drawn out of the thirty-fifth general assembly of the party and out of subsequent discussions. He had merely made a *formal* decision, *in order to keep peace and quiet.*

But a Comrade can be *only* a Marxist-Leninist! To pray to God in the morning and to be a propagandist for atheism in the afternoon is impossible. There neither is nor can there be such a thing as an ideological armistice, no matter what Comrade Lommatzsch may think. He must now make an open and sincere confession of faith. He must make a real decision. And he is not the only one!

As the ultimate alternatives were placed with increasing clarity before the people of East Germany, there were abject surrenders such as that of Comrade Lommatzsch, and there were also heroic professions of faith. Most of these were never known beyond a very limited circle, for the decisions were not always spectacular, nor were they publicized. There was, for example, the bank inspector who was singled out and awarded a financial premium for his excellent work. When it was discovered that he was a Church elder and that he regularly attended Church, his monetary premium was stricken, and he was threatened with the loss of his job if he did not give up his position as a Church elder. He made his decision and lost both his premium and his job. There was also the teacher who refused to allow his daughter to apply for the Youth Dedication. He was released from the school and has been unable to find another job because no one dared to employ a person fired for such reasons. There were those faithful members of the parish in Anhalt who conducted a prayer service in their church every evening for their recently arrested pastor, in spite of the fact that party observers stood very openly in front of the church and noted the name of every individual who entered.

Not all of the decisions of these bitter days were made upon the grounds of Christian conviction or loyalty to the Church. The accelerated ideological campaign of the SED was as incompatible with personal and intellectual freedom as it was with the Christian faith. Many of those who were unable to accept the regimentation of the Communist regime found no other way to preserve their integrity than to flee to the West, though to most responsible men and women the abandoning of home and country was the last and most painful resort.

During 1957 a total of 262,000 refugees left East Germany, an average of more than 700 every day. Most of these were young people and skilled laborers. But during the first half of 1958, under the pressures of the new campaign, the numbers of intellectuals among the refugees rose to an all-time high. Seventy-five university professors, including the head of the University of Jena, sought refuge in the West, as did 85 scientific assistants, more than 600 doctors and dentists, and almost 1,400 teachers. With the "new morality" of the socialistic ethic, proclaimed by the fifth party congress of the SED in July, 1958, neither intellectual nor Christian freedom was able to come to terms.

With this kind of climate developing in East Germany, and with the request of its highest authority, the All-German Synod, for conversations with government leaders deliberately ignored, the EKD prepared to issue a public statement of its own. While the East Conference was in session in Berlin, polishing a preliminary draft prepared by a committee, a letter mysteriously arrived from Prime Minister Grotewohl declaring the government's readiness to receive a Church delegation, providing that such a delegation included only representatives of Churches in the German Democratic Republic. This would exclude both Dibelius and Grueber, and if Bishop Moritz Mitzenheim of Thuringia were included, it should be in his capacity as an East German bishop, and not as a member of the Council of the EKD.

Although the East Conference had approved its own draft statement, it decided not to publish it, but rather to meet Grotewohl's terms in the hope that a conference with State officials might be more fruitful than a mutual exchange of public statements. Since the main issue was education, it was decided to send the committee appointed for that purpose by the synod, and to add the names of Bishop Mitzenheim and Bishop Krummacher.

The first meeting with the prime minister was arranged on June 2nd, and it became immediately apparent that he was not interested in discussing specific questions such as that of education, but rather in the creation of a more friendly atmosphere, based upon an affirmation of loyalty to the State by the Church. For such a general discussion the committee of educational experts was not equipped, but, unfortunately, Church leaders did not feel they could change the membership after the negotiations had begun. Bishop Mitzenheim served as chairman of the Church committee, and a series of three conferences was held, with several minor discussions and exchanges of correspondence between. In his response to Grotewohl's opening statement, Mitzenheim expressed the eagerness of the Church to work for the solution of common problems, and his assurance that such a solution could be found. The tone of this statement and that which Mitzenheim prepared for the second conference was much more conciliatory than the actual situation within the congregations of East Germany warranted. Before the final meeting it was therefore agreed in consultation with EKD leaders that if Grotewohl should ask the committee for a decision which went beyond their competence as educational specialists, they should postpone such a decision until they had discussed the matter with all the bishops of East Germany.

The crucial meeting was held on July 21, 1958, and lasted from eleven o'clock in the morning till four in the afternoon. Grotewohl read his suggestions first, and Mitzenheim followed with the statement prepared by the committee. Noting that there were opposite views represented in the two documents, Grotewohl suggested that his statement be used as a basis for negotiation and that the Church committee make whatever changes it felt necessary. At this point, instead of asking for another meeting, which he was afraid might not be granted, Mitzenheim agreed to a one-hour pause, during which the Church committee prepared suggested modifications. The document, still essentially Grotewohl's statement, was then brought back to the general conference, accepted, and issued as a joint communiqué by the government and the Church.

The Church, it declared, "serves the cause of peace among the nations with the particular means at its disposal, and therefore agrees fundamentally with the peace efforts of the German Democratic Republic and its government. Christians faithfully fulfill their responsibilities as citizens in obedience to the law. They respect the development toward Socialism, and make their contribution to the peaceful upbuilding of the life of the people."

Church representatives agreed to withdraw their complaints that the government had violated the constitution, and the government reiterated its adherence to the constitutional guarantees of full freedom of faith and conscience for every citizen. The government agreed to review the complaints of the Church regarding the educational practices in the public schools, and both sides declared their readiness to engage in further discussions to clarify the specific issues in question.

When the members of the committee returned to West Berlin to discuss with Church leaders the results of the conference, it was already clear that the Church had been maneuvered into an extremely embarrassing position. With the fifth party conference of the SED having categorically stated only a week earlier that the only acceptable world view was that of atheism, and with Party Secretary Walter Ulbricht having just made public his Ten Commandments as the basis of the new Socialist ethic, it was very difficult to understand how a Church committee could subscribe to a statement pledging "respect" toward the development of Socialism in the East German Republic. With all of the flagrant examples of discrimination against school children, students, and Christian laymen because of their refusal to endorse atheism, it was difficult to explain how this committee could withdraw its claims that the state was violating the guarantees written into the constitution. Before withdrawing these well-documented charges, the committee might properly have asked for concrete evidence of a change of policy on the part of the government.

It was Mitzenheim's contention, however, that even the holding of the Church-State conversations had been a triumph for the Church. He believed that the groundwork had thereby been laid for a "new beginning," in which the State would honestly fulfill its responsibilities under the constitution and disputed questions could be settled through mutual discussion. Nothing in the development of Church-State relations in East Germany up to this point affords any reasonable ground for such an overly optimistic judgment.

Mitzenheim had only recently been thrust into a position of leadership among the East German bishops, by the refusal of the government to deal with EKD officials. His Thuringian Church was one of the most homogeneous of all the provincial Churches in Germany, with a membership including well over 90 per cent of the population. With unwarranted confidence in the inner strength of the folk Church, the bishop was apparently ready to hazard a policy of institutional coexistence in the hope of keeping the historic form of the Church extant. Since the policy of direct resistance was seemingly a losing one, if measured in terms of participation in the Youth Dedication, perhaps the way of friendly cooperation and cautious negotiation might hold the line until the political situation should change. Although his fellow bishops reminded him that this had been the fatal formula employed in Nazi Germany and, more currently, in Hungary and Czechoslovakia, Bishop Mitzenheim believed that the Church loyalty of the laity was strong enough to outlast even the power of a totalitarian State.

The immediate problem of the Church leadership in Berlin was how to respond to the communiqué of July 21st, which almost everyone but Mitzenheim felt had been a tragic defeat for the Church. If they gave it their unqualified approval, this would surely be viewed as a capitulation to the East German State. If they issued a repudiation, this would play directly into the hands of the Communists who had long sought to drive a wedge into the leadership of the Church. It was finally decided to issue a statement welcoming the new assurance of religious freedom by the government, but stressing the Church's earnest expectation that through the anticipated series of conferences concrete solutions would now be found for the many specific complaints which had been laid before the State. Leaders of the United Lutheran Church in Germany declared that the value of the communiqué could be judged only after an actual improvement of relationships had been demonstrated.

The East press cited these statements as evidence that reactionary Church leadership in both parts of Germany was attempting to rob the communiqué of its true significance.

The true significance of the July communiqué was by no means clear. Neither Church nor State had committed itself to any clear position. The Church had won from the State a reaffirmation of constitutional guarantees which the State insisted it had never broken anyway. The State had won from the Church a statement that it would "respect" the development toward Socialism, but there was no doubt that the Church intended to await more specific concessions in subsequent conferences with the State. The best one could say of the communiqué was that it had established a very uncertain truce between Church and State; it was dependent upon conditions which neither side could fulfill without betraying its basic commitments.

Very significantly, however, it did set the stage for a painful but long overdue process within the Church of East Germany. For thirteen years since the end of the war, the Evangelical Church in Germany had looked upon the scourge of Communism as a temporary tribulation which would sooner or later pass away. During its period of ascendancy it would assail the Church, interfere with its work, imprison its pastors, and even make inroads into its membership. But eventually the scourge would be removed, and the Church, within a reunited Fatherland, would recoup its losses and resume its honored and protected position as one of the great institutions of German society.

By 1958 it was clear that the "good old days" would never return to East Germany. One might still dream of reunification, but only the dreamers expected any early withdrawal of the Communists from their most western European outpost. In such a situation the Church would have to give serious thought to new ways of ordering its own life, and new counsel to men and women called of God to bear their Christian witness in a Marxist land.

FOURTEEN

THE WAY OF THE CHURCH IN A MARXIST LAND

In the months of discussion and debate which followed the issuing of the communiqué of July 21st, two important facts emerged. The first was that the ideological position of the Communist government of East Germany had crystallized and that in this realm there was no intention of making any concessions to the Church. Leaders of both party and government made this perfectly clear through their open and unabashed championing of atheism as the only foundation for the Marxist-Leninist society. Most Church leaders recognized this, and though they continued to demand respect for the constitutional guarantees of freedom of conscience, they realized that in the fluid world of Marxist dialectic the situation in which such guarantees could be honored had changed, and no amount of logic could ever restore them to validity in East Germany.

The second important fact was that although most Church leaders recognized the openly antagonistic position of the Communists toward the Church, there was a wide divergence of opinion on how best to meet this antagonism. Far too much of the Church's strategy thus far had been based upon a vague hope that better times were coming, when Communism should have run its course in East Germany and the German nation should be reunified. There had been very little careful theological or practical study given to the question of how a Church should order its life and counsel its members in a State that would remain Marxist for an indefinite period to come. More discussion attended this theme after the Synod of Berlin in April, 1958, than had ever been the case before. The fact that viewpoints within the Church varied so widely was in itself a boon to the Communists, who had sought for years to open a breach in the unified front of the Church.

Although the communiqué had pointed toward the holding of a series of Church-State conferences for dealing with the long list of grievances which the Church had accumulated, weeks dragged on into months without the government's displaying any inclination whatever to hold such discussions. Pressures to participate in the Youth Dedication continued unabated, with noncooperating children being excluded from entrance to high schools and their parents finding either job or housing in jeopardy. Official government sponsorship of the Youth Dedication was heralded through the issuance of postage stamps in 1959 commemorating five years of the ceremony. In the newspapers of Dresden, large industrial city of Saxony, the following notice appeared: "In accordance with a decision of the Railroad Administration of Dresden, from the present time on, no apprentices may be employed who have not received the Youth Dedication."

One of the clearest evidences of the hardening of Communist policy toward the Church in East Germany appeared in connection with the parliamentary elections held in October, 1958. There was, as usual, some attempt on the part of the CDU to summon Christians to the support of the peace program of the National Front. There was also, as usual during an election campaign, some relaxation of travel restrictions, even for churchmen. But most significant was a confidential statement made by Albert Norden, Secretary for Agitation in the Central Committee of the SED, concerning the proper attitude of the party toward Church people in the impending elections. His statement reflected clearly the official party attitude toward the Church, and also indicated the grounds upon which the Communists based their optimism concerning the early collapse of the Church. Of those who still belonged to the Church, Norden ventured the opinion that at least 98 per cent were bound to the Church only through traditional ceremonials. These people, not really Christian by conviction, declared Norden, would easily be won for Communism by tact and patience. On the basis of party observations of Church services and Church activities, about 150 out of every 10,000 persons were exceedingly loyal to the Church; with this group he saw little hope of success. Norden claimed that 90 per cent of the youth were already enlisted for Socialism, but he nevertheless warned his party associates to concentrate upon parishes where larger numbers still attended religious instruction and Church services.

For the pastors Norden reserved his bitterest barbs, but thereby also paid them the highest compliments as constant and loyal contenders for the faith. In the past the party had approached the clergy with invitations, visits, and friendly discussions, treating them at times like "prima donnas." "For twelve years," said Norden, "we have sought in vain to win them." Now such tactics were to be shelved. Atheistic propaganda had already unmasked these "pious hypocrites." The people had rejected the "fascistic clericalism" which they represented, and had made them the objects of derision and laughter. Norden advised that they be left alone to putter about in their churches until the day should come when they withered away for lack of air and lack of money. "When in the next few years the last of the old women have died off, the pastors will have to weep their tears alone on the lifeless walls of their empty churches."

Norden recognized that it would be desirable to give every possible encouragement to those pastors who showed "progressive" tendencies. But unfortunately, he admitted, "one must look for them with lanterns, and they are mostly old men who are looking for a quiet and comfortable eve of life."

If Norden's judgments were correct, by far the largest number of pastors would have to be written off by the party as hopeless cases. Apparently the Communists had no expectation of destroying the Church by a frontal attack upon the pastors. They would rather wage an extended war of attrition, capitalizing upon the inherent weaknesses of the traditional and form-ridden folk Church. To meet such an attack the Church would have to find some way, even at a very late hour of the day, to confront its large nominal membership with living and eternal truths rather than forms and ceremonies which could be bartered, if necessary, for more practical things such as jobs and housing and education.

Norden's speech was a confidential statement to the inner circle of the Communist Party. A few weeks later Prime Minister Otto Grotewohl mounted a podium in East Berlin and delivered an equally frank and realistic public addess. It was significant that this speech was delivered by Grotewohl, and not by Ulbricht or Norden or one of the other thoroughgoing Communists of the SED. Grotewohl was an old Social Democrat, and represented the moderate wing in the Communist-Socialist party merger of 1947. Always more interested in his German Fatherland than in the promotion of dogmatic world Communism, Grotewohl had once told a Church representative in confidential conversation that he would rather be a laborer in a reunified Germany than prime minister in a divided Germany.

When Grotewohl, as the official head of the East German government, proclaimed Communist dogma it was clear that the party bosses had determined to cast off all pretense and place the official sanction of the State behind the doctrinal program of the party. Grotewohl had no choice but to speak the bidding of his masters. Socialism, he declared to the assembled artists and cultural experts who made up his audience, aimed to build and educate a "new man," and for this reason the education of the children in Socialist theory must be given first priority. Basic to this theory was Marxist-Leninist science, which fought against "all kinds of fear, prejudice, miracles, and superstitions which convey a false concept of the world." If it opposed these official views, the Church was guilty of forcing citizens of the republic to violate their consciences, and this the government would not tolerate.

Not only did Grotewohl claim for the schools the responsibility for intellectual education in keeping with Socialist science, but for moral education of the children in harmony with Socialist principles. "At the same time that the pattern of the social order changes," he asserted, "the customs and usages of the people, and their understanding of the meaning of Right and Good and Evil, also change. All things are moral which serve the cause of Socialism. This is the foundation of the moral education and training of the youth."

With a statement such as this, the Communist State openly declared its totalitarian intent. The political and economic structure of the country had long ago been brought under complete control. Cultural and artistic expression were under strict supervision. Intellectual education was a State monopoly. Now even the inner realm of moral education was being claimed as a province of the State, and with it the authority to redefine the official meaning of right and wrong. Walter Ulbricht had in all seriousness announced a Socialist version of the Ten Commandments in 1958, and now the government officially placed its full authority and power behind this "new morality." The lines had been drawn before this, but with Grotewohl's speech they were clearly emblazoned before the public eye.

Such evidences of the hardening of the Communist ideological position were quite generally observed and understood by most of the Churches of East Germany. The persistence of the party in stressing the Youth Dedication year after year, the addition of the new Communist ceremonials, and the increasing intensity of atheistic indoctrination in the public schools touched every congregation and practically every family. Real concern had been manifested by the Churches over the steady yearly increase in participation in the Youth Dedication on the part of the young people completing their elementary-school course. In 1955, the year the ceremony was introduced, a maximum of 15 per cent of the children had taken part. In 1956 the number had risen to 25 per cent; in 1957, to 32 per cent; in 1958, to 47 per cent; and in 1959, to 65 per cent. This increase had occurred in spite of the firm position taken by the Churches that anyone who took part in the Youth Dedication could not be confirmed.

As the number of confirmands declined, it became apparent that the Church had chosen to make its stand on an essentially weak position. The rite of Confirmation, never a sacrament in the Lutheran Church, had traditionally been the ceremony marking the end of formal religious instruction and the reception of the young person into full membership in the Church with the privilege of receiving the Lord's Supper. Although the rite itself called upon the confirmed for a personal profession of faith in the Triune God and a promise to live a devoted and active Christian life within the fellowship of the congregation, Confirmation was popularly regarded as an ecclesiastical formality and as an occasion for family celebrations and festivity. Following Confirmation, by far the largest majority of confirmands simply adopted the pattern of indifference toward congregational participation which they had observed in their parents.

As early as the 1830's a reform of the Confirmation practices of the Lutheran Church had been advocated by Johann Hinrich Wichern, and periodically, down to the Synod of Berlin in 1945, the matter had been discussed. But always the traditional practices remained, and pastors went on listening to Confirmation vows from young people, most of whom they knew from decades of their own experience they might see again in church once a year at most.

The Church was therefore simply not prepared to fight a successful battle with the Communist organization on such precarious ground as the rite of Confirmation. For a few years the strength of the tradition would suffice to hold the loyalty of nominal Church members, but if a substitute could be provided, which offered the same opportunity for family gatherings, and which also carried with it some assurance of economic or educational preference, increasing numbers of families were ready to accept the substitute. Only those for whom Confirmation remained as a serious confessional act would eventually resist participation in the Youth Dedication, and, as the statistics indicated, this would be a smaller group each year, until eventually the irreducible inner core of the believing Church had been reached.

As soon as the Youth Dedication was introduced in 1955, pastors began to stress more pointedly in their pulpits and their instruction classes the confessional character of the rite of Confirmation. As the Youth Dedication progressed, a finer and deeper emphasis upon the real meaning of Confirmation therefore also developed within the congregations of East Germany. Young people and their families were confronted with the realization that a Confirmation pledge of loyalty to Christ and His Church might mean the sacrifice of economic or educational opportunities or the loss of friendships. In every case where this realization was faced and understood—and there were thousands of them—the life of the Church was enriched and its roots were driven deeper and deeper into the grace of God as its only source of strength

As the Youth Dedication was supplemented by the other Communist ceremonies and finally given the official sanction of the State, young people and families were also confronted more clearly with the confessional character of the Communist appeal. Just as Confirmation must be seen as an act of allegiance, and not merely a community festival, so also must the Youth Dedication be seen as the first step in a long series of loyalty pledges with the ultimate aim of complete personal commitment to the atheistic values of Communism. It is safe to say that most of those who failed to see in Confirmation an act of exclusive Christian commitment, and therefor joined the Youth Dedication, also failed to regard the Communist ceremony as an act of commitment. Once involved in the Communist net, however, there would be repeated confrontations and renewed demands, with respite afforded only in active commitment or passive conformity.

The problem of Confirmation loomed large in the concern of the Synod of the EKD which convened in Berlin in April, 1958. In view of the critical situation the synod urged its member Churches to give special thought to new methods and forms for all of the work of the Church, but especially in relation to Confirmation. A special committee was appointed to coordinate the work of the member Churches in establishing new and uniform rules for Confirmation.

Out of the discussions which followed in the various Churches came a wide variety of suggestions. One group suggested eliminating Confirmation entirely, since it had no Biblical basis as a separate, formal act. Others suggested admitting children to Communion at the age of ten or eleven, and postponing the catechization and Confirmation until the more mature age of seventeen. Most of them proposed a separation of the single parts of Confirmation, such as completion of instruction, the taking of the vow, admission to Communion, and the granting of congregational rights. All of the Churches adopted temporary procedures to be used in 1959, pending the completion of a unified system. Under these temporary plans all children, whether they joined the Youth Dedication or not, were permitted to continue in the course of instruction up to the end. Then followed an interval of special preparation for Communion and for congregational life, in which serious candidates for Confirmation might participate. At the end of this period the young people would be confirmed and would receive the Lord's Supper. If, after taking part in the Youth Dedication, a child still remained faithful in the life of the Church and indicated to the pastor his desire to be confirmed, he might participate in the course of sacramental preparation the following year and then be confirmed. According to these procedures no child would be deprived of instruction, and opportunity would also be given for those who experienced a change of heart to be confirmed at a later time. Greater emphasis was also placed upon the receiving of the Sacrament, as a work of identification with the confessing Church.

The discussion of Confirmation and Youth Dedication brought to light several basic differences of opinion within Churches of East Germany. The most outspoken advocate of a firm and unyielding policy was Bishop Otto Dibelius, who had entertained no illusions whatever during the past fourteen years concerning the ultimate aims of the Communists toward the Church. Without ever becoming the political lackey of the West, Dibelius had consistently opposed every attempt of the Communists in East Germany to restrict the freedom of the Church and the freedom of the individual, and had earned the distinction of being that regime's most hated churchman. Since early 1957 he had not been able to secure permission to make official Church trips within the German Democratic Republic, and government officials refused even to hold conversations with him.

Prime Minister Grotewohl's speech to the East Berlin Artists and Cultural Experts provided the bishop with an occasion to write an open letter, replying to the Communist intention to make their world view determinative of the total life of people in East Germany. Denouncing Grotewohl's address as "a State-sponsored proclamation of atheistic thinking," which was at variance with the basic Christian convictions of the people, Dibelius protested vigorously the attempt to substitute a new morality for the ancient Ten Commandments. When, for example, members of the armed forces of the German Democratic Republic were called upon by their superiors to hate people of a different persuasion, Christendom in Germany, could only respond with "a definite and everlasting No." Moreover, declared the bishop, Christian parents had the right to insist that their children be reared in the faith of Jesus Christ and in obedience to His commandments, not in a morality based upon dialectical materialism.

As for the Youth Dedication, Dibelius made it clear that the Church in the German Democratic Republic continued to regard

Confirmation and the Youth Dedication as mutually exclusive. Admission to the Lord's Supper could not be granted to any Church member who "has professed his allegiance to another diametrically opposed system of belief. The functions of the Church are not public theater performances accessible to the whim of anyone. They are solemn occasions on which the fellowship of faith is founded."

If such a clear delineation between the basic loyalties of the people of East Germany should eventually lead to a minority Church, made up only of those who were willing to stand firmly for the faith, Dibelius and large numbers with him were prepared to accept this. "Better 20 per cent of the people as real Church members, honest and uncompromising," affirmed another East German Church leader, "than a semblance of a Church in the hands of the State."

Others in East Germany, however, were far less ready to sacrifice the traditional structure of the folk Church, with its impressive statistics claiming 90 to 95 per cent of the population as Church members. The leader of this group was the Lutheran Bishop of Thuringia, Moritz Mitzenheim. He feared that if too strict a policy were maintained by the Church toward those who participated in the Youth Dedication, the Confirmation classes would become steadily smaller, and the numbers of people who looked upon themselves as outside the Church would steadily increase. Even the purely formal tie which these people maintained with the traditional Church would thus be lost, and there would be no future point of contact when an improved climate should permit a more normal program of Church work.

Consequently, when the temporary Confirmation regulations for 1959 were drawn up, Thuringia and its small neighbor Church of Anhalt made very little practical distinction between those prospective confirmands who had participated in the Youth Dedication and those who had not. A similar attitude toward the Socialist name-giving ceremony was reflected in an official order which was circulated in one district of the Thuringian Church, instructing the pastors to baptize all children presented to them, whether they had participated in the name-giving ceremony or not.

It became extremely embarrassing for the majority of the East German Churches that Bishop Mitzenheim was thrust into a position of leadership just at the time this compromising position in respect to the Youth Dedication was developing within his own Church. His leading role in drawing up the unfortunate communiqué of July 21, 1958, further illustrated his apparent conviction that a conciliatory relationship with leaders of the State would ease tensions and provide a better climate for the work of the Church.

The same embarrassing eagerness of the Thuringian bishop to play an independent and friendly hand in dealing with political leaders was demonstrated when he was invited to attend the party rally of the CDU in Dresden in Saxony in October. Although the Bishop of Saxony had already very pointedly rejected a similar invitation, Mitzenheim accepted, and was warmly and publicly greeted by the party leaders when he arrived. The Saxon Church shortly thereafter expressed its disapproval of this affront to its bishop by refusing Mitzenheim permission to speak in one of the large Lutheran churches in Leipzig. Such dissensions within the Church front were naturally observed by the Communists with great satisfaction.

Leaders of other Churches watched with growing dismay as Mitzenheim's "new course" developed. When the Thuringian Synod in November took a more conciliatory position on the Youth Dedication than had been recommended by the EKD, Mitzenheim defended this course by pointing out that his new policy had already produced a considerable improvement in Church-State relations in Thuringia since the communiqué in July. The other bishops admitted that there had been a few local improvements, but sent a letter to the prime minister on November 21st protesting that the government-sponsored campaign to impose atheistic Socialism upon the youth continued unabated in spite of assurances given in the July communiqué.

Following Khrushchev's spectacular November ultimatum to the western powers that they must evacuate Berlin within six months, the political implications of Mitzenheim's new course came to light. On January 10th the Soviet Union proposed a draft of a German peace treaty which it hoped to make the basis of discussions involving both the East and West German governments as well as the great powers. Mitzenheim greeted this proposal warmly, and when Prime Minister Grotewohl wrote to Adenauer suggesting preliminary conversations between the two German governments, the bishop was carried away by the revived dream of German reunification. Completely ignoring Grotewohl's cynical East Berlin speech delivered less than three weeks before, in which the prime minister had stated flatly that whatever served the cause of Socialism was moral, Mitzenheim wrote a letter complimenting him upon having discovered a "new ethos" for human and international dealings. He assured Grotewohl that he would take occasion in churches and in parishes and even in the sessions of the coming Thuringian Synod to voice his approval of the prime minister's line of reasoning. This naïve and tragic letter was cordially received by the government, and care was taken not only to publish it in every newspaper in East Germany but also to pass it out on printed handbills to every traveler on the East Zone Autobahns!

Neither friendly advice nor sharp warning from fellow bishops and churchmen in recent months have served to deflect the Bishop of Thuringia from his chosen course. He has joined with the other Churches in periodic protests and in vain requests for the resumption of top-level conversations, but his tone is always mild and his manner ingratiating. He has by no means adopted a pro-Communist line, nor does he support the cause of the "progressive" pastors, but his public utterances are more distinguished by what they fail to say than by what they say. The bishops of East Germany, eager to prevent an open rift in their ranks, have sought firmly and patiently to speak with a single voice. But they have found it necessary to dispense with Bishop Mitzenheim's leadership in the East Conference of the EKD, and to select the more courageous Dr. Krummacher, Bishop of Pomerania, as their chairman.

Throughout the postwar years there has always been a small group of so-called "progressive" pastors in East Germany, whose leftist political orientation made them sympathetic toward Soviet economic and social policies. These are the outright collaborationists, who would correspond to the "German-Christians" of the National Socialist Movement. The fact that Albert Norden told his colleagues of the SED Central Committee that "one must look for them with lanterns" indicates that even the Communists do not yet regard them as a highly significant group. Their most influential leaders are found among the newer professors being brought into the theological faculties of the state universities; men such as Professors Christoph Haufe and Dedo Mueller of Leipzig, Kehnscherper of Greifswald,

Hanfried Mueller of East Berlin, and the old Socialist Emil Fuchs of Leipzig, together with Karl Kleinschmidt of Schwerin and a few other active pastors.

Not until July 1, 1958, however, was there any formal organization of "progressive pastors." At that time a Saxon pastor named Wolfgang Caffier gathered about sixty pastors from all of East Germany in a little hotel in Leipzig and organized the League of Evangelical Pastors. Claiming that the atheistic character of Communism could actually be blamed upon the failure of the Church to speak to the questions of injustice raised by Karl Marx, Caffier proposed that the Church now make amends by confessing its past sins and joining in the honest efforts of the State to build a society in which the laboring man would no longer be hungry and poor.

Through the columns of their official organ, *Evangelisches Pfarrerblatt*, richly subsidized by the State, the league called upon pastors to pledge their loyalty to the State and its program of peace and Socialism, to guard themselves against the western-influenced leadership of the EKD, and to accept the commitments of the July communiqué. As a sign of its cooperative intentions, the League of Evangelical Pastors joined the National Front and sent its chairman, Pastor Caffier, as a delegate to the third national congress. On the question of Confirmation and Youth Dedication, the "progressive pastors" advised leniency, insisting that there was nothing in the Socialist Youth Pledge which in any way violated the Christian's confession of faith.

Far more complicated and difficult to evaluate is the body of opinion in East Germany which has grown up around the widely publicized letter written by Karl Barth to a pastor in the German Democratic Republic in August, 1958. As a young professor at the University of Bonn in 1934, this great Swiss theologian had provided much of the spiritual inspiration for the anti-Nazi resistance movement of the Confessing Church. He was the author of the famous Declaration of Barmen, in which the German Church served clear and uncompromising notice upon the Nazi State that it acknowledged no authority other than the "lordship of Christ." The Barmen Declaration had provided the rallying point for all those who fought for the integrity of the Church and of the Gospel, and even after the

Nazi regime had collapsed in 1945, it was invoked by the German Churches as their "declaration of spiritual independence."

It was therefore not strange that the intrepid counselor of an earlier Church struggle should be called upon for advice to pastors once more confronted by a government demanding the total loyalty of its citizens. What did seem strange, however, was that the forty-five pages of advice given in 1958 was so diametrically opposed to that given in 1934. Whereas Barth had called for active resistance against Nazism, he seemed to take a much more conciliatory attitude toward Communism. To the extent that Communism sought to induce Christians to renounce their faith or indulge in blind hatred or submission, Barth acknowledged that it ought to be resisted. But he warned his friends in East Germany against thinking of the Communist world as the sole region where active hostility to Christ existed. The so-called "free" West was also under attack from the evil spirits of arrogant wealth and creeping totalitarianism.

With such observations coming from one who himself resided in a western land it would be difficult to take issue. The Devil has never been a respecter of political boundaries. But when Barth entered upon the question of whether or not Christians in East Germany should sign the loyalty pledges which their government demanded of them, he was on shaky ground. Although admitting that he did not know the exact text of these pledges, he "assumed" that they were not so far-reaching as the oath of allegiance demanded by Hitler. Thinking of his own constitutional relationship to the Swiss Confederation, he declared, such a loyalty pledge would imply an acknowledgment of the government without approving every measure adopted by it. Loyalty, in Barth's thinking, also would involve the freedom to disagree with the ideology of the State without suffering reprisals.

Having thus read into the East German situation his own understanding of constitutional freedom, Barth advised his friends, "In your position I would see no difficulty in pledging loyalty to the German Democratic Republic in this sense, and therefore in signing the declaration required of you in all sincerity."

After reading advice such as this to pastors who are being spied upon by unknown agents of the secret police, who are counseling young people being asked daily in their schools to pledge their total loyalty and strength to a system which denies both God and Christian morality, and parents being threatened with the loss of support for their families if they do not dedicate their newborn infants to Socialism instead of Christ, it is difficult to avoid asking the almost impertinent question, Does not Karl Barth know what is going on in East Germany?

But the distance from Basel to Leipzig is not great, and it is safe to assume that the one letter which Barth answered was not the only report he had received from pastors in the German Democratic Republic. Karl Barth knows the East German situation well. But his advice reflects two things. The first is a very well-founded fear that the Christian Gospel may be identified with the "western way of life" and that the political-economic contest between East and West may thereby be exalted to the status of a "holy war" in which all the demons are on one side and God wears an American uniform. It is certainly in keeping with the spirit of Barmen to reaffirm that the Gospel is not the handmaiden of any economic or political overlord, no matter how benevolent it may appear to be. The task of the Church is to proclaim clearly and fearlessly the Word of the Lord, to point out wrong and injustice wherever it appears, and to summon all men to repentance and obedience to His eternal Law. For this timely reminder that the mission of the Church and the Christian Gospel are far greater and more inclusive than a mere crusade against Communism or a mere defense of the American way of life Karl Barth merits thanks.

But in seeking to convey this warning, Barth has vastly minimized the demonic forces that are at work within the Communist structure. Their professed aim is to destroy the Church and the Christian faith of men by subtle and direct assaults, and they are supported by the all-embracing power and machinery of a totalitarian government. It may be perfectly true that the German people are reaping the harvest of earlier sins and betrayals, as Barth pointed out, but this in no way lessens the reality of the present onslaught. Simply because the Communist scourge could be understood as "God's punishing rod" upon the German Church and people for not having recognized soon enough the demons in National Socialism, the first sin of blindness would not be atoned for by repetition in a different setting. Barth's own discernment of the "principalities and powers" at work in Soviet

Communism appears to be as dim as that of large numbers of Germans in 1934.

Some critics have suggested that Barth's own well-known anti-Adenauer politics show through his bitter castigation of the West and his essentially benevolent evaluation of the situation in the Communist world. Many pastors in East Germany have suggested that six months of actual experience in an East German pastorate might alter Barth's judgments of the nature of the conflict being waged in every parish behind the Iron Curtain.

Although his letter of August, 1958, was Barth's first active participation in the East German Church-State controversy, his viewpoints had been represented in West Germany for several years by the so-called *Bruederschaften,* or Brotherhoods of the Confessing Church. Claiming to represent the pure spirit of Barmen, these groups felt that the tendency of the Church in West Germany since the war had been to revert to old ecclesiastical and social patterns and to become the supporter and advocate of government policies both domestic and international.

This was the fatal tendency in the Church, they asserted, which had opened the way for the successes of the Nazis in Germany, and prepared the way for the terrible destruction which they brought upon all of Europe. Determined that this should not happen again, the Brotherhoods opposed German rearmament, NATO, and the entire western defense policy which sought to integrate West Germany into an anti-Soviet bloc. Claiming to exercise the responsibility of the Church announced at Barmen, to warn against public as well as private sin, the Brotherhoods actually became the advocates of such a specific course of political action that they were open to the accusation of confusing the Gospel and politics. And since a pacifistic and neutralized West Germany would have suited Soviet designs perfectly, the Brotherhoods were often criticized for alleged sympathies with the East. Led by Martin Niemoeller and Gustav Heinemann, they worked unceasingly to mobilize Church opinion through synodical resolutions, appeals to the public, and manifestoes adopted by mass rallies or assemblies.

Although the Brotherhoods are largely a West German organization, their actions have had an important relation to the problem of Church and State in East Germany. This has been especially true since the hope of German reunification has practically disappeared, and it has become clear that Soviet Communism will remain as the pattern of public life in East Germany for a long time to come. They have tried to warn the people of the West not to identify Christianity with their particular political and economic systems or to look upon the Christian mission simply as a sterile anti-Communism. They have also raised the counterpart question whether the system of Communism is essentially anti-Christian, or whether it is possible to separate its economic and social doctrines from its professed atheism.

Some of the most stimulating treatments of these extremely current themes have appeared recently in Berlin, where it is still possible to bring together for free discussion scholars and pastors from East and West. Professor Helmut Gollwitzer of the Free University of Berlin, one of the most popular theological writers and lecturers in Germany today, has suggested that the atheistic emphasis in Soviet Communism, real as it is, is not actually essential, except as the foundation for the Communist "messianic" hope of a future perfect society. As long as the goals of social revolution are still in the distant future, Gollwitzer claims, Communism must cultivate the dream of an idyllic "heaven on earth," to be created by man without any need of God. But the closer the Communist Society comes to achieving some of its earthly goals, the less need there will be to stress the "messianic" hope and consequently the less need there will be for an atheistic dogma.

If the Christian congregation could see its mission under Communism as a divine order to enter a new and strange land, and to find new forms of expression and witness, instead of trying vainly to defend the outworn positions of privilege held for fifteen hundred years, a whole new era might be opened in the history of the Church. Gollwitzer suggests that the concern of the Church in a Marxist land should not be simply to outlast Communism, but rather to make a positive contribution in the society where it is placed. Through its congregational life, its worship, and its preaching, it should seek to humanize the society, to protect and improve the dignity and freedom of the individual. Most of all, the congregation should remember that its Gospel is the unconquerable Gospel of Easter. In the final analysis the decision of men against God is helpless in the face of God's decision for man.

To both the detached counseling of Karl Barth in Basel and the theoretic advising of Helmut Gollwitzer in West Berlin, however, pastors and lay people in obscure towns and villages of East Germany raised many questions. In order to enter upon Gollwitzer's new adventure, was it necessary to confess only the sins and neglects of the Church in the past and condemn only the besetting sins of modern western materialism? At the same time must one only speak appreciatively of the professed passion of the Communists for peace and disarmament, and remain silent about their inhumanities, their flagrant injustices, and their broken promises? Should one postpone his defense against militant atheism until a Communist "millennium" was close enough to render atheism obsolete? How many confirmands would have been betrayed into the Devil's hands by that time? How many nursery tots would by then have been given stones for bread? How many free men would have been browbeaten into abject servility?

When "bridgebuilders" such as Martin Niemoeller attended Soviet-sponsored international peace rallies to demonstrate to the Communists that not all in the West have self-righteously judged them to be beyond redemption, the teacher who lost her job because she refused to solicit for the Youth Dedication might properly inquire whether this was a part of the Church's new adventure. And when Professor Heinrich Vogel denounced the atomic rearmament of the western powers in prophetic tones, the young lad who spent five years of his life in East German uranium mines might well ask why he had not raised his voice long ago against atomic rearmament in Russia.

Such questions are neither rhetorical nor theoretical. They are being asked every day in thousands of homes by tens of thousands of people who are seeking to bear a Christian witness in the midst of a Marxist land.

Implicit in such questions is the fundamental problem of setting limits to the authority of the Marxist State. The Church is not called upon to prescribe the forms of political or economic life: it must nevertheless be ready to give advice when its people inquire whether allegiance to the State and obedience to its laws are compatible with the Christain conscience.

For the Christian this has historically been a question of the proper understanding of the Romans 13:1-5, where Paul writes:

Let every person be subject to the governing authorities. For there is no authority except from God, and those that exist have been instituted by God. Therefore he who resists the authorities resists what God has appointed, and those who resist will incur judgment. For rulers are not a terror to good conduct, but to bad. Would you have no fear of him who is in authority? Then do what is good, and you will receive his approval, for he is God's servant for your good. But if you do wrong, be afraid, for he does not bear the sword in vain; he is the servant of God to execute his wrath on the wrongdoer. Therefore one must be subject, not only to avoid God's wrath but also for the sake of conscience.

Christians have been called upon to live under many different forms of government, ranging from heathen dictatorships to theocracies. Paul's words were directed to Christians living under Nero, a bloodthirsty heathen Roman emperor who gave his name to one of the bitterest of the early Christian persecutions. Yet Paul instructed members of the Roman congregation to respect his regime as ordained of God.

German theologians in East and West have agreed that the German Democratic Republic is also a valid government in the sense of Romans 13. The people of East Germany have no other government which is able to perform the necessary functions of maintaining law and order. Diplomatic recognition of that government by the Federal Republic or by the western powers has been viewed as a purely political matter.

The fact that the dominant party in the government is committed to an ideology opposed to the Christian faith has not until recently caused any serious questioning of the authority of the State itself, although in the minds of most churchmen there had always lurked the feeling that this regime was not permanent. This largely unspoken hope had no doubt encouraged Church leaders to avoid discussing the fundamental issues of the ultimate relation of Church and the Christian to a Marxist State. In view of recent developments such discussions at an earlier date would have been highly desirable. After 1957 it became apparent that this question could no longer be settled by a simple reference to Romans 13.

Pastors were being confronted every day by distracted parents and young people asking for advice in specific matters which involved State-sponsored activities. The Youth Dedication was acknowledged as an official State function. The educational process was a State monopoly, in which roads to academic preference were closed to those who refused to conform to State-sponsored atheism. With the rapidly advancing collectivization of agriculture, the State was broadening its control upon economic opportunity, and presently would be able to deprive any person of his livelihood who would not pledge his support of Socialism. The growing successes of the Youth Dedication and the other Socialist ceremonies indicated that this day was not far off.

In his report to the EKD Synod in 1958, Bishop Dibelius voiced the question which burned in many minds: Can a Christian actually find a place at all in the Socialist State? Even if he acknowledges the State as authoritative in the sense of Romans 13, where shall the lines be drawn between Caesar's law and the Law of God, to which the Christian owes his first obedience?

The Council of the Evangelical Church of the Union also raised this question following the appearance of the communiqué of July 21st, and asked the faculty of the Naumburg Seminary to prepare a statement on the meaning of the concepts of Socialism, Justice, and Peace, which were so prominent in the communiqué. Under the leadership of Pastor Johannes Hamel, former student pastor at the University of Halle, the Naumburg faculty drew up a study document entitled "The Gospel and the Christian Life in the German Democratic Republic," which was brought to the Synod of the EKU in February, 1959. The synod in turn commended it to pastoral conferences in all the member churches of the EKU as a basis for further inquiry into the relation of the Christian to government and public life. Special committees to study the question of a State-sponsored atheism in relation to the responsibilities of the Christian were constituted by each of the three major Church federations in Germany, the EKU, the EKD, and the United Lutheran Church.

None of these "Atheism Committees," however, dealt primarily with the question of the nature of the State. All of them assumed the validity of the Socialist State as a power which, regardless of its character or the way in which it originated, commanded the loyalty of the Christian. All of them, however, recognized the great problems being faced by individual laymen in the congregations, who were seeking to be loyal Christians and loyal citizens at the same time. Yet in no case has any Church committee or organization given any encouragement whatever either to revolution or to flight.

One of the most arresting interpretations of the role of the Christian in a Marxist land was that of Pastor Hamel. He advised his fellow Christians in East Germany to accept the revolutionary changes in the world around them and make use of them as an opportunity. "In the face of these powers," wrote Hamel, "God calls His people, treading the path of the cross, to new obedience, new praise, new prayer, new endurance. He calls for the renewal of our Church and for the transformation of her patterns in order that she may serve Him in greater faithfulness."

Instead of arguing whether Marxism is good or bad—and either view could become a denial of the Gospel if it became a primary concern—Hamel advised the Church to bear courageous witness to its absolute loyalty to God and His Truth. It must never admit that its work has been rendered impossible, because its work is the work of God's Holy Spirit. There can therefore never be a situation in which the Church is lost; even the fiercest of persecutions actually become new opportunities to witness for Christ.

For American Church people and pastors who tend to feel a trifle smug in the presence of their material blessings and who may occasionally feel a surge of pious pity for those "less fortunate," it may come as a shock to find a man like Hamel summoning his colleagues in East Germany to accept their situation as an opportunity rather than as a curse. There is something fascinating about regarding the Communists as unwilling and unintentioned "servants of God," calling the Church to a bold witness of the Gospel—not as the "democratic way of life" or as a religious success story—but as the only hope and refuge for men who love truth and hate falsehood. Here is neither a mock heroic nor a plea for pity, but a proclamation of new opportunity for the Church, by someone who really believes that he serves the Lord of the Nations and the Master of History.

There is no doubt that Pastor Hamel's writings provide a healthy corrective for western views of the Church behind the Iron Curtain. But the members of East German congregations—the teachers, the pupils, the laborers, the farmers, the public employees—are clutching after more concrete advice on where to draw the line between the realms of God and Caesar. The fact that Communism provides new opportunities for witnessing does not make that witnessing easy. Accompanying most of these opportunities is a profound struggle of conscience on the part of simple Christians who want to be obedient to both God and the State, but who find themselves torn asunder by the decisions they must make.

For the counseling of these people at the parish level, the guide lines being worked out by the "Atheism Committees" for distribution among the pastors promise more practical help. The committee of the United Lutheran Church, for example, took sharp issue with the highly theoretical views of Professor Gollwitzer on the separability of Communism and atheism. The East German State has declared in plain language that it has renounced the binding character of God's eternal Law and substituted its own standard of right and wrong. There is scant comfort for the Christian farmer in Pomerania, whose farm has been collectivized by force, in the theoretical possibility that some day Communism may lose its atheistic missionary zeal. It is much more realistic to warn the farmer that because the State has made atheism an official doctrine, the Christian must anticipate constant conflict, suffering, and perhaps eventually martyrdom. There is no easy way for the Christian in an atheistic State. He must be prepared to live from day to day on the exceptions and the inconsistencies indulged in by that State—but always with an unflinching faith that he is in God's hand and that God's holy will ultimately will be vindicated.

Some areas of community life could be expected to produce conflicts more readily than others. The Christian layman might, for example, participate with good conscience in an agricultural cooperative or a State-owned factory, and bear a Christian witness through the diligence and excellence of his work. But in view of the ideological character of the schools and of the social law, it would seem very questionable that a person could serve as a teacher or a judge without denying his Christian faith. In an atheistic State active participation by a Christian in the political process would be exceedingly difficult. Membership in a political party such as the SED, which is committed to an atheistic position, would be impossible for an honest and thoughtful Christian. Even the most elementary political act, that of casting a ballot in a general election, the Christian would discover to be fraught with conflicts of conscience. For he would have no choice on election day except to cast his vote for the single slate of hand-picked candidates, all committed in advance to the support of the atheistic principles of the leading political party.

The counsel which a Christian pastor, fortified by such a consensus of his colleagues, might give to his inquiring parishioner could never relieve the individual of his own daily responsibility of decision. No all-inclusive rules can be established to fit every situation, and in very few of these situations are the issues black and white. The frontier of individual Christian decision is, after all, the battle line of the Church in East Germany today. Yet, as Hamel and Barth point out, the urgency of Christian decision is not limited to lands under Marxist rule. Choices of right and wrong confront Christians every day in every land. And upon the clarity and the vigor of these daily decisions depends the real vitality of the Church, whether in East or West.

While committees of the Churches were endeavoring to establish some practical guide lines for the Christian life within the Marxist State, Bishop Otto Dibelius dropped a bombshell into the midst of the discussions. He wrote a letter to Bishop Hanns Lilje of Hannover, as a greeting on Lilje's sixtieth birthday, expressing his conviction that the word *Obrigkeit*, used by Luther in his translation of Romans 13, was no longer appropriate for the modern political State. Because of Lilje's well-known facility in the German language, Dibelius hoped that he might be able to suggest a better word.

In explaining why he felt the need of a new translation, Dibelius gave expression to his own views on the nature of the East German government and the proper relation of the Christian to it. Taking sharp issue with those who held that the Communist State must be acknowledged as a valid authority in the sense of Romans 13 because it provided at least the minimum essentials of external order, Dibelius denied flatly any Christian obligation to the East German government. For him the decisive point was reached when the Communist State declared its intention of ordering all of life in accord with its own standard of right and wrong. No State which thus brazenly attempted to repeal the very foundation of God's

Law and order in the world could have any further claim to being
called "the servant of God," nor could its actions be respected as
being "for the good" of its citizens. For the sake of Christ and His
Church, he, Dibelius, would be eager to see such a regime overthrown.
Not even the traffic laws of East Germany could be considered binding upon the Christian, because they were not based upon justice,
but upon the principle that whatever serves Socialism is right. Thus,
on the Autobahn, "one is apt to see a Soviet car go by at top speed,
followed by an East German government vehicle. They are permitted
to do this; I am not, because I am not a party functionary."

Dibelius hastened to add that if he himself should be apprehended
and asked to pay a fine for exceeding the speed limit, he would do so,
but his obedience and respect for this authority would not be motivated by the injunctions of Romans 13. "Demons remain demons.
They will never become legitimate powers."

Had the birthday letter remained a private matter, it need not have
created such a furor. But Dibelius arranged for a limited printing of
five hundred copies of the letter in an attractive little booklet for distribution among pastors and other friends. When the bishop returned from his vacation, he was greeted with a storm of protest from
friends and foes alike.

Obviously the text of the letter had found its way to political
offices in East Berlin. They simply treated it as confirmation of the
wisdom of the three-year-old government policy of denying entry to
such a dangerous man into the German Democratic Republic. Beyond this the Communist press could find little else to say about
Dibelius which had not already been said many times before.

Criticism of the bishop within the Church was more serious. Quite
apart from the interpretation of Romans 13, on which Dibelius stood
virtually alone, the letter certainly created practical problems for the
pastors in the German Democratic Republic. They would face the
unenviable choice of supporting the bishop's statements, which could
have far more serious effect upon them than upon the bishop, who
lived in West Berlin, or disavowing his position, and thus admitting
a serious cleft between pastors and Church leadership.

In a letter to all its pastors the Church Council of Berlin-Brandenburg actually repudiated the views expressed by its bishop and announced the continued adherence of the Brandenburg Church to the

scriptural requirement of obedience to the "governing authorities" in East Germany. The Weissensee Circle, a group of pastors and theologians who had long been critical of Dibelius' vigorous exercise of the office of bishop, called upon him to explain his controversial action to the Synod of Berlin-Brandenburg. They also proposed to lay before the synod a request that in the future the scope of the bishop's office be more carefully limited.

Many of Dibelius' friends, both in East and West Germany, felt that while the example of traffic regulation was poorly chosen, and while his theological position on Romans 13 was by no means ortho- dox, he had nevertheless called clear attention to the central issue in the controversy between Church and State. In a situation where much concern was being shown over the finding of an acceptable course for the Christian man in a Marxist land, Dibelius reminded his fellow Christians that there must be a point at which "the ever- lasting No" is said. Others might not wish to draw the line at the same point as the bishop, and he had not sought to impose his judg- ment upon anyone. But he was in effect drawing a bold line beneath those apostolic words which appear in the fifth chapter of Acts, and which were not spoken about "the powers that be," but *to* the "powers that be": "We must obey God rather than men."

With the exception of one brief radio conversation with Bishop Lilje, in which he left no doubt that he would stand by what he had said, Dibelius made no attempts to answer his critics until the Pro- vincial Synod of Berlin-Brandenburg convened on January 24, 1960. The largest part of his official report was devoted to a review of his own attempts to reconcile the various State forms under which he had lived with the "divinely ordained authority" of Romans 13.

Almost eighty years old, the span of Otto Dibelius' life had very nearly coincided with that of the modern German State. He had re- ceived his education and begun his career in the Church during the days of the kaiser. In manners and bearing, as well as in politics, he remained a representative of the "old order" which had ended with the German defeat in 1918. The unstable decade of the Weimar Re- public, with its many governmental changes, had been followed by the National Socialist regime, which Dibelius, though himself never a party member, had first accepted as a welcome respite from the fluc- tuations of the uncertain democracy of the twenties. To each of these governments Dibelius had successively accorded his loyalty as "the power ordained by God." But when the Nazis launched their programs of euthanasia and mass execution of the Jews, thus scrapping the moral Law of God, they forfeited in Dibelius' mind all claim to be recognized as a divinely ordained authority. Ousted from his office as General Superintendent of the Kurmark, Dibelius worked actively in the illegal Confessing Church movement, until the Nazi collapse in 1945 when he emerged again into a position of leadership in the Church of Berlin-Brandenburg.

In keeping with Romans 13, he had also attempted to accord his respect both to the Russian occupation and to the German Democratic Republic as authorities under God. Although he was completely unsympathetic toward the social and economic system of Communism, Dibelius felt that even such radical changes as were instituted in East Germany after 1945 did not alter the respect that he as a Christian was bound to show toward that government. But when the Communist regime announced its intention to scrap the Ten Commandments, as the Nazis had also done, and to impose new standards of right and wrong upon the people of East Germany, its divine mandate, as far as Dibelius was concerned, was forfeited.

Advice of this kind did not, as some have suggested, place the Christian citizen in East Germany before the alternative of treason or damnation. This was not a trumpet call either to revolution or to heroics. It was simply Dibelius' clear warning that the demons were at work in East Germany under the guise of government. Instead of stumbling over Romans 13, which did not apply, Christian men could rather find their guidance for life under such a demonic regime in the principles enunciated by Luther in his treatise on the Freedom of the Christian Man. Luther had written: "A Christian is a perfectly free lord of all, subject to none," and paradoxically, "A Christian is a perfectly dutiful servant of all, subject to all." Even though he could not give his respect to the government in the sense of Romans 13, as the instrument for carrying out the orderly will of God in the community, the Christian would, for the sake of the love of Christ and his fellow man, subject himself, and live a quiet and peaceable life.

At the conclusion of his report to the synod, the bishop announced his intention of laying aside all his ecclesiastical offices in 1961, with the expiration of his terms as co-president of the World Council of Churches and as Chairman of the Council of the EKD. Before that time should come, however, he wished to present his final testament to the Church he had served for a lifetime. There was a warm sense of gratitude for the blessings which had enriched his eighty years in the Church. There was a deep concern that the Church remain faithful to its task of proclaiming the crucified and resurrected Christ, because "that is what the Church stands for, and nothing else." Looking back upon the tragedies of the past and into the hazards of the future, the bishop begged his Church "never again to allow itself to be forced into a ghetto, but to remain constantly aware of its responsibilities for the whole life of the German people." The harder the life of the Church should become, the more important it would be that God should strengthen its spirit of unity, "so that it can perceive which things are insignificant and which are important."

In this critical future time, Dibelius frankly anticipated the end of the traditional folk Church with its large nominal membership, and he prayed that the core of loyal and committed Christians might be increased and strengthened to carry on their witness in a changed and hostile world. On behalf of those who were growing weary in the long and tiring struggle, the bishop offered his prayers for renewed courage, with the reminder that the One who first bore a cross had also promised to strengthen those who bore the cross after him.

With an awareness that the life of the Christian is possible only through the forgiveness of sin, the bishop closed his testament with the words of the Stuttgart Declaration, which he himself had written at the end of World War II, confessing that he personally shared in the guilt of his people and his Church. Acknowledging that he should have been more courageous in his Christian witness, "more faithful in prayer, more joyous in faith, and more ardent in love," he begged forgiveness anew, and promised forgiveness to all who had sinned against him.

This was Bishop Dibelius' valedictory. In the councils of his own Church, as in those of the All-German Federation and the World Council, he would, as befitted a patriarch of eighty years, gradually relinquish the reins of leadership. His successors would never restore either the German State or the German Church which Dibelius symbolized. But in the life which lay before it in a land under Marxist mastery, the Church of East Germany would be wise to remember Dibelius' clear warning not to sanctify the voices of demons with the authority of God.

Meanwhile the embattled Church of Christ lives its life and bears its witness in every village and city of East Germany. Through fifteen years of postwar privation, social and economic revolution, and political controversy, it has sought to minister to the physical and spiritual needs of its people and to subject the great public and international issues to the scrutiny of the Gospel. It has been invited, cajoled, and threatened, and on occasion even persecuted by the Communist State in an effort to enlist its influence and support on behalf of political programs. But for fifteen years this Church has maintained its integrity and its independence in contrast to both Catholic and Protestant Churches in Soviet Russia and in other Communist States of eastern Europe.

Thus far no government-sponsored bishops preside over any of the eight provincial Churches within the German Democratic Republic. No subservient synods have mouthed government-dictated resolutions. No hand-picked "Church inspectors" sit on the Church councils. The Evangelical Church in East Germany still speaks with a clear voice and a free conscience.

No one knows how long this will be possible. Since early 1957 there have been no signs of any relaxation of pressures on laity or clergy. All of the devices of hampering, interfering, and restricting the work of the Church—the cynical weapons of the slow war of attrition—are in use today as they have been for fifteen years. The ideological campaign to discredit the Christian faith in the minds of the youth goes on in the schools and through every public medium of communication with the complete and official support of every branch of the government. Pastors and Christian laymen are made to feel the sinister weapons of economic pressure, educational discrimination, defamation, and arrest. The legal machinery is at hand, ready to be employed whenever party leaders feel the time is ripe, for the elimination of all religious instruction in East Germany, for the closing down of all religious publications, and for the restriction of all religious life within the four walls of the village or city church.

These are not fairy stories, but facts of which the world should be apprised. They have not been recounted to elicit a cheap pity from those who allegedly have it better. No one knows what plans God has for His Church in East Germany.

Already there have been signs of a deepened spiritual vitality in this area which many German churchmen have evaluated as historically the least vigorous portion of German Protestantism. Voluntary Christmas gifts from the Churches of East Germany for the world's hungry and needy people totaled four million marks in 1959, in comparison with prosperous West Germany's ten million. The gospel of sharing has gripped many hearts within these embattled Churches. Pastors report that while government policies make it more and more difficult to gather the formal assessments from nominal Church members, voluntary offerings in all congregations are higher than they have ever been.

Great numbers of people are either forced or induced by party pressure each year to sever their formal ties with the Church, but at the same time the convictions of even greater numbers are being sharpened by the daily conflict. Christian people are being required more and more frequently to defend their convictions in the public arena. This process may reduce the formal membership of the Church drastically, and impose upon it the unfamiliar pattern of a minority group. Both pastors and laity in East Germany are facing this possibility, not with pessimism and despair, but with the realization that the true Church of Jesus Christ has always been a minority in the world. More importantly, this Church of Jesus Christ, the body of those who truly believe in Him, is no human institution which depends for its survival upon human strength or frailty. Outer forms may change, but the living Church is the work of God's Holy Spirit in the hearts of men. Against this the Lord of the Church has promised that even the gates of hell shall not prevail.